The Foreign Politics of The Communist Party of Vietnam

A Study of Communist Tactics

Ton That Thien

Published under the Auspices of
The Information and Resource Center, Singapore

CRANE RUSSAK
A Member of the Taylor & Francis Group
New York · Philadelphia · Washington, DC · London

USA	Publishing Office:	Taylor & Francis New York Inc.
		79 Madison Ave., New York, NY 10016-7892
	Sales Office:	Taylor & Francis Inc.
		242 Cherry St., Philadelphia, PA 19106-1906
UK		Taylor & Francis Ltd.
		4 John St., London WC1N 2ET

The Foreign Politics of the Communist Party of Vietnam

Copyright © 1989 Taylor & Francis New York Inc.

First published 1989
Printed in the United States of America

Library of Congress Cataloging in Publication Data

Ton-That, Thien
    The foreign politics of the Communist Party of Vietnam / by Ton
That Thien.
        p.   cm.
    Bibliography: p.
    Includes index.
    ISBN 0-8448-1572-1.
    1. Vietnam—Foreign relations.   I. Title.
DS559.912.T66   1989
327.59—dc20   89-7651
                                                                    CIP

Contents

List of Maps

Abbreviations

ARG .... Annamite (Vietnamese) Revolutionary Government (designation of Ho Chi Minh's government in August 1945 by Admiral d'Argenlieu)

ASEAN .... Association of Southeast Asian Nations

CGDK .... Coalition Government of Democratic Kampuchea (anti-Heng Samrin)

CMEA .... Council of Mutual Economic Assistance (COMECON)

Comintern .... Communist International (Third International)

CPC .... Communist Party of China

CPF .... Communist Party of France

CPI .... Communist Party of Indochina

CPK .... Communist Party of Kampuchea

CPL .... Communist Party of Laos

CPS .... Communist Party of Siam (Thailand)

CPSU .... Communist Party of the Soviet Union

CPV .... Communist Party of Vietnam

DRV .... Democratic Republic of Vietnam

ECCI .... Executive Committee of the Communist International

GBT .... Gordon, Bernard, Tan (an OSS group)

FBIS .... Foreign Broadcast Information Service

HCM .... Ho Chi Minh

KPNLF .... Khmer People's National Liberation Front (headed by Son Sann)

LFSVN .... Liberation Front of South Vietnam

LSDCSVN .... Lich Su Dang Cong San Viet Nam (History of the Communist party of Vietnam)

NUFSK .... National United Front for Salvation of Kampuchea (Heng Samrin)

NUFINPCK .... National United Front for an Independent, Neutral, Peaceful, and Cooperative Kampuchea (headed by Sihanouk)

OSS .... Office of Strategic Service

Introduction

In deciding to undertake this study, two thoughts came to my mind, one from Pascal and one from Confucius. According to the well-known French thinker, everything has been said, and one always comes too late. The great Asian philosopher, for his part, has warned that we should beware of those after us.

Anyone seeking reading material on Vietnam soon learns that there is a vast literature on the subject, especially on the decades preceding 1975. However, most of the writings that cover Vietnam before the conquest of the southern part of the country by the Communists dealt essentially with the war, and more particularly, with the involvement by the United States in the war. Moreover, these works were largely emotional and polemical. It is only in recent years, especially since the Communist victory in April 1975, that a number of scholars, fascinated by the spectacular and apparently easy success of the Vietnamese Communists, have decided to look closely at the phenomenon of Vietnamese communism as such.

The result has been the appearance of a number of interesting studies on certain aspects of Vietnamese communism: its history, its organization, its rise to power, its place in the Vietnamese nationalist movement, and so on . . . . These studies were methodical, searching, detailed, and clearly reflected the desire of their authors to avoid polemics, especially the antiwar and anti-American polemics that had marked earlier publications.

The studies concerned tended, however, to dwell too much on one aspect: the nationalism of the Vietnamese Communists. The Communist party of Vietnam (CPV) was depicted as a party of true nationalists who were able to seize power with relative ease, to hold on to it, and to extend it steadily, thanks to their superior organization and political skills, their dedication, integrity, and determination; in a word, to what the Communists themselves called "the subjective factor." By contrast, heavy stress was laid on the fact that the other nationalist groups lost because they lacked dedication, were organizationally weak, divided, inept, corrupt, too dependent on foreign support, and so on . . .

The above bias had material as well as methodological origins. The "success" of the CPV cannot be fully understood in terms of the subjective factors alone. What the Communists called the objective factors, in particular the external factors, are at least as important as the subjective factors. To cover fully both the subjective and the objective aspects of the CPV's "success" would require a more extensive and much more careful study, and this is not always easy or possible.

The CPV has certainly achieved success, but only from the point of view of the interests of the party and of international communism, in particular those of the Soviet Union. From the point of view of the Vietnamese people, whose real aspirations were for a peaceful, freer, and better life, the success is not so obvious, especially in the light of what has become undisputable since 1975. In fact, since the CPV established its dominion over the whole of Vietnam, its record has appeared increasingly one of failure, currently as well as retrospectively.

Seen from the vantage point of 1985, the failure of the CPV has to do with the real aims it had pursued since its foundation. These aims, as appear clearly in this study, were global, set against the background of international communism and taking full account of this factor, which is an objective factor. The success of the CPV must therefore be viewed against the background of the influence of this objective factor.

A study of the CPV's foreign politics is necessary for a full understanding of Vietnamese communism, and of the Vietnam question generally. This aspect has not been dealt with extensively or adequately so far in writings on Vietnam. Pascal's statement, when applied to Vietnam, is therefore not correct. All has not been said about that land, and one does not come too late. There still is something to be said about Vietnam. A gap exists.

The gap concerns the foreign politics of the CPV, in particular, about how international developments were viewed by the CPV and how, at certain crucial moments, the CPV took advantage of the situation, and more particularly, manipulated certain people to achieve its true ends; specifically, to accelerate the coming of world revolution, i.e., the establishment of communism—the dictatorship of the proletariat—on a world scale; or how it was prevented from achieving its ends because of adverse international developments, or of its misreading of the international situation. Naturally, the way the CPV looked at international developments and tried to exploit situations and manipulate people stemmed from the basic philosophical ideas of its leaders. An examination of these ideas and how they had been acquired—i.e., the training aspect—must therefore form an important part of a study of the CPV's foreign politics.

This study is an attempt to fill a certain gap on Vietnam by examining the above aspects of the politics of the CPV. My aims, however, are quite modest. I make no claim regarding comprehensiveness or exhaustiveness, originality, or finality. This study is essentially exploratory, an attempt to use an approach different from the one adopted generally so far, which consists of viewing the CPV as a fierce champion of Vietnamese national interests rather than as a zealous servant—wittingly or unwittingly—of international communism.

My study is restricted essentially to one particular aspect of Vietnamese history—Vietnamese communism—and within these narrow limits, it focuses on only one aspect—its foreign *politics*. It does not deal with the broad range of the CPV's foreign policy or foreign relations. For these broader aspects I rely on work already done by others. If there is originality in what I try to do, this would lie rather in the special and close attention given to the doctrinal consideration and to the strategy and tactics applied by the CPV to particular situations, especially to crucial people at crucial moments, and viewed in the light of what the CPV leaders themselves have said about their past actions, and of the stream of Vietnamese publications available since 1975.

This last point deserves stressing. It relates to Confucius' warning. The student of Vietnamese communism, and of Vietnamese affairs in general, enjoys as of 1985 a great advantage over those working in these fields before 1975. He or she has available more illuminating facts. Indeed, since 1975 the Communist government of Vietnam has displayed a behavior, pursued policies, and made statements that throw much, and new, light on what it had really sought to achieve, how, and why, since the early days of the CPV in Canton in 1925.

The student of Vietnamese communism and of Vietnamese affairs in general also has available a mass of documentation put out by Hanoi, especially since 1975. Having won total victory, and not being subject any longer to tactical propaganda constraints, the leaders of the CPV now feel not only quite free, but also happy and proud, to reveal their true intents and objectives, the true motivations and methods of their past actions, partly in self-praise (for their intelligence, farsightedness, and cleverness), partly as lessons for the countries of the Third World (as recipes for defeating Yankee imperialism).

Whatever the reasons for those revelations, they help students of Vietnamese affairs to gain a better insight into the behavior of the CPV leaders. At the same time, they should incite those trying seriously to understand and to interpret Vietnamese communism and Vietnam in its various aspects, including the nature of the Vietnam wars and the respective roles of the CPV, France, and the United States in those conflicts, to engage in an extensive and thorough revision. From this revision one is likely to obtain a more balanced and more accurate picture of what really happened in Vietnam before 1975, as well as a clearer understanding of what has been happening since then, not only in Vietnam, but also in Indochina and Southeast Asia. Thus Confucius was right: those who come later can know better.

This study is not a history of contemporary Vietnam, or of the Vietnam wars, or of Vietnamese nationalism, although, inevitably, it touches upon these aspects and on many others of the Vietnam question. In particular, I am not concerned with the domestic politics of the CPV—its exploitation of the internal situation of Vietnam and its manipulation of the Vietnamese people—or with its internal politics—the struggle between tendencies, factions, individuals, however interesting or fascinating these aspects may be. I am quite happy to leave them to the "Hanoiologists" and Vietnam watchers. I shall hold the basic view that since the CPV, as a good Communist party by Third International standards, operated fully on the basis of democratic centralism, any decision of the central committee, politburo, first secretary, or chairman of the party represented a decision of the party and expressed its collective will.

A knowledge of the day-to-day occurrences in the CPV, in particular, of the power struggle going on inside the party, is necessary, but much more so to the policymakers and political forecasters concerned with Communist Vietnam than to the historian, who is mainly interested in basic trends and whose views are essentially retrospective. I believe that unless one has a good knowledge of those trends—the basic thinking, beliefs, modus operandi, strategy, and tactics—of the CPV, one would not be able to understand clearly its behavior and decisions at particular moments, and still less make accurate predictions about its courses of action over the long haul, which is what really matters.

It is the ignorance, or neglect, of the basic trends that has led, for example, to the widespread views, or rather myths, that the Vietnamese Communists were "nationalist first and Communist second," that Ho Chi Minh was "above communism," that the National Liberation Front of South Vietnam was not a creation of Hanoi, or that "the ultimate aim" of the Vietnamese Communists is the establishment of the Federation of Indochina, and so on . . . whereas, as we see later, a careful examination of the pronouncements of the leaders of the CPV clearly reveal that none of the above views corresponded to reality, and that, in contrast, the Vietnamese Communists avoided calling themselves nationalists, making it perfectly clear that they were patriots totally committed to proletarian internationalism and to the overthrow of imperialism led by the United States, to world revolution, to the establishment of communism—the dictatorship of the proletariat—on a world scale.

The propagation, deliberate or involuntary, and especially the belief in such myths, had very important moral, and hence political, consequences: they put the Communists in the right, and those who oppose them in the wrong. The Vietnam war was therefore "dirty"; to wage war against the National Liberation Front of South Vietnam and against North Vietnam was "immoral," and to oppose the Vietnamese Communists was "reactionary." For the United States, a big and powerful nation, to wage war against North Vietnam was "cowardly."[1] My primary purpose, however, is not to discuss this question, although I have something to say about it in my conclusion.

One more thing should be said about the subject matter of this study. Since the CPV's foreign politics should be viewed against the setting of international politics, in particular, of the CPV's connection with the Third International, the latter is an integral part of this book. Indeed, the CPV's foreign politics could not be fully understood if one does not constantly keep in mind the fact that the CPV was a party that adopted without reservation the brand of theory and practice of politics—bolshevism—that Lenin tried hard to spread throughout the world, through the Communist International (Comintern), which he deliberately created for that specific purpose.

Concerning the sources, since this study is not a history of Vietnam or of the Vietnam wars in both their domestic and international aspects, or of Vietnamese communism per se, I draw freely from the works already done, of which there are many, a great many indeed. It would be tedious to list them here, even selectively. My great debt to their authors is acknowledged in the appropriate places.

With regard to the specific subject of my study, the collected speeches and writings of the leaders of the CPV, in particular, of the key political strategies (Ho Chi Minh, Truong Chinh, Le Duan, Vo Nguyen Giap, Pham Van Dong, and others), the History of the Communist Party of Vietnam, the account of Fifty Years' Activities of the Party, the white paper on Sino-Vietnamese relations, are extensively used, as they are of prime importance in providing insight into the thoughts and deeds of the leaders of the CPV. Some of these publications were available to me in Vietnamese, some in French, some in English. Preference was naturally given to the Vietnamese texts. If a publication was available to me only in French, I translated into English the parts quoted. The French title given in the reference shows that the publication used was in French.

The memoirs of certain foreign officials involved intimately in dealing with the CPV leaders at certain crucial moments, in particular those of Jean Sainteny and Archimedes L. Patti, respectively, heads of the French and American missions in Hanoi in August 1945, are of very great importance, and are used extensively. These two men were the first Allied officials to arrive in Hanoi that August. They had very close personal relations with Ho Chi Minh and played a key role in helping the CPV seize and consolidate power in a crucial period, and their memoirs provide extremely valuable insight into the foreign politics of the CPV, in particular into Ho Chi Minh's manipulation of key people at crucial moments to achieve his ends.

With regard to China, the testimonies of the Chinese officials who played a key role in North Vietnam during the crucial period 1945–1946, in particular Chang Fa-kwei and Hsiao Wen, I rely largely on the excellent book by K. C. Chen, who has interviewed them and made a searching study of Chinese official records.

With regard to Laos and Cambodia, certain Laotians and Cambodians who had closely witnessed developments in their countries, such as Sissouk Na Champassak, Prince Mangkra Phouma, Amphay Doré for Laos, Norodom Sihanouk for Cambodia, provide very valuable testimonies on the politics of the CPV leaders concerning those countries. The white, or black papers, published by the various governments involved in those countries also provide very important material.

With regard to the ASEAN countries, which really became involved with Vietnam only after 1975, the radio broadcasts from those countries and from the Indochinese nations, as monitored by FBIS,[2] are major sources, in addition to the official publications of the governments of those countries.

Concerning the divisions of this study, there are ten chapters. Chapter one describes the setting against which the foreign politics of the CPV are to be examined. This chapter is intended for those who approach Vietnamese studies for the first time and need an overview of the country's history from 1885 to 1985. Those who have already acquired a fair background on Vietnam should simply start reading from chapter two, which concerns Ho Chi Minh as master and leader of the party. Chapter three covers the party itself, describing its basic views and ideas concerning history, the world, politics, party aims, and the ways and means it planned to use to achieve them. These first three chapters form a whole and constitute part I of this study.

Next are five chapters on the United States, France, China, Laos and Cambodia, and ASEAN, respectively, showing how, concretely, the CPV manipulated particular situations, and especially particular people, to achieve its ends, and how successful or unsuccessful these manipulations have been. These chapters constitute part II of this study.

Chapter nine concerns the Soviet Union, showing how the CPV's connection with it, in particular with the Comintern, has affected its politics, the fate of Vietnam, and the Vietnamese people. In a final chapter, I offer a few personal reflections on the CPV and Vietnamese history. Chapters nine and ten form part III of this study.

In this book, I have chosen a topical rather than a chronological approach, and my cut-off point is 1985.

This study would not have been undertaken had it not been for two persons in particular: Professor Jacques Freymond and Professor Harish Kapur. Jacques Freymond, now retired director of the Graduate Institute of International Studies at Geneva, had, over a period of more than thirty years, encouraged me to keep up my interest in international studies, even when pressing patriotic obligations or practical considerations had kept me off the active pursuit of such studies.

Harish Kapur, currently a professor at the same institute, has been a friend and intellectual companion since our student days in 1954. We have had many lively and stimulating discussions over the years about many things, in particular about the writing of this book. In 1983 he finally succeeded in persuading me to undertake this study in spite of my great reluctance to embark on such a venture, as I knew that I would have to work under extremely heavy constraints: I would be very isolated geographically and would receive no material aid from any source. These constraints, I feared—and rightly—were bound to cause interruptions, delays, and naturally great frustrations. Without the persistent prodding and encouragement of Harish Kapur, I would probably not have completed the present work.

I also thank Mr. Nguyen Khac Ngu for helping with the maps.

Finally, I wish to record my very sincere thanks to the Information and Research Center, Singapore, for its encouragement, and for its help in the publication of this book.

I fully realize that this study is very imperfect. But, on the other hand, I am convinced that it will help clarify certain aspects of the Vietnamese question, including the Vietnam wars, and the frightful state of poverty, misery, and continued warfare in which the Vietnamese people have found themselves mired since 1975. This is an attempt at getting at the truth about Vietnam. Of course, the truth, the real truth, all of the truth, about Vietnam will not be known for a long time, if it will ever be known. But we must search for it, as objectively and, especially, as honestly as possible, if we want to really know Vietnamese communism, in the Confucian sense of really knowing:

To know that one know what one knows.

To know that one does not know what one does not know.

That is really knowing.

Trois Rivières, Québec, Canada
Summer 1987

Postscript: This book was completed in the summer of 1987. Since then, a number of events have occurred in Southeast Asia, especially in relation to Cambodia. However, these events have not invalidated my interpretations. I have therefore found that modifications to the book are unnecessary.

Trois Rivières
Autumn 1988.

1

The Setting

In the second half of the nineteenth century, taking advantage of Vietnam's weakness, France annexed the southern part of the country (Cochinchina; see map 1) and imposed a French protectorate on the rest. By the treaty of June 6, 1884, France took away defense and foreign affairs from the Vietnamese emperor, but left him in control of the country's internal affairs.[1] However, in 1885 the French authorities blatantly deposed the Vietnamese emperor and replaced him with a man of their choice, thus extending French direct rule over the whole of Vietnam. (The deposed emperor, Ham Nghi, was exiled to Algeria where he died during World War II. He was replaced by Emperor Dong Khanh, grandfather of Emperor Bao Dai.) These actions caused the outraged Vietnamese intelligentsia to start a series of rebellion movements, which had their ups and downs but which never completely ceased until French rule was fully terminated in 1954.

NATIONALIST MOVEMENTS

The first movement, named *Can Vuong* (Support the King) and led by the Vietnamese Confucian scholars-mandarins, was monarchist in character. The most prominent of these scholars-mandarins was Phan Dinh Phung. For all the heroism and exertions of its members, the movement failed to shake French rule, and it lost much of its strength when Phan Dinh Phung died in 1895.

The nationalist torch was picked up a few years later by another Confucian scholar, Phan Boi Chau, who wanted to regain independence for a Vietnam under a monarch. But at the same time, he advocated modernization and seeking external aid. He thus launched the *Duy Tan* (Mod-

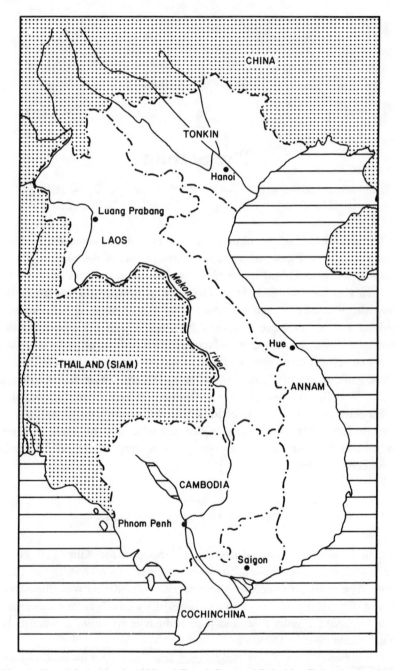

Map 1. French Indochina in 1939 and French Proposed Indochina Federation in 1946.

ernization) movement; actively recruited young people and sent them secretly to Japan for military training, as part of the *Dong Du* (Go East) movement; and sought Japan's support. He himself also went secretly to Japan in 1904. He first obtained some support there, but in 1908 he was expelled by the Japanese at the request of the French government.

While in Japan, Phan Boi Chau came into contact with Chinese revolutionaries, in particular Liang Ch'i-ch'ao. After leaving Japan, he went to China, where he tried to enlist the support of the leaders of the Chinese revolutionary movement, including Sun Yat-sen. From China, Phan Boi Chau continued his agitation against French rule. He also set up bases in Thailand. But his movement did not make much headway, and it practically came to an end when, betrayed by the Vietnamese Communists (reportedly by Ho Chi Minh; see Chapter 2), he was arrested by French authorities in Shanghai and brought back to Vietnam in 1925. He died in 1941.

Until the 1920s, Phan Boi Chau was considered the country's greatest national hero. Another national hero of Vietnam of that period was Phan Chu Trinh, who, unlike Phan Boi Chau, advocated republicanism and the achievement of national independence through cooperation with France and acceptance of French tutelage for a time. His name was associated with the *Dong Kinh Nghia Thuc* (Scholars' Modern Schools) whose aim was to give the Vietnamese a modern education. In spite of his advocacy of cooperation with France, Phan Chu Trinh was jailed by the French authorities for his evoking of independence. In 1911 he was released from jail but was exiled to France. In 1925 he returned to his country, a national hero, and died there in 1926.

The two Phans did much to keep the flame of Vietnamese nationalism burning during the first quarter of the twentieth century. They represented the nationalism of the Vietnamese Confucian elite. With the disappearance of these two men from the scene, the Vietnamese nationalist movement came under a different kind of leadership. Instead of looking to the East, the new leaders looked West, as they belonged to the Western-educated and Western-orientated intelligentsia. These new leaders had gone to schools set up by the French authorities in Vietnam to replace the traditional Confucian schools, or had acquired French ideas and values in France in French schools or through contact with the French, especially during and after World War I.

The new nationalists divided into two groups, a division that was to last for the following decades: those who rejected Western colonialism but accepted Western democratic ideas and values, and those who rejected both Western colonialism and Western democratic values and adopted the Marxist-Leninist ideology. In Communist terminology: those in favor of bourgeois democracy, and those in favor of Socialist democracy.

The most important of the non-Communist revolutionary organizations was the Viet Nam Quoc Dan Dang (VNQDD), founded in 1927 and patterned closely on the Chinese Kuomintang. The revolutionary Marxist-Leninist party was, of course, the Communist party of Vietnam (changing its name afterward to Communist party of Indochina), founded in 1930 and accepting the leadership of the Third Communist International. Both were secret organizations subject to extremely severe repressions by the French colonial authorities; both were practically wiped out as a result of unsuccessful insurrections in 1930–1931.

The VNQDD insurrection, commonly referred to as the Yen Bay revolt, occurred in February 1930. Its failure led to the arrest of thousands of its members, including almost its entire leadership. After this devastating blow, the VNQDD practically ceased to exist as an effective revolutionary nationalist organization capable of being a serious threat to French rule. Those who escaped arrest fled to China and continued to operate from there under the protection of the Chinese Kuomintang.

The Communist party of Indochina (CPI), for its part, staged a series of "Soviets" in the provinces of Nghe-An and Ha-Tinh in 1930–1931. As a result of their failure and of the savage repression by the French colonial authorities, the CPI also suffered near extinction. But thanks to the help of the Comintern, it was able to reconstitute itself by 1934. Nevertheless, like the VNQDD, it ceased to be a real challenge to French rule until 1945.

In addition to the VNQDD and the CPI, there were other, less important nationalist organizations. However, most of them were reformist and did not favor political separation of Vietnam from France. There was also a Trotskyite group, led by Ta Thu Thau, which competed with the CPI for support among the population.[2]

Internationally, the period 1885–1939 was one in which France was an acknowledged great European power. Its vast colonial empire was second in importance only to the British empire. On the other hand, as a result of its victory over Germany in 1918, of the U.S. relapse into isolationism, and of Russia being crippled by internal disturbances, France became a leading world power as well. In the colonies, no power was capable of challenging its position, except Great Britain, and for an obvious reason—imperial solidarity—the latter had no real interest in mounting such a challenge.

France's colonial position was made still more secure by the treaties signed in Washington in 1921. Under the Four Power Treaty, the United States, Great Britain, France, and Japan pledged to respect the *status quo* regarding their colonial possessions in the Pacific, whereas under the Five Power Treaty, a ceiling was placed on Japan's naval strength. Thus France's sovereignty over Indochina was fully protected.

Under the circumstances, the Vietnamese revolutionary nationalists, having no strong organization, no armed forces, no powerful and firm allies, could not hope to terminate French rule. For the Vietnamese Communists, in particular, defeating imperialism, even in Vietnam alone, was a remote possibility, a very remote one indeed. The high hopes that Lenin had entertained in 1917 about the coming of the world revolution had been dashed by 1921. That year, Lenin began to speak about the existence of a "state of equilibrium" and about the "zigzag line of history."[3] In 1927 Zinoviev, one of Lenin's trusted lieutenants, talked about the inevitability of the "ebb and flow" of the revolution."[4] That year, Communist revolutionary hopes in Asia were dashed when Chiang Kai-shek dealt devastating blows against them in China. In 1928 Stalin made "socialism in one country" the official policy of the Soviet Union.

In Europe the following twelve years witnessed the spectacular rise of fascism and the evaporation of Communist hopes of seizing power in a number of countries, in particular in Germany. Hitler's rise to power there in 1933 and his ruthless suppression of communism, together with his avowed intention of seeking "living space" in the East, posed a serious threat to Soviet Russia, the fortress of the world revolution. This danger was compounded by the linking up of Germany, Italy, and Japan by the Anti-Comintern Pact in November 1936. The growing danger posed by the Fascist powers led Stalin to impose the united front tactics on the Comintern, to seek a rapprochement with the Western powers, and to give firmer support to China, especially after Japan's invasion of that country in 1937.

The international situation in 1928–1939 thus did not favor the Vietnamese nationalist revolutionaries. Yet, the upshot of the revolutionary activities between 1885 and 1930, and of the abortive revolts of 1930–1931, followed by the trials and executions of nationalist leaders, national heroes, was that a climate of widespread unrest and a strong spirit of rebellion persisted throughout those years. This situation was to greatly benefit all nationalist revolutionaries from 1939 onward, when the world underwent a complete change as a result of the outbreak of World War II.

WORLD WAR II

As elsewhere in Southeast Asia, World War II was to produce great up-heavals in Vietnam. In particular, it gave a strong boost to Vietnamese nationalism. France had its hands tied up in Europe and could not main-tain a strong position in Indochina. On the other hand, deprived of sup-port from France, Indochina found itself in a precarious position vis-a-vis Japan, whose ambitions regarding Southeast Asia were well known.

Japan moved swiftly in June 1940, when the French armies were crushed by Hitler's forces. Paris fell on June 14; the French government asked for an armistice on June 16. Three days later, Japan struck in Indochina. Tokyo demanded the right to set up a Japanese mission in Hanoi to ensure the effective control of traffic on the Haiphong-Kunming railway to pre-vent war supplies from reaching the Chinese forces. This move followed an earlier demand that the railway be closed to the transport of war ma-terial to China. General Georges Catroux, then governor general of In-dochina, yielded to Japanese demands.[5]

To the Vietnamese nationalists, the French decision conveyed a clear message: the French were weak and no longer in full control in Indochina. The weakness became still clearer in September when the Japanese de-manded the right to use airports and to move troops into northern Indo-china, starting from the 22nd of that month. Again, the French authorities in Indochina, now headed by Admiral Jean Decoux, who had chosen to place the colony under the authority of Marshall Petain instead of General de Gaulle, capitulated on orders from Vichy. But, whether as a result of a misunderstanding or as a deliberate warning to the French authorities, the Japanese forces in southern China attacked the border town of Lang Son and inflicted heavy casualties on the French garrison there.

Following the attack, the Communists launched a series of uprisings against the French. These actions were serious mistakes. The uprisings were premature and, naturally, they were ruthlessly put down by the French authorities. France was down but not yet out. In an agreement with Japan on August 17, 1940, France had conceded the right to use military fa-cilities and to station troops in Indochina; but, in return, it had secured Japan's formal recognition of French sovereignty over Indochina, thus giving the French authorities there a free hand to deal with the Vietnam-ese nationalist revolutionary movements as they saw fit.

However, the Japanese authorities gave protection to the Vietnamese friendly to Japan whose security was seriously threatened by the French police, and fostered the growth of pro-Japanese parties, in particular, of

the Dai Viet. On the other hand, the Japanese humiliating behavior toward the French—unrestrained, insolent, brutal, and especially public—
whether accidental or deliberate, convinced more and more Vietnamese
that France had become impotent, and its days in Indochina were num-
bered.

French impotence became more and more obvious. This was further
demonstrated by the conclusion of a series of agreements under which
France made more and more concessions to Japan, with far-reaching im-
plicatitons, economically and especially militarily. These culiminated in
the Joint Defense Agreement of July 29, 1941. In the eyes of the Allies,
this formally placed Indochina squarely in the enemy camp. For the Vietnamese, it meant the formal end of French sovereignty. The combined
effect of these two reactions was to make a smooth and full return of
France to Indochina impossible in 1945.

The logical consequence of the Franco-Japanese agreement of July 29
was the Japanese demand, in the form of an ultimatum on March 8, 1945,
that the French forces be placed under effective Japanese command. When
the ultimatum expired, the Japanese struck: the French forces were dis-
armed, and the French administration was eliminated on March 9. On
March 11, Emperor Bao Dai declared the Treaty of 1884 terminated, and
with it, the French protectorate. Thus the Japanese accomplished with
great ease, in just one day, what the Vietnamese nationalist revolutionaries, Communists included, had been trying very hard, but in vain, to
do for almost a century: the ending of French rule in fact as well as in
law.

Logically also, the Japanese had acted primarily not in the interests of
the Vietnamese but in those of Japan, more particularly, for the implementation of their grand imperial design of "Greater East Asia Co-Pros-
perity Sphere."[6] It is thus not surprising that, for Vietnam, independence
could be only nominal. Japan retained control not only of foreign affairs,
and especially of defense, but also of administration. It refused to turn
over immediately to the Bao Dai government control of Cochinchina.
Worse still, unlike the policy it pursued toward the Philippines, Burma,
or Indonesia, it did not allow this government to have an army or even
a ministry of defense. These restrictions were to prove fatal to the Bao
Dai government when Japan suddenly surrendered to the Allies on August
15, after the atomic bombing of Hiroshima and Nagasaki. The use of the
atomic bomb against Japan by the United States on August 6 and 9, and
the removal of the French administration in Indochina by Japan on March
9, 1945 are two of the four most decisive external factors in the shaping

of events in Vietnam in the next four decades. (The other two are France's defeat in 1940, and the U.S. presidential order to American military authorities in China to block all attempts by the French to reenter Indochina in August 1945.)

THE POSTWAR STRUGGLE

On August 15, 1945, an extraordinary situation emerged in Vietnam. Japan's sudden surrender had caught everyone by surprise. The Bao Dai government found itself unprepared and impotent: it had had not enough time to establish itself firmly, and worse still, it had no armed forces at its disposal. The French troops were still interned by the Japanese, and the French officials, including the supreme head of the French administration in Indochina, Governor General Admiral Decoux, were still under detention by the Japanese; General de Gaulle was absorbed by pressing French and European affairs, and the French Expeditionary Corps was still being formed 13,000 miles away. The Japanese were no longer interested in exercising effective authority in Indochina, and the Allied forces were still weeks away. A total military, political, and administrative vacuum prevailed in Vietnam.

The vacuum could be filled by any group that was on the spot and had the organization, preparation, and leadership to take full advantage of the situation. The CPV was that group, Ho Chi Minh was that leader. A good student of Lenin, Ho Chi Minh had watched the international situation closely, and he fully realized that the United States played a key role at this time in the determination of the fate of Vietnam. For the achievement of his purpose, it was therefore vital for him to have the Americans on his side. For this he must manipulate them will skill. He did so with great success. As a result, only a few days after Japan's surrender, he was able to seize effective power, hang on to it, and consolidate it in the crucial following months.

Ho had a lead, even a long one, on the French. But the latter were bound to catch up and pause a major problem for him and his party. President Franklin Roosevelt, who had planned to place Indochina under international trusteeship, died in April 1945, and the trusteeship idea died with him. There was no mention of it at the San Francisco conference on the United Nations in June. In August General de Gaulle obtained President Harry Truman's acceptance of the idea of Indochina's return to

France. By the end of October, the American officials in Hanoi had been notified about the change of American policy and instructed to abandon "neutrality" in favor of "cooperation" in regard to the French. Those considered "too friendly" to Ho Chi Minh were firmly moved out of northern Indochina.[7] To Ho Chi Minh and his disciples, the meaning of those events was quite clear. France was to return to Indochina with the blessings with the Allies.

Meantime, in early September, Chinese troops arrived to disarm the Japanese forces north of the 16th parallel, as part of the Potsdam agreements (see map 2). With the Chinese troops came the leaders of the VNQDD and the Dong Minh Hoi and their armed followers. (The Dong Minh Hoi was a party created in China during World War II under the auspices of General Chang Fa-Kwei, commander of the Chinese troops in southern China.) While in China, these leaders had been opposed to communism, and to Ho Chi Minh in particular. They were now determined, with Chinese (KMT) support, to prevent Ho from gaining or keeping power in a Vietnam free from French rule.

The Chinese were, however, bound to leave sooner or later. Under an agreement concluded by the Chinese and French governments in Chungking on February 28, 1946, in northern Indochina the Chinese troops were to be replaced by French troops. Earlier, on October 8, 1945, France had concluded an agreement with the British; Great Britain was to restore to France control over Indochina south of the 16th parallel. These two agreements thus restored French sovereignty over all of Indochina, at least in theory.

In practice, however, since Ho Chi Minh's government had considerable influence on the nationalist elements fighting the French forces in southern Vietnam, and what was still more important, full de facto control over northern Vietnam, a return of France to the north, in particular a landing of French troops there even for the purpose of replacing Chinese troops in the name of the Allies, must have the agreement of Ho's government if it was to be peaceful. Negotiation was therefore inevitable.

For Ho Chi Minh, too, there was no alternative to letting the French troops land peacefully. Willy nilly, the Chinese would have to leave. On the other hand, for military as well as diplomatic and political reasons, Ho was not yet ready for war. His forces were still very weak and especially ill-equipped. The Chinese Red Army was thousands of miles away, and in his rear Ho still had to face the Kuomintang forces. His government had no international status. And what is more important than

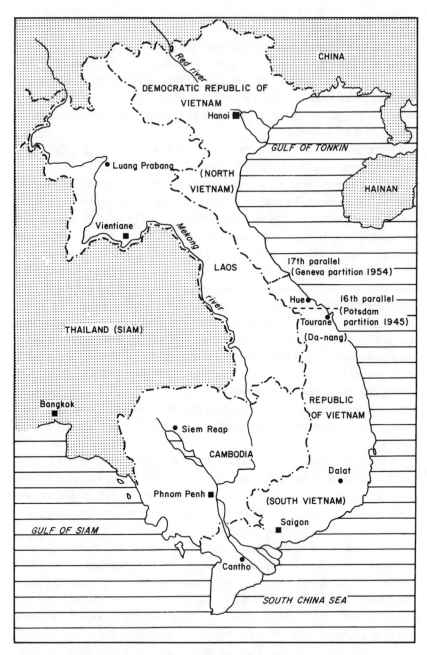

Map 2. Indochina in 1945/1946 (16th Parallel) and in 1954/1975 (17th Parallel).

everything else, he had not yet fully secured his government's acceptance as a nationalist government representing all the Vietnamese people. For this, he needed time for more maneuvering.

Ho's needs coincided with those of General Philippe Leclerc, commander of the French forces. Leclerc wanted French presence restored in northern Vietnam. To him, entering Hanoi was to be "the last stage of the liberation."[8] But he wanted to do so without having to fight, at least not before French troops had entered Hanoi.

The consequence of the convergence of Ho's and Leclerc's desires was the conclusion of the Franco-Vietnamese agreement of March 6, 1946. As subsequent events were to prove clearly, these agreements, one political and one military, were only tactical moves, with mental reservatitons on both sides.

The political agreement, which recognized the Democratic Republic of Vietnam (DRV) as a free state within the Indochinese Federation and the French Union, did not solve the real issue.[9] What Ho wanted was a fully independent and unified Vietnam, naturally under Communist control and free to choose its own international alignment, the natural choice being alignment with Moscow. France, on the other hand, wanted to retain sovereignty and exercise substantial powers in Vietnam through control of the Indochinese Federation and the French Union (see map 1). In any case, it wanted in Vietnam, if not a submissive, then, at least, a friendly and reliable government, and it firmly refused to entertain the idea of a Communist Vietnam in a French Union headed by a France allied to the Western powers.[10] Thus nothing was really settled. Further negotiations were necessary.

The continued negotiations were held, first at Dalat in April, then at Fontainebleau near Paris in July–September. Naturally enough, they produced no result. The two sides, for obvious reasons, talked past each other. A last-minute attempt by Ho Chi Minh and Marius Moutet, the French minister for Overseas France, to save the situation by the signing of a modus vivendi on September 14 did not lead to any improvement, and the real talk was left to the canons.[11] This began on the night of December 19, 1946.

For a time, Ho Chi Minh's government suffered a number of disadvantages. It was isolated diplomatically, weak militarily, and in a precarious position politically. One of Ho's major concerns before he entered Hanoi in August 1945, or even while he was still in China or in the jungles of the Sino-Vietnamese border, was to secure international recognition, not only as a de facto and exclusive authority in Vietnam, but as the official and legal government of all Vietnam, Cochinchina included. Although the position of his government had been strengthened by Bao Dai's abdication and transfer of power on August 25, 1945, its international position remained uncertain. The March 6 agreement was only preliminary. For foreign countries, especially for the United States and China, France still exercised sovereignty over Indochina. The Soviet Union was far away, and Stalin was more concerned about extending Soviet power and influence in Europe than about improving the fortunes of a small Communist party in Asia.

Militarily, although Vo Nguyen Giap, commander of the armed forces of the DRV, had been able to build up an army of 60,000 men by December 1946, it was still in its formative stage, lacking arms and especially ammunitions. It was in no position to defeat, or even seriously challenge, the French Expeditionary Corps. The Chinese Communists was still three years away, and in December 1946, there was no clear indication as yet that they could defeat the Kuomintang forces and extend their control to all of China, down to the border of Vietnam. The DRV had no safe rear base, an essential condition for waging a guerilla war successfully.

Politically, although Bao Dai had transferred the "mandate of Heaven" to the DRV, and although the CPV, through the Viet-Minh (Viet Nam Doc Lap Dong Minh–Vietnam Independence League–front for the CPV, set up by Ho Chi Minh in 1940) had a large following thanks to its heavy play on the Vietnamese people's burning desire for immediate and total independence, and to its skillful exploitation of its American connections, it had not been able to secure unanimous support among the population. Furthermore, if Ho Chi Minh had obtained French recognition for his government, as far as the French were concerned, it applied only to the Democratic Republic of Vietnam (i.e., Vietnam north of the 16th parallel).

Finally, Bao Dai had by this time clearly put distance between himself and Ho Chi Minh's government by staying in Hongkong, and moves were being made by other political groups to put up an anti-Communist government headed by him to challenge the legitimacy of the government led by Ho Chi Minh. If Bao Dai could wrest from the French what Ho had been unable to do—national unification of the country and full independence, or even a substantial measure of real independence—the Viet-Minh might collapse as a natitonalist front, appear more obviously Communist, and consequently isolated and vulnerable.

Ho Chi Minh had therefore to hang on in the hope that the Left in

France would emerge victorious in the French coming elections and form a government that would be favorable to the RDV and make it more natural for Vietnam to stay in the French Union; or until the Chinese Communists could gain control of all China; or for a change in official Soviet policy; or for the French government to make disastrous mistakes.

The first eventuality did not materialize, and in the spring of 1947, the Communists were out of the French government. But the three other possibilities did, and this opened up tremendous avenues for the CPV.

The total victory of the Chinese Communist party (CPC) and the arrival of Chinese Communist troops on the Vietnamese borders in late 1949 provided the DRV with a colossal ally and a safe rear base. The Soviet switch of policy, from accommodation to confrontation with the West, was signalled by Zhdanov's famous speech at the founding of the Cominform in Poland, in September 1947.

Moscow's new policy put the CPV's intransigeant policy in line with that of Moscow. Likewise, the elimination of the Communists from the French government made the adoption of a tough policy by the CPV look good in the eyes of the French Communist party (CPF). Finally, the French government ruined Bao Dai's and the Vietnamese anti-Communists' chances in the spring of 1947 by refusing them the political weapons they needed—immediate and total reunification and independence—in their competition with Ho's government for popular support both at home and abroad.

The combined effects of those four factors was that, now, not only the DRV was linked geographically with a vast Communist camp stretching all the way from the frontiers of Vietnam to the borders of West Germany, but also the CPV could be certain that its policy was in harmony with that of the entire Communist camp. Internally, through the Viet-Minh, which it controlled, it now fully gained the psychologically very attractive and politically very rewarding image of a nationalist party leading a people in a fierce fight for national independence. Defeat was no longer to be feared, and victory now became virtually a certainty.

The certainty became clearer after the French suffered a series of resounding reverses along the Sino-Vietnamese borders in the autumn of 1950.[12] Psychologically, for Ho's government the war was practically won because to the majority of the Vietnamese, especially the peasants who had remained skeptical or uncertain, it had now been proved that the French were beatable and that in supporting the Viet-Minh, they were sure of supporting the winner, always an extremely important consideration for the naturally cautious Vietnamese.

France could now hope to defeat the DRV only if it had strong national will, and especially the necessary means, in particular manpower, and it had neither of these.[13] The obvious solution to the problem of manpower shortage would be bringing the anti-Communist or non-Communist Vietnamese nationalists into the fight, by offering them immediate real independence. This the French government would not, or could not, do. Instead, after lengthy negotiations with Bao Dai, which started in the summer of 1948, France concluded an agreement on March 8, 1949, which imposed many restrictions on Vietnam's sovereignty.[14] Even so, this agreement, often referred to as "the Elysee agreement," was not ratified by the French National Assembly until January 29, 1950.

The Elysee agreement convinced many Vietnamese that they had only the choice between fighting against France, which meant joining Ho Chi Minh's forces, or abstaining. Many abstained; those already in the fight fought harder. Thus, militarily and politically, the DRV's position now became more secure. Diplomatically also its position became stronger, after its recognition by Communist China and the Soviet Union in the latter half of January.

Ho Chi Minh's recognition by the Soviet Union and Communist China did not change the basic situation of Vietnam internally, but it introduced a new element internationally for, following the Soviet and Chinese move, the United States and other Western nations extended diplomatic recognition to the Bao Dai government in early February. The struggle in Vietnam now became international, a contest between two camps, East and West, which had emerged since 1947 as contestants in a "cold war."

The contest was intensified by the outbreak of the Korean War in June, when the United States became involved in Indochina as a result of President Truman's decision to accelerate the delivery of American military assistance to France and the Associated States of Indochina. The U.S. administration now accepted the French view that, in Korea and in Indochina, the United States and France were fighting the same war against the same enemy in two different theaters.[15]

For Ho Chi Minh and the CPV, America's involvement meant that, to win the war, not only would they have to fight harder and longer, but they also must have the firm and total support of the Communist states. It was clear that they would be able to continue their fight only so long as this support remained firm and total. As they were to find out, such was not always the case. Soviet and Chinese support was not, and could not be, absolute. China's and the Soviet Union's interests were not always the same as those of the DRV. They had their own, and larger, interests to protect, and they made this plain in 1953–1954 by seeking a compromise peace with the West in both Korea and Indochina.

NORTH AND SOUTH VIETNAM

The Korean War was brought to an end by the signing of an armistice at Pan Mun Jom in July 1953. In the case of Vietnam, peace was restored at the Geneva Conference in July 1954. At this conference, Ho Chi Minh and the RDV had to settle for half a victory, although they had won a resounding military victory at Dien Bien Phu in May, and their position seemed quite strong. The DRV was given control of half of Vietnam north of the 17th parallel. Control was total, but it extended to less territory than before the start of the war in December 1949, when Ho Chi Minh's government had effective control of a territory extending at least to the 16th parallel (see map 2). Furthermore, Viet-Minh troops had to evacuate Cambodia as well as Laos.

If to Ho Chi Minh and the CPV total control of Vietnam and Indochina was highly desirable, to their senior partners, the Soviets and the Chinese, avoiding a wider war—in which they would be involved—was a more imperative consideration. An extension of Communist control to all of Vietnam through a continuation of the war could be achieved only at the risk of a war in which the United States would be directly involved, and in which China itself could become a victim, at a time when, after an exhaustive war in Korea, it wanted a respite to devote all its time and energy to internal development.

The Soviet Union, too, had more urgent domestic problems to resolve in the wake of Stalin's death. Moreover, it was tied to China by a defense treaty. Above all, it wanted to prevent the conclusion of a European defense treaty, which was being pressed on France by the United States. This treaty would formalize the rearmament of Germany. To Stalin's successor, preventing German rearmament—viewed as a threat to the Soviet Union in Europe—continued to be more important than total victory for a small Communist party in Asia, especially as achievement of this victory carried with it the risk of involving the Soviet Union in a war.

On the Western side, France was too tired, and especially after the recognition of full independence to Vietnam by a Franco-Vietnamese treaty signed on June 4, French public opinion saw no sense in continuing to make sacrifices in Indochina to defend a French Union that had ceased to exist as a result of the recognition of Vietnam's full independence. As regards the United States, an effective denial of victory, or even of half a victory, to the Communists would clearly require American direct military intervention in Indochina. This intervention would be impossible without formal French invitation and full British cooperation, and neither of these was forthcoming.[16]

The negotiations held at Geneva ended on July 20. They resulted in the conclusion of what has commonly been referred to as "the Geneva Agreements": three separate cease-fire agreements for Vietnam, Laos, and Cambodia, and a Final Declaration, which bore no one's signature. In strict international law, such a declaration is binding for no one, a fact that was to have very important consequences.

According to the Final Declaration, the two Vietnamese parties, the Democratic Republic of Vietnam (North Vietnam) and the State of Vietnam (South Vietnam), were to hold talks from July 1955 onward to determine the modalities of the elections that were to take place in July 1956 and lead to a peaceful reunification of the country. These talks did not occur because the government of South Vietnam, headed by Ngo Dinh Diem, refused them, as his government had not signed and was therefore not a party to, and thus not bound by, the Geneva Agreements, a perfectly valid point in international law.

Since there were no talks, there were no elections, therefore no Communist victory—a victory that practically everyone had expected—and no reunification. And since the Soviet Union did not want to press the case, and no major power, China included, wanted to have war at that time, Ho Chi Minh and the CPV would have to wait and find other ways or, in Communist parlance, other forms of conquering the rest of Vietnam. This is what they were going to do in the next two decades, with great success but at horrendous costs to the country and its people.

In those two decades, Ho Chi Minh and, after his death in 1969, his disciples had to maneuver within a new and very complex international context.[17] There were many major obstacles in their path; one was the presence of John Foster Dulles at the head of U.S. diplomacy. Dulles had favored strong measures including military, "massive retaliation" among them, to stop Communist expansion. He had seriously warned China against intervention in Indochina and pushed hard for the establishment of a military alliance, the South East Asia Treaty Organization (SEATO).

Another major obstacle was Soviet policy. In the wake of Stalin's death (March 1953), a power struggle took place in the Soviet Union. It led to the emergence of Nikita Khrushchev, who advocated de-Stalinization at home and peaceful existence abroad. This meant seeking detente with the United States and avoidance of armed conflicts, which could generate tensions or escalate and lead to direct confrontation between the Soviet Union and the United States.

Since any armed action in South Vietnam would require approval and backing by Moscow, the CPV would have to find a way of winning Soviet approval of an interpretation of the peaceful coexistence policy that would permit the CPV to pursue revolutionary, including armed, action in South Vietnam without thwarting Krushchev's desire for detente with the United States. In this it had the support of China, whose leaders did not share the views on peaceful coexistence put forward by Khrushchev at the Twentieth Congress of the Communist party of the USSR in 1956, and at the meetings of the Communist parties in 1957 and 1960.[18]

The conflict between the USSR and China and the necessity for Moscow to compete with Peking in maintaining its image as the leader of the world revolution gave the CPV room to maneuver. Since Moscow did not want an open break, and since Peking objected to an interpretation of peaceful coexistence as the freezing of all revolutionary activities, especially in the Third World, the CPV was able to use an interpretation of peaceful coexistence that would combine the maintenance of peace between the Soviet Union and the United States with the continuation of revolutionary struggle where conditions were favorable.

The way was open to the CPV to pursue a forward policy in South Vietnam by means and at a level that, in its view, would not provoke direct U.S. intervention in South Vietnam. From 1957 onward, the CPV accordingly added military action to political agitation, but on a limited scale, while waiting for an opportunity to escalate its military operations.

The opportunity was provided in 1960 by events in Laos, where the breakdown of a precarious peace led to a resumption of the civil war. Although Khrushchev did not want to get involved there, he had to reckon with China's militancy. China used the occasion to prove that, unlike the Soviet Union, it would not hesitate to support revolutionary movements. The CPV asserted the right of Communist parties to pursue a forward policy where a revolutionary was considered to exist. In the view of the CPV, such a situation existed in 1959, and still more so in 1960.

The resumption of the civil war in Laos led to the convening of an international conference at Geneva in May 1961. This resulted in the conclusion of an international agreement in July 1962, which forbade SEATO intervention in Laos. North Vietnam could now open a corridor along the border of Laos and Vietnam through the territory controlled by the Pathet

Lao, which was under the control of Hanoi. Through this corridor, North Vietnam could freely send troops and supplies in increasing quantities to South Vietnam to intensify its operations against the government there. Furthermore, with Peking's help, it was able to obtain from Prince Sihanouk permission to use Cambodian territory to set up passageways and bases from which to mount attacks against the South Vietnamese forces, and sanctuaries to which its troops could retreat for refuge and recuperation.

U.S. INVOLVEMENT

Hanoi's decision to embark on a forward policy in South Vietnam was based on its assessment that the situation there was "ripe" for revolution, but also, and much more, on its conviction that the United States would not intervene directly and would accept for South Vietnam the same solution as for Laos.

Hanoi's belief was based on two decisions by President John Kennedy. On the one hand, Kennedy refused to intervene directly in Laos and accepted a coalition government there as part of an international agreement reached at the Geneva Conference on Laos in July 1962. On the other hand, and this is more important still, during the conference, Kennedy authorized Averell Harriman, chief of the American delegation, to meet secretly with the North Vietnamese delegation and discover whether they were prepared to accept for South Vietnam the same solution as for Laos, i.e. a coalition government.[19]

To the leaders of the CPV, Harriman's approach was a clear indication that the United States was seeking for a way to disengage from Vietnam, as it had done in Laos. It followed logically that if they pressed on, they would have a very good chance of conquering South Vietnam without running too much risk. Their guesses were correct, as, according to people close to Kennedy and to the White House, the U.S. president planned to disengage from Vietnam in 1965, after his reelection.[20]

The CPV's chances for a quick victory in South Vietnam were tremendously improved by the elimination of President Ngo Dinh Diem by the United States in November 1963. Diem had been the major obstacle to a Communist takeover. With his removal, the road to Saigon was wide open to the CPV. However, three weeks after Diem was killed, Kennedy himself was assassinated, and his plan of disengagement could not be implemented, for President Lyndon Johnson, who succeeded Kennedy, had different ideas. Johnson was determined not to allow a Communist takeover of South Vietnam, through a coalition government or otherwise.[21]

However, the South Vietnamese situation looked good to the CPV leaders in late 1963. Following the removal of Diem, South Vietnam was plunged into a state of chaos and disorganization, which facilitated Communist agitation in the cities and military operations in the countryside. By early 1965, after a series of major military reverses, South Vietnam was on the brink of collapse.

President Johnson was faced with the painful choice between letting South Vietnam fall into Communist hands or intervening more directly. He chose not only to intervene in the South, but also to attack the North. By ignoring Khrushchev's warning, the CPV leaders had brought war to North Vietnam and raised the prospects of widening the Vietnam war, with complications for China and the Soviet Union.

However, like Kennedy before him and Nixon after him, Johnson would not, or could not, do what was needed to win the war in Vietnam. Whereas the CPV fought a *total war for world stakes,* Johnson chose to fight a *limited war for local stakes.* Whereas the CPV fought for the victory of world communism, the United States fought only for the withdrawal of North Vietnamese troops from South Vietnam. Johnson made it clear, through various channels and in various ways, that he did not want a war with China and a confrontation with the Soviet Union, and especially he did not want the destruction of the Hanoi government.[22]

Moscow and Peking were thus free to continue to give backing to their Vietnamese allies. This, obviously, prolonged the war, as so long as Hanoi continued to receive military and other supplies from China and/or the Soviet Union, so long it could continue to wage war. Whereas China, in furtherance of its policy of forcing the United States to seek its cooperation, encouraged Hanoi to pursue the war, the Soviet Union under Khrushchev wanted to see the war ended so that it could improve its U.S. relations. Fortunately for the DRV, Khrushchev was ousted in October 1964, and the new Soviet leadership, under Brezhnev, increased Soviet aid to the DRV to enable it to cope with U.S. intensification of the war. The situation was thus stalemated.

The stalemate lasted until February 1968, when North Vietnam, in flagrant violation of the Lunar New Year's (*Tet*) truce, staged a surprise attack against all the cities of South Vietnam, including Saigon, the capital. The spectacle of the counteroffensive waged by South Vietnamese, and especially by American, troops to eject the Communists from Saigon and other cities, and of the vast destruction inflicted by the fighting brought directly into the bedrooms of America shook American opinion. But, above all, the audacity of the attack, and the fact of the attack itself, brought about the collapse of American morale, including that of the American Commander-in-Chief, President Johnson. Earlier, the morale of the American secretary of defense, first Robert McNamara, then Clark Clifford, had already collapsed—a remarkable situation indeed!

As a result of the Communist Tet offensive, in March 1968 Johnson decided to stop the bombing of North Vietnam, and to seriously seek peace, an "honorable peace." This was an admission of defeat, for to seek peace in such circumstances meant to be ready to give in to the enemy's major demands, with some device for saving appearances.

In May, during the American presidential campaign, Hanoi agreed to meet with U.S. negotiators. Paris was chosen as the site for the talks. In early November, on the eve of the U.S. presidential elections, Hanoi announced its readiness to start negotiations. Due to Saigon's stalling, these negotiations began only after the inauguration of the new American president, Richard Nixon.

Nixon took over in 1969 and pursued the peace negotiations, but at the same time he applied a policy of withdrawal of American troops under the guise of "Vietnamization." The American armies were leaving the battlefield before an agreement was reached in negotiations. Only defeated troops leave the battlefield before the war is over. No one was blind to that fact, least of all the CPV leaders. They knew they had definitely won the war. Now, it remained only for them to decide how to finish it off, quickly and economically. The Paris negotiations were to serve that purpose. Through these talks, they secured the total withdrawal of American troops on the one hand, and, on the other, the establishment of a coalition government in South Vietnam, and especially their right to retain their own troops there.

COMMUNIST VICTORY

The result of the negotiations was the Paris Peace Agreement of January 23, 1973, which laid the ground for North Vietnam's final assault on South Vietnam in 1975. But, in the meantime, the CPV leaders had to reckon with a major obstacle: the possibility of a resumption of American bombing. But luck was on their side. On November 7, 1973, the U.S. Congress passed a War Powers Resolution, which seriously limited the

U.S. president's powers to commit American armed forces to action abroad. In August 1974 a major political scandal (Watergate) forced the resignation of President Nixon, the man who would not hesitate to bomb North Vietnam savagely. Last, sentiment was growing in the U.S. Congress for total disengagement from Vietnam, including financial disengagement. This would mean turning over the South Vietnamese to Communist rule.

The combined effect of these developments, which were carefully watched and analyzed in Hanoi, was to prompt the CPV leadership to launch a massive military offensive in the spring of 1975 for the final kill.[23] It started with a surprise attack on the highland town of Ban Me Thuot on March 10. Strategic and tactical mistakes made by South Vietnam's president Nguyen Van Thieu and his generals opened the way for a Communist quick drive toward Saigon with a force of five well-equipped divisions sent in from North Vietnam. On April 23, on the eve of the final assault against Saigon, Gerald Ford, the new U.S. president, declared that for the United States the war was finished. This, plus a refusal of the U.S. Congress to extend further financial aid to South Vietnam, was the final massive blow that completely broke the morale of the already badly shaken South Vietnamese armed forces, and it sealed the fate of the country.

The Communist forces captured Saigon on April 30. For the first time, the CPV exercised total control over all of Vietnam. A key country of Southeast Asia fell completely into Communist hands. The CPV achieved an end they had pursued since 1930, and that, as many people were soon to learn to their astonishment or their sorrow, was only part of a larger purpose: world revolution.

After capturing South Vietnam, the CPV lost no time in extending its control over neighboring Laos and Cambodia. With its help, or rather under its direction, the Lao Communists seized total power in that country, abolished the monarchy, and set up a full-fledged Communist state by the end of December. On July 17, 1977, the rulers of this new state signed with the Socialist Republic of Vietnam (SRV)—new name for the Democratic Republic of Vietnam—a treaty establishing a "special relationship" between the two countries, as well as a boundary treaty whose terms were kept secret. In addition, the SRV maintained some 40,000–60,000 troops in Laos.

Attempts to exercise the same kind of control over Cambodia, however, failed. Moreover, a dispute between Cambodia and the SRV over the demarcation of the borders between the two countries, and suppressive measures taken by the Cambodian leaders against the pro-Vietnamese elements of the Communist party of Kampuchea (CPK), led to armed conflict between the two countries in 1975–1978, and to full-scale war in the late 1979. The SRV invaded Cambodia in force, occupied Phnom Penh, where, on January 8, it set up a puppet government under Heng Samrin, a Communist who had fled earlier to Vietnam to avoid liquidation by Pol Pot, head of the Communist government and party of Cambodia. On February 17 the SRV signed with the new Cambodian government a treaty that established between Vietnam and Cambodia the same kind of "special relationship" as that existing between Laos and Vietnam.

The blatant invasion of Cambodia and its total domination brought the SRV into conflict with China. Sino-Vietnamese relations had deteriorated since Peking reversed its policy of enmity toward the United States and invited President Nixon to China in 1972. They deteriorated still further after the CPV victory in 1975, which was followed by conflict between the two countries over the delimitation of their borders and over Vietnamese policy toward Chinese residents in Vietnam. Moreover, China strongly and clearly objected to Vietnam's total and exclusive control over Laos and especially Cambodia, whose government had placed itself under Chinese protection. Vietnam's massive invasion of Cambodia with some 180,000 troops was followed by Chinese massive attack along the northern borders of Vietnam in February–March 1979.

To forestall a Chinese attack, the SRV had earlier secured assurances of Soviet support, first by joining Comecon in June 1978, then by signing a treaty of "friendship" on November 3. The treaty contained clauses of a clearly military character and was obviously directed at China. The SRV had now placed itself squarely on the Soviet side in the Sino-Soviet conflict, and had become an enemy of China.

The SRV invasion of Cambodia and establishment of a puppet government there had another consequence: it brought the SRV into conflict with the Association of South East Asian Nations (ASEAN), in particular with Thailand. To secure full control of Cambodia, the SRV had to send troops to the Thai border. Sooner or later these forces would be involved in armed clashes with Thai forces. In such a situation, Thailand naturally had to seek the support of its ASEAN fellow members, as well as that of China. It obtained both.

Although some ASEAN countries, in particular Malaysia and Indonesia, feared and distrusted China and saw in Vietnam an obstacle to China's march southward, they could not refuse to support Thailand against Vietnam. This was a matter of principle as well as self-interest. The SRV's blatant invasion of Cambodia was an act of aggression, and what the SRV did in Cambodia could well be repeated against other ASEAN members.

The ASEAN governments therefore denounced the SRV's invasion of Cambodia in increasingly strong terms and demanded the withdrawal of Vietnamese troops from that country. On the other hand, to prevent the SRV from consolidating its hold on Cambodia, they extended diplomatic support to the anti-Vietnamese Cambodian government, and political and military aid to the Cambodian forces battling the SRV occupation troops.

In giving full support to Cambodia, the ASEAN countries had become de facto allies of China, with which, through Thailand, they coordinated their actions at the United Nations and elsewhere. With such support given the anti-Cambodian forces, the SRV could not hope to establish full control over Cambodia in a short time, if ever. The SRV was therefore getting bogged down in a long war in Cambodia, and likewise in Laos, where anti-Vietnamese forces backed by China and Thailand were also operating.

Involved in another protracted war, just after thirty years of already devastating war against France and the United States, the SRV could not continue for long and without total exhaustion without external help. And the only country from which it could obtain help for war to extend its power in Southeast Asia was the Soviet Union. But the Soviet Union would not give something for nothing. In return for its aid, Moscow extracted political and economic, as well as military concessions: full alignment on the Soviet Union's position in foreign policy, economic integration into the Soviet bloc through Comecon, and in particular, use of air and naval bases in Vietnam by the Soviet Union. The SRV had no choice but to bow to Soviet wishes. This introduced Russian military presence into Southeast Asia for the first time in history. It is clear, however, that even with extensive Soviet help, the SRV could not easily finish off Cambodia.

Meanwhile, the development of the country, which had seriously been neglected during the previous thirty years of war, could not be pursued successfully. After ten years of CPV rule, Vietnam became the poorest country in Southeast Asia, and one of the poorest countries in the world. The prospects of rapid, or even moderate, improvement were extremely poor so long as the CPV leaders persisted in pursuing policies that kept the SRV at war and isolated in the world.

It is against this setting that the foreign politics of the CPV must be considered. Particular actions taken by the CPV leaders at particular times in regard to particular individuals or groups of people especially must be viewed.

In the next two chapters, we examine the backgrounds and basic views of the men who were responsible for formulating and implementing CPV policy, first Ho Chi Minh, then the other leaders of the party.

2

Founder, Teacher, and Leader—
Ho Chi Minh

Ho Chi Minh has been acknowledged by his disciples as "the founder, organizer, teacher, educator, and leader" of the Communist party of Vietnam, as "the supreme leader" of the party, "the man who has guided it in its efforts to develop its forces and to forge its victories."[1] On the day of his funeral, these disciples, through the voice of Le Duan, secretary general of the party, vowed to become "worthy disciples of President Ho Chi Minh."[2] Thus even after his death, Ho Chi Minh continued to guide the CPV's thoughts and actions.

Without a good knowledge of Ho Chi Minh's life, thoughts, and personality, it is not possible to have a full understanding of Vietnamese communism. It is appropriate, then, to begin a study of the foreign politics of the Communist party of Vietnam with a study of Ho Chi Minh himself. This is not an easy task, for Ho Chi Minh, true to Lenin's teaching about the necessity of secrecy, always took great care to surround himself with mystery. Those who have devoted much time to the study of Ho's biography bemoan the fact that there are many obscurities and uncertainties concerning his life.[3] Some of these can now be eliminated thanks to recent Vietnamese publications,[4] but many others are likely to remain for some time.

EARLY YEARS

The uncertainties start with Ho's birth date. No one can say with absolute certainty when Ho was born. Several dates have been given: 1895, 1894, 1892, 1890.[5] But in 1983 two Vietnamese scholars, going through the French National Archives, section Outre Mer, stumbled on a letter written by Ho (then Nguyen Tat Thanh) to the French minister of colonies and the French president of the republic, on September 15, 1911, requesting admission to the French Ecole Coloniale (School for Colonial Administrators).[6] In the letter Ho stated that he was born in 1892. This is probably his real birth date, as, under French colonial rule, fraudulent declarations concerning one's personal data were severely punished.

Ho's name at birth was Nguyen Sinh Cung. When he was ten or eleven, according to Vietnamese custom, this name was changed by his father to Nguyen Tat Thanh (Nguyen who will surely succeed). This was one of many names, up to seventy-six, that Ho was to carry during his lifetime.[7]

The province where Ho was born, Nghe An, was reputedly one of the poorest in the country, and his village, Kim Lien, in the district of Nam Dan, was the poorest in the province. In spite of its gentle name, Kim Lien (Golden Lotus) had a high proportion of beggars. Ho's father, Nguyen Sinh Sac (or Huy), belonged to one of the poorest families of the village. Sac had become an orphan at the age of three and had to live with a half brother. Bright and hard working, he attracted the attention of a teacher from the village of Hoang Tru. Hoang Xuan Duong took him home, gave him board and education, as well as a daughter (Loan) in marriage when she was only thirteen. It was at Hoang Tru that Ho was born, the third of four children.

Nguyen Sinh Sac passed the *Cu Nhan* (master's degree) in 1894, but failed his *Tien Si* (doctorate) in 1895. He was to try again in 1898. To prepare for it, he took his family to Hue, the imperial capital. There, Sac and his wife led an extremely hard existence. Young Ho was to experience the pains, and especially the humiliations, of extreme poverty. In 1901 as a result of the death of his wife, Sac had to take his family back to Kim Lien.

In 1904 Sac passed the difficult examination and received the title of *Pho Bang* (doctor, grade II). It was the first time in the history of the village of Kim Lien that it had a *dai khoa* (highest degree graduate). Against traditions, Sac declined to join the mandarinate. This was the signal of a scholar's desire to keep his distance from the ruling authorities. But at the end of 1904, Sac was formally commanded to serve in the administration. He therefore had no choice but to go Hue, taking his family with him.

Ho, who until then had been tutored in Confucian studies, now received a "franco-indochinese" education. He was bright and eager to learn. In 1907 he was admitted to the prestigious Quoc Hoc College (National College).

During his stay in Hue, Ho came into contact with French civilization, in particular with the uglier side of colonialism. He witnessed the brutal and humiliating way in which the French treated the Vietnamese people, including students. This was to instill in him an intense hatred all his life, not only for French, but also for Western, civilization.

The time of Ho's stay in Hue was also a time of intense nationalist agitation and popular discontent. Ho was naturally affected by these events. In 1908 a widespread anti-high taxes movement broke out, and it took a nationalist turn. There was agitation among the students, who went on strike. Ho was among them. As a consequence, he was expelled from Quoc Hoc College in May 1908.

Meanwhile, his father was assigned as chief of the district of Binh Khe, in Binh Dinh province. Binh Khe was considered a difficult district, with a traditionally rebellious population. Popular discontent there was high in 1908, and Sac was considered lacking in firmness in dealing with it. As a result, he was dismissed. Afterward, he moved to southern Vietnam (Cochinchina), where he eked out a living by practicing oriental medicine. He died there in 1930. Ho was then out of the country. He never forgave France for what it had done to his father. He was to tell Louis Arnoux, responsible for watching the Vietnamese in France, during a meeting between the two men in 1920: "How could I ever forgive France for such crimes!"[8]

It is not clear what Ho did from 1908 to 1909, but in late 1909 he moved south, stopping at Binh Khe to visit his father. His next stop was Phan Thiet, where he got a job as a teacher at the Duc Thanh school in 1910. Some time late that year, unannounced, he left Phan Thiet for Saigon. There he did odd jobs, then entered the Ba Son trade school for the training of marine personnel.[9] Again, Ho quit after three months. And again, he did odd jobs to survive. But he was burning with the desire to go abroad, to go west, in order to see and learn. Being penniless, the only way he could do so was to enlist for work on a ship. And so, on June 2, 1911, Ho sought out the captain of *Latouche Tréville,* of the Messageries Maritimes Company, asked for a job, and was accepted. On the following day, he started work under the name of Ba.[10] On June 5, he sailed for Europe on the same ship.[11] He was not to see his country again for thirty years.

SHAPING IDEOLOGY

As noted earlier, on September 5, 1911, only two months after his arrival in France, Ho sought admission to the Ecole Coloniale. It is clear that, like every intelligent and ambitious Vietnamese, he was anxious to obtain an education by any means. Yet, one can speculate what would have happened to him and to the history of Vietnam and other countries involved with Vietnam—Laos, Cambodia, France, the United States, China, all of Southeast Asia—if Ho had been accepted to that school and had joined the ranks of those whom he was later to call "traitors" marked for the assassination squad.

Ho spent a brief period at Saint Adresse, Le Havre, where he worked as a gardener for the captain of the *Latouche Tréville* and took advantage of the respite to improve his French with the help of the French cook in the same house. Then he went out to sea again, visiting many countries of the Middle East and Africa, as well as the United States, where he briefly worked in a restaurant in Boston, and visited New York (Harlem and Brooklyn) and San Francisco.[12]

At this time, there was no indication that Ho had any revolutionary plan in mind. He still showed great respect and admiration for Phan Chu Trinh, who was a well-known reformist. His letters revealed a great sensitivity to international developments. Thus when World War I broke out, he wrote with great perceptiveness for someone with little formal schooling: "Five great powers are fighting one another. Nine countries are involved in war. . . . Destiny will reserve us many surprises and it is impossible to predict who will win . . . Japan seems to want to get involved. I think that in three or four months, the situation in Asia will undergo big changes. . . ."[13]

In the meantime, the main and urgent problem for a penniless young man was to work in order to survive. Thus Ho did odd jobs. He worked as a snow sweeper in a school; then as a boiler attendant in a workshop; finally as a cook hand at the Carlton, a high class London hotel, where he had the good luck of catching the eye of Escoffier, the chief cook, who moved him from dishwasher to pastry assistant.

Ho's main purpose in going to London was, however, to learn English. And English he did learn; he spent most of what he earned on English lessons with an Italian teacher. This was to prove a very good investment in 1940–1945 in South China, when, in the competition with other Vietnamese nationalists for control of the Viet-Minh, and especially for American support—a key factor in winning this control—his good knowledge of English gave him a commanding advantage.

As usual with Ho, one day he suddenly disappeared from London. There is no known record of what he did between August 1914 and 1917, but it is well established that he was in Paris on December 3, 1917. There his career as a revolutionary was to begin. On Ho's first days in Paris, we now have testimony of Michele Zecchini, a member of the Socialist party assigned to look after Ho by Paul Vaillant Couturier, a senior party member.[14] Zecchini met Ho for the first time in July 1918; Ho was then already on close terms with senior members of the party: Charles Longuet, Marcel Cachin, Paul Vaillant Couturier, Léon Blum, and Edouard Herriot.

Ho lived in a furnished room on rue de Charonne in Paris, and his security was precarious because he lacked the necessary military papers and the *gendarmerie* was searching actively for deserters and draft dodgers. Zecchini put him up with a Tunisian named Moktar in a small apartment in the thirteenth precinct, where Ho could hide while the party tried to obtain the necessary papers for him and while it checked his identity before admitting him to the party. To avoid the police, Ho had to stay indoors most of the time. Eventually, Zecchini found a small apartment for him at 9 Impasse Compoint, in the seventeenth precinct.

During this time Ho acquired a nickname that intrigued many of his compatriots, and it remained unexplained until Zecchini's revelation. The nickname was "Monsieur Ferdinand," used by Maria Leoni, a member of the party and later companion of the Italian communist leader Palmiro Toggliatti. Leoni was in charge of foreign workers, and therefore had much to do with Ho. What was striking about Ho, said Zecchini, was his eyes, "which literally popped at you" and which scared Leoni. They reminded her of a person in a cheap novel, an Asian criminal who, to escape the attention of the police, tried to give himself the appearance of a European and took the name of Ferdinand. One day, on returning from a meeting at the Palais Mutualité with Zecchini, Couturier, and Ho, she could not help confiding her fear to her companions. Everybody laughed, and Couturier said: "If that can rid you of your fright, why not call him Ferdinand?" Obviously, no one ever took the trouble of explaining this to Ho's Vietnamese companions.[15]

Ho made his living as a photo retoucher, first for newspapers, then for his own account. Contrary to widespread belief, Ho did very well and earned good money, according to Zecchini. At the end of 1918 he was admitted to the party.

Ho made his mark in the nationalist movement by presenting a petition to the Allies who were meeting at Versailles. That was in early 1919, and he took the name of Nguyen Ai Quoc (Nguyen the patriot), a collective pen name used by a group of Vietnamese nationalists in Paris (among them Tran Van An). The petition was not received by the Allies, but it was printed in the *L'Humanité* on June 18. Compared with the demands he was to make later, in 1945–1946, these were very mild, but in view of the conditions prevailing at the time, Ho's act was considered courageous and instantly brought him to the attention of the Vietnamese nationalist circles. Two years earlier, he had founded the Association of Vietnamese Patriots. Founding organizations was then, as for the rest of his life, his favorite tactics for tying up people.

In July 1920, through *L'Humanité,* Ho became acquainted with Lenin's "Theses on the National and Colonial Questions." This entirely changed his outlook, his life, the history of Vietnam, and much else. Ho's reactions to the reading of Lenin's theses have been much publicized. Ho himself has told how he was moved to tears, and alone in his room, shouted aloud as if he were talking to large crowd: "Oppressed and suffering compatriots, this is what we need, this is the road of our liberation. From that day, I have made my choice: I approved of the Third International, and completely followed Lenin."[16] Ho became then a total believer in Lenin.

For the rest of his life, Ho was to retain an unshakable faith in Lenin and Leninism, and instill it into his disciples. One of his last thoughts when writing his testament in 1969 was about the anticipated pleasure of going to a meeting, not with his Vietnamese ancestors, but with "the venerable Marx and Lenin,"[17] an obvious violation of the country's traditions.

In December 1920 at the Eighteenth Congress of the French Socialist party at Tours, Ho Chi Minh sided with those who voted in favor of joining the Third Communist International, becoming in the process a founding member of the French Communist party (CPF), and Vietnam's first Communist as well. He underwent a total transformation: from being merely a Vietnamese nationalist, to a convinced international Communist. National independence now became just a stage on the road to world revolution, and his first loyalty was to the Comintern.

In return, Ho acquired a base, and political, financial, and material support (refuge, travel papers, safe quarters, and operational facilities abroad, etc.). As revealed by Zecchini, immediately after his decision to side with the CPF "he had funds at his disposal to make speaking tours throughout France and the African colonies."[18] In April 1921 he began writing in the *Revue Communiste.* In October, with the help of the CPF, he founded the Union Coloniale. In 1922 he founded *Le Paria.*

1922 was to be the last year of what Lacouture has called "the first French cycle" of Ho's revolutionary career.[19] In the summer of 1923, again unannounced and secretly, Ho left his friends of *Le Paria* for an undisclosed destination. The destination turned out to be Moscow.

LIFE IN THE SOVIET UNION

Writing in 1967, Lacouture said that the date of Ho's departure from Paris and his arrival in Moscow were still "enigmas."[20] But, today, they are enigmas no more, thanks to Ho himself and to the CPV. In an interview by Charles Fourniau of *L'Humanité* in 1969, Ho was precise concerning his secret departure for Moscow in 1923.[21] With the help of the CPF, he left Paris for Berlin by train on June 18, 1923, disguised as a rich cigar-smoking capitalist traveling first class, after elaborate plans to deceive the French police agents assigned to his surveillance. He left Berlin on a Soviet ship on June 27 and registered in Saint Petersburg on June 30, according to the chronology of his activities in *Toan Tap*.[22]

Here, we should mention a very important fact: Ho's practice of deliberately misleading others. In his biography written by Tran Dan Tien, who was none other than himself, it is said that he arrived in Saint Petersburg without papers at all and had to wait there for some time until his identity could be checked out with the CPF members in Moscow, in particular with Vaillant Couturier, whose name he had given as a reference. Couturier came to Saint Petersburg to fetch him and bring him to Moscow. Ho said he arrived in Moscow "in the midst of winter," just after Lenin's death.[23]

In 1980 a book was written by Hong Ha on Ho's life in the Soviet Union.[24] Obviously, the author had been given access to the Soviet archives. He reprinted several Soviet official documents showing that Ho's trip had been carefully planned in conjunction with the Soviet authorities, and the Soviet mission in Berlin provided him with all the necessary papers, as well as arrangements for his travel to the Soviet Union. Under the name of Chen Vang, born on February 15, 1895, he received his papers on June 16, 1923, arrived in Saint Petersburg on June 30, "on a nice sunny day, with temperature of 18 degrees Celsius" and was lodged at the international hotel Astoria.[25]

Surely, those were major, even momentous, events in Ho's life. How could he have forgotten them? The obvious answer is that he wanted to give the impression that his arrival in Moscow was a fortuitous event and that he did not have so close a connection with the Comintern.

In Moscow, Ho worked at the Communist International and studied at the Lenin University.[26] He took an active part in the Congress of the Peasants' International (Kresintern) and was elected to the executive committee of that body. He stayed at the hotel International, later renamed "Lux," located not far from the Kremlin and reserved for foreign guests. It was there, on January 24, 1924, while breakfasting with a number of Communists from Asia, that he was stunned to hear the news of Lenin's death.[27] Ho was very grieved by this untimely death, for it deprived him of the great excitement of meeting his hero, and this, he said, had been "the greatest regret" of his life.[28]

In July 1924 Ho took part in the Fifth Congress of the Comintern as a delegate of the CPF. He made a long speech in which he insisted on the importance for Communist parties, in particular the CPF, to devote more attention to the colonial question. He was appointed a member of the eastern bureau "directly in charge of the southern bureau."[29] He also took part in the meetings of the International Workers' Relief, the Women's International, and the Youth International.

At the end of 1924, Ho was sent to China "to do work in the advisory mission to the government of Sun Yat-sen headed by comrade Borodin."[30] A Soviet study said that in the autumn of 1924, the executive of the Comintern instructed Ho to "arrange contacts between the Comintern and revolutionaries in Indochina. . . . as Comintern plenipotentiary in organizing revolutionary forces in Vietnam and the whole of Indochina."[31] Zecchini, for his part, revealed that before his departure, Ho had confided in a letter to Maria Leoni that "the Comintern had assigned him to be an interpreter to Borodin and to General Galep" (Vassili Blucher).[32] For his work in Canton, Ho took the name of Li Suei, and for his security, he resided in the Soviet mission's quarters.

From mid-December 1924, the time of his arrival in Canton, to mid-April 1927, the time of his precipitate departure to avoid arrest by the Kuomintang, Ho proved a very eager and good agent of the Comintern. He sent the executive committee and various agencies affiliated with it frequent letters containing reports, requests for instructions, or for funds.

Ho also lost no time in carrying out his assignments regarding Vietnam. In early 1925 he started the first training course for Vietnamese Communist cadres. In June he founded the Viet Nam Thanh Nien Cach Mang Dong Chi Hoi (Association of Vietnamese Revolutionary Youth) and a paper, *Thanh Nien*. He cofounded and became secretary of the Union of Oppressed Peoples of Asia. During that time, he set up the first secret cell of the CPV, with nine members. All this was duly reported to the ECCI. In a letter dated February 19, 1925, he asked for $5,000—a large sum at the time—to carry out his work. In the same year, he wrote *Le Procès de la colonisation française,* a scathing denunciation of French colonialism, in which he gave vent to all the hatred accumulated since his youth. In 1927, to provide study material to his students, Ho wrote *Duong Cach Menh* (The Road of Revolution).[33]

It was during this period that Ho allegedly betrayed Phan Boi Chau to the French police for 100,000 piastres.[34] Nguyen Khac Huyen, in his biography of Ho, speaks of "Ho's ruthless methods of operations and his readiness to sacrifice any man to achieve his objectives," and gives the following account of the betrayal. To finance his revolution in Vietnam, Ho needed funds. One day he came up with "a perfidious idea." He invited Phan Boi Chau to discuss matters of common interest and to attend the foundation of the Vietnamese branch of the World Federation of Small and Weak Nations. Full of hope and enthusiasm, Phan accepted the invitation. As he arrived at the Shanghai railway station en route to Canton to meet Ho, French agents, who had been informed about Phan's whereabouts, seized him and took him to the French concession in Shanghai.

By betraying Phan Boi Chau to the French police, Ho achieved the following purposes:

1. He got rid of an influential national leader, a dangerous rival to the Communists in their scheme of control of the anti-French movement.
2. He used ransom money for a good cause: the promotion of communism.
3. The arrest, trial, and execution of Phan Boi Chau would arouse the Vietnamese people against the French and intensify their resistance.

"This reasoning," says Huyen, "should dissipate any doubt one may entertain about Ho's ruthlessness."[35]

The story of Ho's selling of Phan Boi Chau to the French police has been naturally denied strongly by the CPV and its sympathizers. Thomas Hodgkin, for example, has called it "a fantasy, delighting the heart of . . . the counter-revolutionary academic cabal."[36] But David Halberstam, another sympathizer of the CPV, although attributing the idea to one of Ho's companions, does not exonerate Ho himself, for Halberstam says, "Ho gave his agreement."[37] And Bernard Fall, also a CPV sympathizer, has said: "Ho knows how to be pitiless when he deems it necessary for the success of the revolution, *his* revolution. The assassinations, not only of thousands of nationalists, but also of Vietnamese Trot-skyites are proof of that."[38]

Later in Ho's career, in the period 1940–1945, similar, although less spectacular maneuvers occurred to get rid of rivals to secure control of the nationalist movement. But in the meantime, in addition to the task of laying the foundations for the establishment of a Communist party in Indochina, Ho was entrusted with a second one: to report on the peasant movement and help establish a peasant-worker united front in China. In May 1925, with a number of Chinese Communists, Ho organized the First Peasant Congress of Kwantung and the Second Worker-Peasant Congress with a view to setting up a United Front of Workers and Peasants in China.[39] On July 31, 1925 Ho was entrusted by the executive of Kresintern with the mission of organizing the peasants of China and "a number of other countries."[40]

In April 1927, forewarned about an impending action of Chiang Kai-shek against the Communists, Ho secretly fled from Canton to Hongkong, Shanghai, and found a way back to the Soviet Union.[41] In June he was back in Moscow, then went to the Crimea for a period of recuperation.

FOUNDING THE PARTY

Ho did not stay long in the Soviet Union. In August he was sent to Berlin to help establish the Anti-Imperialist League. In 1928 he was sent to the Congress Against Imperialism at Brussels, then to Germany, Switzerland, Italy, and Ceylon. On his return from Ceylon, he went secretly to France; in the autumn of that year he was dispatched to Thailand.[42]

From 1928 to the end of 1929, Ho operated in Thailand among the Vietnamese population there under the guise of a Buddhist monk bearing the name of Thau Chin (Uncle Chin).[43] In late 1929 Ho was ordered by the Comintern to Hongkong to help unify the three warring Vietnamese Communist factions into a single party. He succeeded, and on February 3, 1930, the Communist party of Vietnam was born. In his appeal to the Vietnamese people following the foundation of the party, Ho himself said that he had "received instructions from the Communist International to resolve the problem of revolution in our country" and had successfully accomplished this task.[44] Moscow was pleased with Ho. According to Reznikov, "The Comintern emphasized the outstanding services of Ho Chi Minh as founder of the Communist party of Indochina."[45]

In addition to militating among the Vietnamese, Ho was also assigned the task of reorganizing the Comintern's network in Southeast Asia.[46] He was the only obvious candidate after M. N. Roy had fallen out with Stalin in 1927, and Tan Malaka, the Indonesian, had been anathemized as a Trotskyist in 1928.[47] And so, in March he was back in Thailand, and in April he went to Malaya "to carry out the mission entrusted to him by the Comintern."[48] He also went to Singapore and then to Hongkong. Soon, however, Ho was to fall on evil days.

On June 6, 1931 under the name of Sung Wen So, Ho was arrested in Hongkong by British police, on information supplied by a French Communist, Joseph Ducroux, a Comintern agent in charge of liaison between the CPI, Moscow, and the CPF, who had been arrested earlier in Singapore. Thanks to the energetic help of a British lawyer, Frank Loseby, who took charge of his defense, Ho was cleared for lack of evidence that he was an agent of the Comintern. But he faced the danger of deportation to Indochina where a death sentence awaited him, and where the French colonial authorities wanted him extradited.

Again, Ho was saved by Loseby, who helped him escape from the hospital where he was being treated for tuberculosis and go into hiding, first in Hongkong, then in Amoy. He stayed in hiding there for several months before moving to Shanghai to find a way of getting back to the Soviet Union. Vaillant Couturier, who happened to be passing through Shanghai, put him in touch with the Chinese Communists, who helped him get on a Soviet ship sailing for Vladivostok and, from there, take the train for Moscow.[49] That was in the spring of 1933. Meanwhile, Loseby, to distract attention from him, spread the news that he was dead. Colonial police heaved with relief, his comrades in the CPV cried, and Communists all over the world held memorial services.[50]

In October 1934, under the name of Linov, Ho entered Lenin School, reserved for Communist high cadres; at the end of the year, he entered the historical section of the Institute for the Study of National and Colonial Questions. From 1934 to 1938, Ho was to spend "the most peaceful and the most studious of his life."[51]

There has been a great deal of speculation to the effect that Ho was "in temporary disgrace" for his failures since 1930,[52] or that he had "fallen out of favor with the current Comintern leadership," that his authority over the CPV had declined, and this was "a direct consequence of the Comintern's adoption of ultra-Left policies" at its Sixth World Congress in 1928.[53] This view is contradicted by several facts.

First, as we have seen earlier, on May 12, 1931 the Eastern Bureau had sent Ho a letter congratulating him on the results of the Nghe-Tinh

Soviets and on his contributions related to the leadership of the CPV. Next, Stalin, in his report to the Sixteenth Party Congress in mid-1930, commended the experience of the Indochinese revolutionaries to other Eastern peoples. "When one recalls," McLane says, "that Stalin rarely made reference to the Southeast Asian colonies, some significance may be attached to his singling out Indochina in this instance."[54] Last, according to Nguyen Khanh Toan, who was in Moscow in the 1930s, Ho played a leadership role and controlled both groups of Vietnamese who were studying in Moscow at that time;[55] and the official chronology says that when Ho attended the Seventh Congress of the Comintern in 1935, he did so "as representative of the Far Eastern Bureau."[56] He was far from being "under some kind of preventive detention" in Moscow, as Huynh Kim Khanh has suggested.[57]

The truth is probably that at this time Ho was ordered to lie low for a while to put the police of the colonial powers off his track. For this reason, the news of his death in prison in Hongkong floated by Loseby was not denied in Moscow, where Ho had already returned in the spring of 1933. Second, because of the new threat to the Soviet Union represented by the rise of Hitler in Germany, the Soviet government was seeking a rapprochement with France, and it was considered impolitic to give the French government cause for suspicion by reminding it that there was a Moscow-backed Indochinese revolutionary on the loose.

According to Dominique Desanti, at the Seventh Congress of the Comintern, the presence of Chou En-lai and Mao Tse-tung in ECCI was noted, but Ho Chi Minh could be found under none of his usual pseudonyms. However, there was an Indochinese named Cha Yen. Plausibly, following closely on the agreements that the Soviet Union had just concluded with Laval, it was thought better not to place among the executive of the International the chief of the "Indochinese subversion" who had so many times been condemned to death by French courts.[58]

Desanti also reported that at the special section of the dining room reserved for important Communists at the restaurant of the hotel Lux, there was "an Indochinese, a former photographer from the XIII precinct of Paris," who each day shifted place because there was no napkin and that was the only way the man could wipe his mouth and his goatee with a clean cloth. His shifting was spread over thirty days, as the tablecloth was changed only once a month because of a shortage of soap. Although one Hanoi source said Chayan was Le Hong Phong, the references to "a former photographer from the XIII precinct of Paris," and to a concern for cleanliness—Ho's well-known habit—strongly suggest that the man was Ho Chi Minh and that he was an important figure in Moscow then.[59]

In addition to the theory put forward by Huynh Kim Khanh, there was another, suggested by Lacouture, to the effect that Ho "remained aloof" from the quarrels and the purges that were tearing up the CPSU and the International in the mid-1930s.[60] Ho thus emerged unscathed from Stalin's bloody purges of almost the entire leadership of the Comintern. Yet another theory is that Ho was himself a Stalinist and had the favor of Stalin. This theory is more plausible for two main reasons.

First, as early as 1924–1925, Stalin "bolshevized" the Communist parties by setting up alongside their leaderships a parallel apparatus composed of his own agents. Ho was surely one of these agents, as until his definite return to Vietnam in 1945, he was charged with important Comintern missions, never occupied a position in the CPV leadership, obviously played the role of a supervisor, and spoke with the authority of the Third International behind him.

Second, the CPV's resolutions frequently referred to Stalin, whose wisdom it praised, and in the drafting of these resolutions Ho had an important part. It is interesting to note this connection that Bernard Fall, after putting forward the Ho "in disgrace" theory in 1963 in *The Two Vietnams,* switched to this diametrically opposite view in 1967 in *Last Reflections on a War,* and said that Ho "probably was unconditionally loyal to Stalin, and Stalin knew it."[61]

That Ho Chi Minh had the confidence of Moscow has been confirmed by Reznikov, who wrote that Ho's services in training Marxist-Leninist fighters for his country were "exceedingly great," and the transition of the patriotic movement to Marxism-Leninism in Indochina took place "with the active assistance of the Comintern," which operated "in close contact with the great patriot and internationalist Ho Chi Minh." Reznikov added that the Comintern rendered its aid to the incipient Communist movement in Indochina "through the good offices of Ho Chi Minh," and the decisions of the Comintern relating to the activity of Communists and the liberation struggle of the Vietnamese "were drafted with his participation and sent to him first of all."[62]

In 1938 Ho was sent back to the East. A report sent by him to ECCI in July 1939 shows that he was charged with two missions, or, rather, one mission with two facets: help China in its fight against Japan—the immediate but secondary task—and prepare Indochina for the coming war against Japan—the most distant but more important task.[63]

The dispatch of Ho to the East followed the crucial Seventh Congress of the Comintern, which stressed the Japanese danger and which laid down the united front line for Communists all over the world.

Ho went to China, again, as in 1924, in relative security. The CPC, following the Comintern line of united front, was cooperating with the Kuomintang government, which Stalin strongly supported so that it could continue its fight against Japan.

Ho first stopped at Sian, then moved to Yenan. At this time, he took the name of Ho Quang (Hu Kwang). He stayed at Yenan for some time, then joined the Chinese Communist Eighth Army as a private, and moved first to Kweilin, where he was manager of the club of an army unit, then to Henyang, where he was secretary of a party branch in charge of radio monitoring.[64]

Ho's main aim was, however, to find a way to return to Vietnam. In 1940 under the name of Tran Vuong, Ho reached Kunming where, in June, he met Pham Van Dong and Vo Nguyen Giap. He advocated "maintaining close contact with the Comintern."[65] He sent Dong and Giap to Yenan to study at the Chinese party school there. But, on hearing the news of the capitulation of France, he countermanded the order and instructed Dong and Giap to backtrack, join him and a number of others at Kweilin to discuss the question of their immediate return to Vietnam to make preparations for setting up a base in the jungles on the Sino-Vietnamese border, and await the opportunity to seize power. Ho himself went to Chungking to discuss the situation with the central committee of the CPC.[66]

In December he was at Tsing Tsi, a small town on the Chinese side of the Sino-Vietnamese border. On February 8, 1941, he crossed the border at Pac Bo, in Cao Bang province. He was back in Vietnam, for the first time in thirty years. Ho immediately made preparations for the convening of the eighth plenum of the party to prepare for the coming seizure of power.

The plenum met on May 10–19, 1941, just over a month before Hitler launched his armies against the Soviet Union. Party documents stated that Ho convened and presided over this meeting "as representative of the Communist International."[67] The plenum decided that the immediate task of the revolution was national liberation, and the enemies against whom it must direct its forces were "the Nippo-French fascist aggressors."[68] It decided also, on Ho's proposal, to found the Viet Nam Doc Lap Dong Minh (League for the Independence of Vietnam), better known as Viet-Minh. This league was to "support" the Laotians and Cambodians in setting up similar leagues and form a United Front of Indochina.[69] At this time Ho took the name of Ho Chi Minh, which he was to use officially from then on.

On August 13, 1942, as representative of the Viet-Minh and the Vietnamese section of the International Anti-Aggression League, Ho went to China, ostensibly to pay his respects to Marshall Chiang Kai-shek, but in fact to contact the CPC in Chungking.[70] On crossing the border, he was arrested by Tai Li, head of the Chinese intelligence service. Ho was to be detained by the Chinese for thirteen months. He was taken from jail to jail in exhaustive marches and under terrible conditions. By cleverly manipulating the Chinese generals Chang Fa-kwei and Hsiao Wen and thanks to the interventions of Chou En-lai and of the OSS, he was released on September 13, 1943. Meanwhile, his companions thought that he had died in jail.

In March 1944 Ho attended a Chinese-sponsored Congress of the Viet Nam Cach Menh Dong Minh Hoi (Vietnam Revolutionary League) at Liuchow, and in July he was back in Vietnam. In October he issued a message to the Vietnamese to prepare them for the coming events. In December he was in Kunming to attend the Congress of the Alliance against Fascism.

In early 1945 Ho was back at Pac Bo. In March immediately after hearing the news of the Japanese coup against the French administration on the 9th, Ho convened a special meeting of the politburo. At this meeting, March 9–12, it was decided to change the slogan "Drive out the Japanese and the French" to "Drive out the Japanese" and to accelerate at all speed the preparations for the general insurrection. In May at the news of the capitulation of Germany, Ho moved his headquarters to Tan Trao in Tuyen Quang province, to be nearer Hanoi in order to better direct the planned coming insurrection. On August 16, two days after the capitulation of Japan, Ho held a national congress and launched the appeal for general insurrection to seize an opportunity "which occurs only once in a thousand years."[71] This was the start of "The August Revolution."

Within two weeks, power was in the hands of the Viet-Minh, that is, of the CPV. On August 26 Ho entered Hanoi in great secrecy. A provisional government was set up. On September 2 Ho declared Vietnam's independence and proclaimed the establishment of the Democratic Republic of Vietnam, of which he became president, a position he would hold until his death on September 3, 1969.

Although the rest of Ho's life is generally well known, the crucial period 1945–1946, one aspect of his activities, has been little noted in CPV publications; that is, his diplomatic activities aimed at obtaining material aid and political support for his movement from the Chinese, and especially from the Americans. Another important fact should also be mentioned here: from 1940 to 1951 Ho took great care to conceal or downplay his communism and his connection with international communism, in particular his association with Moscow. It was only when victory seemed certain, after the resounding defeat inflicted on the French forces at the Chinese border in the autumn of 1950, thanks to massive Chinese aid, that Ho publicly admitted his communism and proclaimed that the DRV "definitely stands" in the international Communist camp.[72] This is one of the basic elements of Ho's intellectual makeup and of his teachings to his disciples.

Ho Chi Minh was Vietnam's first Communist, but more particularly, he was an unconditional believer in Leninism, and with it, in the Third International. Ho had come to Leninism step by step, but once he thought he understood it and had made his choice, his belief was total, without qualification or reservation. As he wrote in 1960:

> At first, it was patriotism, and not yet communism, which led me to trust and follow Lenin and the Third International. But, step by step, through struggle and through the study of Marxist-Leninist theory, and through practical work, little by little, I came to understand that only socialism and communism can free the oppressed peoples and the workers of the world from slavery.[73]

From his conversion to Leninism in 1920 until his death in 1969, Ho never deviated from it, and he took great care to ensure that his disciples did the same. He constantly insisted that they did their utmost to preserve the purity of Leninism, in particular its basic tenets: world revolution and proletarian internationalism—always maintaining solidarity with the international Communist camp. This is one of the most important aspects of Vietnamese communism.

Ho's addresses to the CPV rank and file and to the Vietnamese people are replete with urgings and admonitions that they must know, understand, and remember what Lenin meant to Vietnam. Three days after Lenin's death, Ho said: "When he was alive, he was our father, our teacher, our comrade, and our counselor. Now he is the bright star showing us our way to the social revolution. Lenin will live for ever in our work," and the best way to express love for him would be "to do what he has insisted upon."[74] If the peoples in the West considered Lenin a teacher, the peoples of the East feel for Lenin deep love, respect him "like their father and mother," Ho said.[75] In Confucian Asia, this is the strongest expression of supreme respect and deepest love.

When Ho organized his first courses for the first group of Vietnamese in Canton in 1925–1927, to provide his students with study material, he wrote *Duong Cach Menh* (The Road of Revolution). William Duiker has said of this book that it was a "primer," in essence "a highly simplistic application of the Marxist revolutionary process to Asian society," and to those familiar with the complexity of the Marxist doctrine, his explanation of Marxist class struggle is "even more primitive," and his arguments are "simplistic, even misleading," but he adds that "they probably possess an inner logic for many frustrated individuals."[76] To judge from what Ho's disciples have said of it, this "primitive" little book had an immense influence.

The bulk of Ho's book deals with the future of the revolution. This is precisely the most important thing about it, especially from the vantage point of 1926–1927. According to Pham Van Dong, *Duong Cach Menh* has "laid the foundation of the future program of the party," and it has "a great influence on the future of the Vietnamese revolution."[77] *Duong Cach Menh* defined the general line and the strategy and tactical moves of that revolution. "In it, President Ho Chi Minh deals mainly with the radical revolutionary ideology. He points out that in order to live we must make revolution . . ."[78] *Duong Cach Menh* deals with "the qualities of the revolutionary," that is, with revolutionary morality."[79] This is perhaps the most important contribution of Ho Chi Minh to the success of the CPV. In the first chapter of the book, Ho said: "The arguments and hope of this book can be reduced to two words: Cach Menh! Cach Menh! Cach Menh!!!" ("Revolution! Revolution! Revolution!").[80]

THE HO LEGACY

One of the remarkable things about Ho Chi Minh is his great sensitivity to international developments. This sensitivity was heightened by his training in Moscow and through his contacts with the Comintern. In 1930 he already spoke of the coming second world war.[81] Ho's closest associates and students recall that they were astonished by his wide knowledge of international affairs, and in his conversations or lectures he always insisted on the necessity for them to pay close attention to international developments.

Two of the most important things in which Ho had learned to believe totally as a result of his training in Moscow were world revolution and proletarian internationalism. According to Ho's official biography, "He (Ho) has shown . . . that the Vietnamese revolution is an integral part of the world revolution, aligns itself on the Communist International, and has close relationships with the French revolutionary movement and the national liberation movement in the other colonies."[82]

Ho constantly insisted on the necessity for the members of the CPV to be imbued with the idea that the fate of the Vietnamese revolution is bound up with that of the international Communist movement, and in particular, with that of the Soviet Union. From the beginning, in *Duong Cach Menh,* Ho stressed that "to be successful, the Vietnamese revolutionaries must rely on the aid of the Third International."[83] From the day of the foundation of the party in 1930 to his death in 1969, Ho constantly reminded his disciples of the necessity of staying close to the Communist International, and of working hard to maintain the unity of the international Communist movement. In an article written for *New Times* (Moscow) in 1965, twenty-two years after the dissolution of the Comintern, he said that one of the lessons of twenty years of struggle was that "we must be absolutely loyal to proletarian internationalism."[84] One of his last thoughts before his death, in his testament, was the hope that the party would "do its best to contribute effectively to the restoration of unity among the fraternal parties on the basis of Marxism-Leninism and proletarian internationalism.[85]

At the same time, Ho insisted that they had international obligations, and must strive their hardest to fulfill them. Ho's official biography says that "in calling on our people to struggle for its sacred national rights, the president reminded them ceaselessly of their international obligations."[86]

From 1965 onward, the main international obligation became defeating "American imperialism." This was not only a matter of obligation but also of "honor and glory," Ho told DRV's national assembly in April 1966.[87]

In addition to the importance of internationalism, Ho told his disciples pay great attention to theory, for "it is only by adopting a vanguard theory that a revolutionary party can fulfill a revolutionary obligation."[88] In an address to the students of the first course on theory at the Nguyen Ai Quoc school in September 1957, Ho stressed the necessity of "improving our knowledge of Marxism-Leninism."[89]

Among the important lessons Ho taught his disciples, three others need mention. One is the need for secrecy. "Secrecy, never forget it, always secrecy: let the enemy think that you are in the West when you are in the East," Ho told Vo Nguyen Giap.[90] He advised his disciples to observe the rule of "three nothings" (see nothing, hear nothing, know nothing) when a stranger asks questions.[91] Nguyen Luong Bang recalls that Ho insisted on the need to remain undetected, and Ho himself took "all imaginable precautions" to erase all traces after him.[92] This goes a long way toward explaining why so little was known about Ho Chi Minh by his enemies, friends, or even companions.

The second lesson is the need to win a person's confidence first, before starting propaganda. In his training courses, Vu Anh recalls, Ho told the students that they must "win the sympathy of people before starting an organization."[93] And Le Manh Trinh recalls how, when he had trouble in propaganda work among the Vietnamese in Thailand, he was told by Ho that he must begin by winning the confidence of the people among whom he worked. "If you win the esteem of those people, Ho told him, you will succeed."[94] Ho himself was to apply this rule, with devastating effectiveness, in his relations with the Chinese, French, and Americans in 1940–1946.

The third lesson is the insistence on thoroughness and willingness to pursue a long struggle and endure sacrifices. Vo Nguyen Giap recalls that, while in China, in the preparation of courses for the cadres, Ho saw to it that the student was always asked the question: "After the first step, what is the next?" and if the second step was not clear in everybody's mind, "everything had to be done all over again, explanations as well as discussions."[95] Ho himself has said that as a professional revolutionary, his itinerary was "always carefully" planned.[96] He told his disciples in 1928 to expect that the revolution in Vietnam would be "a long march, full of difficulties,"[97] and in 1940 that "between the enemy and us, it is a struggle to the death, and we must endure everything, overcome the worst difficulties, fight through to the end."[98] He also told them to see "far and wide" and to "decide quickly, and decide at the right moment."[99]

Two traits about Ho are strictly his own. The first is his remarkable flair for avoiding disastrous action, or for the right and precise moment to seize a favorable opportunity with rapidity and decisiveness. As an example, one can cite two major cases. One is his stopping of the central committee's decision to launch a general insurrection in 1944. If it had taken place, the French colonial authorities would have crushed it and put the CPV back where it was after the Nghe Tinh Soviets in 1930–1931. Another is his decision to launch the general insurrection on August

16, only one day after the announcement of Japan's capitulation to the Allies. Like Lenin, Ho was a master of revolutionary tactics, and it is this rare quality that enabled him to exercise unchallenged authority in the CPV all through his life.

The second is Ho's personality, or his use of it, his personal strategy and tactics, in the manipulating of people, or the cultivating of a certain image of himself for the achievement of his purposes. What struck everyone coming into contact with him was the impression he generated: a frail, timid, seemingly harmless and vulnerable nice old man, "an awfully sweet guy," as the Americans on the OSS team working with him in 1945 described him. This was, of course, a totally wrong impression, as they were to find out after counting the costs—material, political, and moral—of a confrontation with him in 1965–1975. But the Americans were not alone in making this error. The French, too: politicians like Sainteny or journalists like Lacouture or well-meaning ordinary Frenchmen were conquered, "envoutés" (bewitched), to borrow a term used by Lacouture about himself.[100]

Ho obviously possessed a natural simplicity, and this surely helped. But he also engaged in deliberate acting and, in the long run, the acting somehow showed. Lacouture, for example, in spite of his bewitchment by Ho, has said that Ho practiced "duplicity with sincerity," that what was remarkable about him was "the inimitable mixture of wiliness. . . . and affectionate spontaneity."[101] Sainteny, another Frenchman bewitched by Ho and who was his strong defender for many years, eventually had second thoughts about his hero. Writing after Ho's death, he said: "At what moment did I face the true Ho Chi Minh? At what moment a personage made up for the necessities of the occasion was placed between us? Even today, more than twenty years after our first meeting, I find it hard to answer this question with certainty."[102]

What Ho could not hide also was his ruthlessness. As Nguyen Khac Huyen says in his biography of Ho: "Undoubtedly, Ho Chi Minh was one of the most cunning, ruthless Communists the world has yet known."[103] Bernard Fall's mention of how "pitiless" Ho could be has already been noted. Several other authors concurred. R. Harris Smith in *OSS* says that during the American OSS team's march with Ho's troops to Hanoi in August 1945

the Americans had a chance to see Ho's sensitivity, and his ruthlessness as well. As the entourage advanced, a group of Viet Minh soldiers moved ahead of the main body to make certain that all was "secure." The OSS officers later came across villages where buildings had been burned to the ground and village chiefs executed. They were told that the countryside had been ravaged by the retreating Japanese. But the Americans knew that the carnage had been carried out under orders from Ho to ensure the support and "cooperation" of the villages.[104]

However, as Philippe Devillers has noted, the resort to terror occurred as early as 1943. Through terror, says Devillers, the Viet-Minh was able to force the population in a large number of districts to join the party and help it its procurement of supplies, its movements, its work, and its gathering of intelligence. "Those who refused to join were looted and dispossessed; those who worked against the party by providing information to the administration were assassinated without fuss."[105]

General Yves Gras has given perhaps the best description of Ho Chi Minh as a person. Ho, says Gras, exercised on all who approached him "a strange fascination." He "concealed an inflexible will under an appearance of sweetness and gentleness." He was capable of the most delicate sentiments, and knew how to charm by his courtesy and his kindness, and, by his good-heartedness, play a reassuring role." He loved to charm. But he has shown himself to be pitiless, and to shrink from nothing, even from assassination, when the interests of the party and of the revolution were at stake. Duplicity is, definitely, clearly visible as the dominant trait of his nature."[106]

Nguyen Khac Huyen speaks of "two-faced Ho" and calls him "old fox."[107] This, no doubt, is the main reason behind the fact bemoaned by Huynh Kim Khanh and for which Ho had much to do: "The Janus face of Vietnamese communism has been the central difficulty of those who seek to identify its nature."[108] To all that, one should add that the really most distinctive feature of Ho's character is: he tolerates no opposition to his schemes. This can be summarized by Ho in his own words: "All those who do not follow the line laid down by me will be broken."[109] These words remind us of Lenin or Stalin!

3

The Party and Its Basic Thinking

Officially, the Communist party of Vietnam was founded on February 3, 1950, although, as in the case of its founder Ho Chi Minh, there have been uncertainties about the exact date, place, and circumstances. The Vietnam Workers' party (Dang Lao Dong Viet Nam) officially adopted February 3, 1930 as the date at its Third National Congress in September 1960. However, on two occasions, 1951 and 1957, Ho Chi Minh gave the date of January 6, 1930.[1] The discrepancy was probably caused by the mixing up of the lunar and solar calendars.[2]

The place and circumstances of the founding of the party have been the subjects of rather fanciful stories. Lacouture says that if one refers to "the most serious sources" of the history of the CPV, the party was probably founded "on the stands of the Hongkong Stadium while a soccer match was going on."[3] Bernard Fall said that the meeting took place in Hongkong, "in the bleachers of a stadium while a soccer game was in progress and probably went on for three weeks."[4] An article in *Tap Chi Cong San* in 1980 set the record straight. It said that the meeting took place "in the small room of a worker in Kowloon," and "lasted five intensive days."[5]

THE FLEDGLING PARTY

The Vietnamese Communist movement was actually born in early 1925, with the founding of the Vietnam Revolutionary Youth Association (VRYA) by Ho Chi Minh. In a letter to the ECCI on February 2, 1925, less than two months after his arrival in Canton, Ho reported that he had organized a secret group of nine members, five of whom were already candidates for membership of the party.[6] This was the secret *Thanh Nien Cong San*

Doan (Communist Youth Corps), which was to operate under cover of the VRYA. Between 1925 and 1927, Ho was to train some 200 other members, some chosen for further training in Moscow, and the rest sent to Vietnam to spread the Communist message there. Under the guidance of Ho Chi Minh, himself guided by the Comintern, these men were to be responsible for the introduction of Marxism-Leninism to Vietnam.

The circumstances leading to the founding of the CPV are generally well known.[7] After Ho Chi Minh became a member of the French Communist party (CPF) and of its committee on colonial questions in the early 1920s, he sought to plant the seed of communism in Indochina by having Communist literature smuggled into the colony by French sailors who were members of the CPF. According to Alain Ruscio, in 1927, on the initiative of the C.G.T.U., an organization called the Cercle international des marins (International Seamen Club) was founded. This club "played a central role in the smuggling of this subversive press" into Indochina.[8] Later, Ho could draw on the resources of the Comintern through Vietnamese sailors in Hongkong and Shanghai.

It was not until the late 1920s that the Communist movement in Vietnam really began to take shape, following a decision of the Sixth Congress of the Comintern in 1928 that a Communist party should be set up in each colony.[9] A number of the members of the VRYA were stirred to action by this decision. The first Communist cell on Vietnamese territory was formed in Hanoi in late March 1929 with the express purpose of working secretly to transform the VRYA into a Communist party through the convening of a national congress of the association.

The planned congress was held in Hongkong in May 1929, but the result was a split of the organization. Two rival Communist parties emerged: one was the Indochinese Communist party (Dong Duong Cong San Dang), formed in June 1929, grouping the VRYA members of northern Vietnam; the other was the Communist party of Annam (An Nam Cong San Dang), formed in October and grouping those of southern central Vietnam. In January 1930, the members of a nationalist party from central Vietnam, the Tam Tam Xa (Heart to Heart Association), decided to form yet another Communist party with the name of Indochinese Communist League (Dong Duong Cong San Lien Doan). All three parties sought recognition by the Comintern. Faced with this situation, the latter ordered Ho Chi Minh, who was then operating in Thailand, to bring together the three factions into a single Communist party.

The Comintern's instructions, set out in a letter dated October 27, 1929, were quite specific and peremptory. The letter said that a party must be set up "urgently" in Indochina, and this party must be the only one in the country. It stressed that "only the organizations which totally recognized the decisions of the Communist International shall be recognized as organizations belonging to the Communist party of Indochina and having the right to attend the coming National Congress of the Communist party," whereas the organizations that did not recognize the decisions of the Communist International "must be expelled." It also said that the party must be established before the meeting of the national congress, that "all the old names (Vietnam Revolutionary Youth, Tan Viet, and others) must be abandoned," that all the secret activities of the party and of the organizations depending on the party "must be carried out in the name of the Communist party of Indochina."

The letter finally enjoined the CPI to "stay in constant touch with the Communist International," to "establish contact" with the members of the Chinese Communist party in Indochina and "ensure their participation in practical and revolutionary work in Indochina," and "to maintain liasion systematically with the French Communist party and keep the latter informed of its activities."[10] This explains much of the politics of the CPV in later years, in particular its total obedience to Moscow, and its strong dependence on the Chinese and the French Communist parties.

Upon receiving his instructions from Moscow, Ho Chi Minh proceeded posthaste to Hongkong and convened a conference there on February 3–7, 1930. He had the full authority of Moscow behind him. As Milton Sachs put it, he had "a mandate from Moscow."[11] The result was the establishment of a single party.

In October of the same year, on order from Moscow, the name was changed to Communist party of Indochina (CPI), to make clear that the party covered Laos and Cambodia as well. This was the name carried by the party until it was "dissolved" in November 1945. This "dissolution" lasted until February 1951, when the party resurfaced as the Vietnam Workers' party (Dang Lao Dong Viet Nam), to be replaced again in December 1976 by that of Communist party of Vietnam (Dang Cong San Viet Nam). As we see in chapter 7, after 1945 the CPI was reconstituted in fact under another form. Meantime, it was recognized as an independent section of the Comintern by the eleventh plenum of the ECCI on April 11, 1931, and as a national section by the Seventh Congress of the Comintern on August 20, 1935.

According to an article published in *Le Courrier du Vietnam* in 1984, before its recognition as an independent section by the ECCI in April 1931, the CPV was a section of the French Communist party. The foundation of a Communist party for Indochina was suggested at a plenary session of the sixth congress of the Comintern on August 17, 1928, by Nguyen Van Tao, a Vietnamese who was a member of the Central Committee of the CPF.[12]

On the other hand, the Soviet author Reznikov revealed that in 1927 the VRYA requested the central committee of the Communist party of China to enable it to set up a Vietnamese Communist cell in Canton, but "the request was turned down." The CPC said that the Vietnamese "should first complete a national revolution," that the Vietnamese groups were still weak, and that "the Vietnamese would do better to join the Communist party of China." The Vietnamese repeated their request "several times more," but that they "invariably got the same response."[13]

On the relations of the French Communist party with the Vietnamese Communist Movement, Reznikov said:

> The Comintern section and its French Section maintained contact both with the League (VRYA) and with the Communists operating and extending their positions within it. In March 1927 a meeting was held in Canton in which representatives of the Comintern, the French Communist Party and the League took part. The last named was Ho Chi Minh. It was planned to hold a conference of representatives of communist groups functioning in Vietnam itself in December 1927 in Canton. But the delegates from Vietnam arrived from Vietnam in the city right at the height of the uprising of the Canton proletariat. So the conference did not take place; many delegates ended up in prison.[14]

Reznikov added that in May 1927 the ECCI eastern secretariat had prepared "the first recommendations to Communists in Indochina," advising them to unite the different groups into a single party. Ho Chi Minh played an important part in the drafting and execution of the decisions of the Comintern on Vietnam, as these decisions "were drafted with his participation and sent to him first of all."[15]

The growth of the party was rapid. When it was founded in 1930, it had a membership of 211. When it seized power in 1945, it had a membership of 5,000. In 1976, one year after it had taken South Vietnam, it had a membership of 1,500,000. Five years later, at its Fifth National Congress in 1982, the party had 1,727,784 members.[16]

PARTY LEADERSHIP

In addition to rapid growth, the CPV had a remarkably stable leadership. If we examine the memberships of the politburo in Table 1, we see that,

Table 1
Full Members of the Politburo

1984	1976	1960	1953	
1. Do Muoi	Le Duan	Ho Chi Minh	1. Ho Chi Minh	11. Ton Duc Thang
2. Dong Sy Nguyen	Truong Chinh	Hoan Van Hoan	2. Truong Chinh	12. Le Van Luong
3. Le Duan	Pham Van Dong	Le Duan	3. Nguyen Chi Thanh	13. Tran Dang Ninh
4. Le Duc Tho	Pham Hung	Le Duc Tho	4. Le Duan	14. Hoang Van Hoan
5. Pham Van Dong	Le Duc Tho	Le Thanh Nghi	5. Vo Nguyen Giap	15. Le Thanh Nghiem
6. Pham Hung	Vo Nguyen Giap	Nguyen Chi Thanh	6. Pham Van Dong	16. Tran Van Hoan
7. Truong Chinh	Nguyen Duy Trinh	Nguyen Duy Trinh	7. Le Duc Tho	17. Nguyen Duy Trinh
8. Van Tien Dung	Le Thanh Nghi	Pham Hung	8. Nguyen Luong Bang	18. Pham Hung
9. Vo Chi Cong	Tran Quoc Hoan	Pham Van Dong	9. Hoang Quoc Viet	19. Ung Van Khiem
10.	Van Tien Dung	Truong Chinh	10. Chu Van Tan	
11.	Le Van Luong	Vo Nguyen Giap		
12.	Nguyen Van Linh			
13.	Vo Chi Cong			
14.	Chu Huy Man			

apart from replacement of those who died, a dozen men had run the CPV practically without interruption until 1976, and continued to do so until the first big shakeup at the Fifth National Congres in 1982.[17]

Truong Chinh was first secretary from 1940 to 1956, when he lost his position as a result of his mismanagement of land reform. He was replaced by Ho Chi Minh. However, Ho held the position only nominally; the de facto replacement of Truong Chinh was Le Duan, who was confirmed in that position in 1960 and who held it without challenge—at least without *public* challenge—until 1979.

In 1979 it became known that Le Duan's authority, or at least policies, had been challenged by a number of members, some veterans of the party. The information came from Hoang Van Hoan, for many years a member of the politburo, an old guard party member, a man known to be close to Ho Chi Minh and trusted by him, a former ambassador of Vietnam to China, and vice chairman of the standing committee of the national assembly.

Hoan defected to China in August 1979 and denounced Le Duan and his "clique" in vehement terms. But that was after Ho's disappearance from the Vietnamese political scene. While Ho was alive, he was chairman of the party, and his authority was unchallenged. This is particularly true in the realm of foreign affairs. We examine this aspect later, after having dealt with matters related to the theoretical orientations of the party.

Ho had passed on to his disciples the "wonderful weapon" that he had discovered in Soviet Russia. It gave his followers a new faith, which was to guide them not just in the performance of the particular action (anti-French revolution) to achieve a particular aim (the national independence of Vietnam), but which would command their every action, their whole lives, and much more. This new faith was also, and particularly, to affect the whole destiny of Vietnam. It would impose on the Vietnamese people a world view that extended far beyond their national horizons and objectives that went far beyond their national aspirations, their national needs, and especially their national means.

The "wonderful weapon" was the bolshevik theory and practice. Bolshevism was a term for which Ho and his followers seemed to have a strong predilection, for they frequently used it in party documents between 1930 and 1939, and as late as 1955.[18]

The leaders of the CPV constantly repeated that their party was Marxist-Leninist and that the victories won by the party were victories of Marxism-Leninism. The Third National Congress of the party in September 1960 stressed that "The great victories of the past nine years. . . .

are the victories of Marxism-Leninism in a country oppressed and exploited by imperialism."[19] The August revolution was viewed as "the first victory of Marxism-Leninism in a colony."[20] In the same vein, the Fourth National Congress of the party (1976) said in one of its resolutions that the primary reason for which the party had been able to lead the people in the achievement of a grandiose revolutionary enterprise was that "above all it had Marxism-Leninism and has remained absolutely faithful to it."[21]

In 1982 the party issued a separate reprint of the political theses of its first congress in October 1930. The reprint carried an introduction that recalled that "right from its inception," the party was "an authentic Marxist-Leninist party," and that "today, our party continues to hold high . . . the banner which was already flying high from the day of the adoption of the theses of 1930."[22] This is a very significant claim indeed.

Let us now examine how Marxism-Leninism has influenced the CPV, theoretically and operationally. We focus only on those aspects that bear directly on the CPV's foreign politics.

When the Vietnamese analyze the world, like Asians with a long tradition of Chinese culture behind—or rather inside—them, they take a historical, long view. The Vietnamese Communists have followed this tradition. One can say that, partly at least, they were drawn to Marxism-Leninism because of this tradition. In addition to giving explanations that seem quite illuminating about imperialism and its connection with the wretched conditions of the colonial peoples, Marxism-Leninism takes a historical, long view of the world. It is thus with great intellectual, as well as emotional, comfort that the leaders of the CPV looked at the world through the Marxist-Leninist prism. Marx's view of history, with its emphasis on the inevitable evolution of mankind from feudalism to capitalism and socialism, and Lenin's view of the history of our epoch, with his prediction of the ineluctable collapse of imperialism, were sweet music to the ears of the leaders of the CPV.

Another point that deserves stress is that, if generally the Vietnamese intellectuals have a rather strong inclination for theory, those who have chosen the Communist road feel a still greater need for it, especially for a good theory for defeating French colonialism. Thus Lenin's statement that "Without revolutionary theory, there can be no revolutionary movement" has been elevated by the CPV to the status of "an immortal statement."

Of the two aspects of Marxist-Leninist theory—the pure aspect (theory as such) and the applied aspect (operational techniques)—Ho was interested essentially in the second. He preferred to think of it as "weapon."

To his disciples, however, Marxism is "the highest summit of human thought,"[23] or "the torch illuminating the way for the international working class, the oppressed peoples and the whole of mankind."[24]

It is then not surprising that the world's view of the leaders of the CPV was that of Lenin. In fact, this view seems to have been lifted out of Lenin's *Imperialism* and other writings. Thus, said Le Duan, mankind is going through the epoch of transition from capitalism to socialism on a world scale and

> the epoch when the class struggle to the death between agonizing capitalism and triumphant socialism, the epoch when anti-imperialist forces are rising up to make revolution, directly liquidate imperialism, making socialism triumph, first in several countries, then extending victory to other countries, until imperialism is swept away and socialism triumphs on the entire surface of the earth.[25]

The vision of class struggle to the death between capitalism and socialism on a world scale leads naturally to the view of a world divided into two camps. Speaking at the same congress, Truong Chinh said that great changes had occurred in the world since the end of World War II, and he painted the following picture of the new world:

> The socialist system is expanding and consolidating whereas the capitalist system is contracting and weakening.
> The balance of forces between the democratic camp and the imperialist camp has changed to the advantage of the former.
> The democratic camp has become the pillar of world peace and of democracy struggling against mongering imperialism . . .
> The socialist countries and the popular democracies have become more powerful and prosperous each day. . . .
> On the contrary, the imperialist countries have been going through a new crisis; to escape from this crisis, the imperialists are actively preparing for a new world war. At the same time, they are engaged in local wars in order to get rid of their stocks of arms and ammunitions and make it possible for the gun-makers to get richer.[26]

From this passage one can see how, rightly or wrongly, the leaders of the CPV viewed the world. Truong Chinh, let us not forget, occupied the key position of first secretary from 1940 to 1956; he was a leading theoretician of the party, and remained an important figure in the party's apparatus even after he lost his position in 1956.

The leaders of the CPV firmly believed in the correctness of their analysis and in the inevitable collapse of imperialism, just as they firmly
believed in the necessity of destroying it for the sake of peace, democracy, and freedom. Thus, said Le Duan, whereas the Socialist camp is
becoming "the decisive factor of the development of human society," the
general crisis of capitalism is entering a new phase and "world imperialism is going through a process of inevitable collapse,"[27] and it is "only
when socialism has triumphed on the whole globe that it will be possible
to suppress radically the social and national causes of all wars."[28]

In a world neatly divided into two camps, the choice of the CPV leaders
was unequivocal and firm. Said Truong Ching in 1951:

> The world is divided into two camps: the camp of peace and democracy
> and the camp of war-mongering imperialism. The Democratic Republic of
> Vietnam stands on the side of peace and democracy against the war-mon-
> gering imperialists. The Vietnamese revolution is an integral part of the
> world movement of peace, democracy, socialism.[29]

To the Vietnamese Communists, "the camp of peace and democracy"
means "the international communist camp," or "the Soviet camp," and
there is hardly any major speech by a leading member of the CPV from
which the sentence "The Vietnamese revolution is an integral part of the
world revolution" (or democratic camp) is absent. CPV leaders repeatedly
stressed that they fought for the victory of socialism on a world scale and
that they were proud to be the shock troops of the world revolution. As
early as September 1946, when the conflict with France still looked very
much like a fight only for national independence, and at a time when Ho
Chi Minh was trying very hard to avoid being associated with international communism, Truong Chinh said:

> it is not only for us that we fight, but for peace and democracy and national
> independence in the world. . . . the Vietnamese people have become aware
> of their international obligations in the post-war period. They are deter-
> mined to fulfill these obligations to the end, in spite of obstacles.[30]

And two years later, after the conflict with France had developed into
full-scale war:

> Our Republic of Vietnam is an integral part of the democratic forces of
> the world. More important still, it is a vanguard element of these forces
> . . . our people is shedding blood in the fight for its salvation and at the
> same time for peace and democracy in the world.[31]

Three years later, after the RDV had been recognized officially by Communist China and the Soviet Union, Truong Chinh was still more explicit: "At present, our country has become the forward post of the democratic camp."[32]

The Vietnamese Communists thus considered themselves essentially internationalists, proletarian internationalists to be exact. They never used the word "nationalist" when referring to themselves among themselves, but they did use "patriotism," which was always accompanied by "true." And to them, "true patriotism" was equated with socialism. "True patriotism is totally different from the "chauvinism" of the reactionary imperialists. True patriotism is an integral part of internationalism, so said Ho Chi Minh.[33] In 1976 after the reunification of Vietnam under Communist rule, Le Duan declared in his report to the Fourth National Party Congress: "Now that our country has become completely independent, nation and socialism are one and the same thing."[34]

In the eyes of the CPV leaders, since socialism and patriotism are one and the same, a Communist is perforce a patriot, and a genuine one, compared to Vietnamese who are not Communist. Thus Pham Van Dong said in 1960: "In our country, to be a patriot means to love socialism; patriotism is closely linked to socialism, and the communist is the most genuine patriot."[35] It follows from the CPV's assertion that, since patriotism is socialism and to love one's country is to love socialism, and since the Soviet Union is the fatherland of socialism, for a Vietnamese real patriot, who ipso facto must be a Communist, the Soviet Union must therefore also be his or her fatherland. Indeed, the resolution of the First Congress of the party at Macao in 1935 said that "it is necessary to make the masses understand that the Soviet Union is the Fatherland of the proletarians and the oppressed peoples of the whole world."[36]

Not only did the CPV leaders reject nationalism, but they took resolute steps to fight it, both inside and outside the party. The political platform adopted in October 1930 noted with satisfaction that the most important development in the revolutionary movement in Indochina was that the struggle of the masses of the workers and peasants was "no longer subject to the influence of nationalism as previously."[37] The same platform enjoined party members to fight "the narrow nationalism" that was prevalent in other organizations.[38] The resolution of the First National Congress in 1935 called for "the extirpation of the influence of nationalism among the peasants."[39]

Nationalism had to be fought and extirpated because it is "bourgeois," and bourgeois nationalism "cares only about the resistance of one's own nation and remains indifferent to the movement in favor of peace, democracy, and independence in the world," said Truong Chinh.[40] In a party document dated October 30, 1936, members were reminded that they must consider themselves internationalists and not nationalists. It said: "We follow internationalism, not nationalism. . . . the form of our struggle is nationalist, but the content of this struggle is internationalist."[41]

It was Ho Chi Minh who had brought many Vietnamese "from little bourgeois and bourgeois view of nationalism over to the leninist view of patriotism," said Truong Chinh.[42] On the occasion of the twentieth anniversary of the DRV, Ho told party members that they must be "absolutely faithful to proletarian internationalism."[43]

To be absolutely faithful to proletarian internationalism means, for the CPV, first and foremost, to carry out fully its obligations as a section of the Communist International, when this organization was still in existence (i.e., until 1943), and after that date as a member of the international Communist movement, which believed in Leninism, and hence in monolithism, and accepted the leadership of the Soviet Union. As Le Duan stressed in 1960, "the unity of the socialist countries is a monolithic bloc."[44]

The history of the party contains frequent reminders to the members that the party must respect the policy laid down by the Communist International and remain "a bolshevik party." For example, in a decision of the central committee plenum of October 1930, it was stressed that "from now on the party must be bolshevized . . .," and the party must carry out its work "in accordance with the decisions, letters, and instructions of the Communist International . . ."[45]

In a decision of the First National Congress of the party in March 1935, it was said that the success of the party was due to its adoption of "the correct marxist-leninist line of the Bolshevik party under the leadership of comrade Stalin."[46] The party was told to "preserve the purity of marxism-leninism," to maintain "iron discipline," and to "resolutely eliminate" the elements who went against the general political line of the party and of the Communist International and refused to correct their mistakes."[47] A year later, party members were reminded that "the Communist party of Indochina is a section of the Communist International; the ultimate strategy of the party is the strategy of the Communist International."[48] Ho's followers were told from the beginning (1927) in *Duong Cach Menh* that the congress of the Communist International had the power to "make decisions on all matters for the parties in various countries," that the national parties "must obey the orders of the executive committee," that the Communist International was "a world party," and that the Communist parties "must not act without orders from the Communist International."[49]

PARTY STRATEGY AND TACTICS

Let us now turn our attention to the question of modus operandi, of strategy and tactics. Here, even more than in their world outlook, the leaders of the CPV have shown how good they could be at absorbing Leninism, and particularly at applying it effectively, or as they liked to say, "creatively." To those familiar with Lenin's writings on strategy and tactics, the theoretical pronouncements of the CPV leaders seem to be merely reproductions of pages torn out of the major works of the Russian leader on those subjects: "What is to be done?" "Two tactics of social democracy in the democratic revolution," "Marxism and insurrection," and, in particular, "On compromise" and "Leftwing communism—an infantile disorder." This *internalization of Leninism* is particularly striking in the case of Truong Chinh and Le Duan, the acknowledged theoreticians of the party. For practically every statement made by them, one can find a corresponding one in Lenin's writings.

The first problem to which the CPV leaders applied Leninism was power. To them, the object of engaging in revolution was to seize power. As Le Duan said, "Marxism-Leninism teaches us that the fundamental problem of every revolution is the problem of power."[50] And Truong Chinh: "The essential aim of revolution is to seize power and consolidate it."[51] And Pham Van Dong: "Power is the essential problem of revolution. The purpose of engaging in revolution is to conquer power, conserve power, consolidate power. . . ."[52]

All CPV leaders believed firmly that "the only correct way" to conquer power is the use of violence. Said Truong Chinh:

> Since its foundation . . . our Party has asserted that violent revolution is the only correct way. . . . Our Party has understood very early and deeply the theory of violent revolution of Marxism-Leninism, and has consistently followed the path of violent revolution, which is the only correct way not only for the conquest of power but also for the defense of revolutionary power. [53]

Once the CPV leaders had decided that violence was the only correct way to conquer and hold on to power, there remained the question of what strategy to adopt for that purpose, especially in regard to the external aspect of the problem. But, first, how did they view strategy and tactics?

Revolutionary strategy has for its objective the overthrow of the enemy of the revolution "at each stage," whereas revolutionary tactics only aims at "winning victory in a struggle or at a particular moment," said Truong Chinh.[54] Revolutionary strategy is "the science of the knowledge of the enemy."[55] It must "determine the principal enemy, discern allies, elaborate plans for the development of the revolutionary forces, rally allies, and isolate in the highest degree the principal enemy."[56] For its part, tactics must "define exactly the line of conduct for each period, choose the form of struggle and organization, the propaganda slogans for each period and situation, and combine the various forms of struggle and organization . . . according to the ebb and flow of the revolution." Tactics is an integral part of strategy, to whose success it contributes.[57] We are very far from the usual military-oriented concepts of strategy and tactics!

The strategy favored by the CPV leaders was the offensive, step-by-step strategy. Le Duan described it as follows:

> . . . in the fight against imperialism, the revolutionary forces must put into action an offensive strategy, display extreme caution, advance with measured steps, give their action a degree of power corresponding to the concrete situation, that is, apply a mode of struggle consisting in forcing imperialism back step by step, in destroying it piece by piece.[58]

In this kind of strategy, whereas one must maintain the rule of strict intransigence as regards principles, one must at the same time practice "flexible and moving tactics" in order to "exploit fully the contradictions and differentiate to the maximum the ranks of imperialists, to isolate in the highest degree the most dangerous enemy."[59] Thus it will be possible to "force the enemy back step by step, enable the revolution to win one victory after another, defeat the enemy, and win complete victory."[60] In this kind of strategy, identification of the principal enemy is of extreme importance.

Once the principal enemy has been identified, he must be isolated and made the main target. In order to lead the revolution to victory, said Truong Chinh,

> . . . our Party must know who is the enemy to overthrow at each strategic stage (or sometimes at each period of a stage), it must constantly aim at the concrete and immediate and not at the enemy in general, isolate the immediate and principal enemy to overthrow him, exploit the contradictions in the ranks of the enemies to differentiate them in the highest degree, concentrate the fire of revolutionary struggle on the principal and immediate enemy.[61]

Furthermore, one must know how to concentrate the forces of the revolution to "attack the enemy at his most vulnerable point, at the moment when he least expects it." However, one must also know how, "in certain concrete circumstances," to go on the defensive, to discourage the enemy, build new forces, and prepare new offensives.[62]

The next step is to decide who is the principal and immediate enemy at a particular moment. He is "aggressive imperialism." But the aggressive imperialist is not always the same. From 1930 to 1936, he was "French imperialism." From 1936 to 1939, he was "the French Fascists and colonial reactionaries in Indochina." From August 1940 to March 1945, he was "the Japanese Fascists." From 1945 to 1954 he was "the French colonialists and also the American imperialists." From Dien Bien Phu (May 1954) onward, he was "American imperialism."[63] After 1978, a new principal and immediate enemy appeared, this time from the ranks of socialism. He was "the reactionary clique in the Peking ruling circles,"[64] "expansionism and great power hegemonism in mad collusion with imperialism."[65]

On the other hand, at each stage for each revolution, said Truong Chinh, the party must have in view "all the possible allies" in order "to rally those who can be rallied, neutralize those who can be neutralized, the essential thing being to isolate in the highest degree the concrete and immediate enemy and to gather together the large revolutionary forces to overthrow him."[66]

In regard to political alliances, however, there are "durable alliances for a whole strategic stage of the revolution, and temporary alliances for a given period of the revolutionary stage, and alliances for the purpose of neutralization."[67]

Related to the question of identifying enemies and allies is the question of knowing enemy and self. "We must be perfectly informed about the situation prevailing in the enemy's camp as well as in our camp," said Le Duan, and "correctly assess the enemy's intentions, activities and possibilities, and assess with precision the changes which have occurred in his ranks . . ."[68]

For the CPV leaders, if revolutionary violence is the only way to ensure the defeat of the enemy, this violence takes various forms: military, political, diplomatic. Of these, armed struggle is "the fundamental form of struggle."[69] It plays "a decisive role; it directly decides the annihilation of the military forces of the enemy," and "military victory is indispensable to guarantee the success of the resistance," said Vo Nguyen Giap.[70]

Political struggle is another "fundamental form of struggle"; it is the basis of armed struggle, and, at the same time, "a mode of offensive against the enemy . . . it unmasks and defeats the political maneuvers of the enemy, perturbs his rear . . . it is constantly combined with armed struggle and developed into armed struggle."[71]

Diplomacy is yet another form of struggle, a front to be coordinated with the political and military fronts to achieve complete victory.[72] To the CPV leaders, negotiation is not a method of settling conflicts by give and take, but "an instrument of political warfare," and more precisely, "a method of psychological warfare," says Henry Kissinger, who knows something about it after negotiating with the Vietnamese Communists for five years.[73] As General Giap has said candidly: "While delegations are discussing, we go on with the war."[74] On this front, the step-by-step strategy was also applied. This is what Sainteny, another negotiator with the Vietnamese Communists, calls "the policy of successive encroachments," of (moving up) "successive landings," and of "nibbling."[75]

It is natural that the CPV leaders' views on peace, compromise, and peaceful coexistence reflect their belief in the virtues of revolutionary violence. To them, peace is not a renunciation of war, the acceptance of compromise, but only the result of total victory. "We love peace, but not peace at any price, not peace by compromise. Peace for us could mean only total victory," Vo Nguyen Giap told Oriana Fallaci.[76] In the same vein, Pham Van Dong said: "Real peace must be based on the victory over the aggressor."[77] Since the CPV accepted nothing but total victory, for them there is no compromise either. "In a fight (against the Americans), there is no room for agreement. Either we win or we lose," says a captured document.[78]

One should therefore not expect the CPV leaders to accept real peaceful coexistence either. Indeed, peaceful coexistence was viewed by them just as a form of struggle that would permit the destruction of imperialism while avoiding a general war in which the Soviet Union would be directly involved. This is what the CPV leaders meant when they talked about "preserving peace." It is very important to keep this in mind, for since 1945 CPV leaders have constantly talked about peace, but since 1945, of all the nations of the world, Vietnam under their rule has been constantly at war.

The CPV leaders have been quite candid about their views. Peaceful coexistence is "a form of struggle" between socialism and capitalism, said Le Duan. This class struggle must be conducted "in every field— political, economic, ideological—but not in the form of war."[79] The aim of peaceful coexistence is to strengthen the Socialist camp, weaken imperialism and, eventually, destroy it through the intensification of revolutionary struggle in the capitalist countries, especially in the colonial and dependent countries. More specifically, said Le Duan,

> Peaceful coexistence does not mean the negation of the struggle between the two opposite social systems. . . . Neither does peaceful coexistence mean limiting the class struggle in the countries of the capitalist system or the movement of liberation of peoples against neo-colonialism and colonialism in the countries subject to the oppression and aggression by imperialists. . . . Peaceful coexistence is a form of class struggle between socialism and capitalism. . . .[80]

Thus peaceful coexistence does not mean accepting to live peacefully together, to recognize other peoples' right to exist, to live and let live. It only means creating the conditions that make general war between the camps of socialism and capitalism impossible, at the same time seeking to destroy capitalism by pushing forward revolution in different countries. In the absence of a world war, and even with the necessity of preserving world peace, said Le Duan, revolution can always break out and triumph.

It is in the zones of Asia, Africa, and Latin America that the intensification of the anti-imperialist revolution must be carried out, for this zone is "the converging point of a very large number of contradictions in the world":

> Here, imperialism has suffered, and is suffering the most violent blows. Here, an immense revolutionary force has risen up heroically, like a mounting tide. And here the apparatus of domination is relatively weak. Here the bourgeoisie does not possess a developed economy, or a strong political structure, a solid culture and a powerful organisation as in Europe and North America. It is clear that it is precisely in this zone of Asia, Africa and Latin America, which constitutes the weakest link in the imperialist and capitalist chain, that one finds the place which is easiest to pierce in the imperialist and capitalist chain.[81]

Peaceful coexistence thus does not contradict Lenin's thesis on the inevitability of war, and makes possible the continuation of the struggle against imperialism, more exactly "imperialism headed by Yankee imperialism," without putting the Soviet Union at risk; it is another form and a safer way of achieving the ultimate aim, which is "to build socialism and communism throughout the world."[82] The relentless pursuit of this aim, although it may not lead to general war, means involving Vietnam in ceaseless warfare.

When the Vietnamese Communists fight, they do so according to the doctrine of "revolutionary war." This doctrine, first expounded by Truong Chinh in 1946 and later developed by Vo Nguyen Giap,[83] is well known and there is no need for us to dwell on it here, except in one or two respects of special relevance to this study. According to this doctrine, the war will be a protracted, total, and revolutionary, a people's war in which the aim is total victory, no matter how long it will take and how high the costs.

The concept of protracted war, borrowed from Mao Tse-tung and adapted to Vietnamese conditions, is one in three stages: strategic defensive, equilibrium of forces, strategic counteroffensive. It seeks to prevent the enemy from exploiting his advantages, in particular, his superiority in weaponry and mechanized equipment, to generate division in his ranks, deprive him of political support at home and abroad, and in the long run, tire him and force him to give up. At the same time, the whole population of Vietnam is mobilized and its fighting spirit inflamed through the full exploitation of nationalism, and, in the case of peasants, who form the majority of the population and of the armed forces, through the exacerbation of their discontent. Over time, the enemy will become weaker, the revolutionary forces stronger.

Such a strategy will be costly to the country in terms of destruction, and to the population in terms of lives. But the CPV leadership viewed these losses with equanimity. In 1945 Ho Chi Minh said that he was determined to achieve his ends, even if Vietnam, from north to south, would be reduced to ashes, "even if it meant the life of every man, woman, and child."[84] A year later in Paris he warned the French that he would not shrink from a costly war, that it would be "a war of tiger against elephant" in which he was prepared to trade "ten Vietnamese for one Frenchman."[85] In 1946 Truong Chinh already evoked the somber prospect of "mountains of bones" and "rivers of blood."[86]

Vo Nguyen Giap, for his part, was unmoved by the thought of large number of lives lost and the length of time required for the achievement of his ends. To a French officer, Major F. F. Fonde, he said: "Destructions . . . what does it matter! . . . Losses. . . . a million Vietnamese, no importance at all. . . ."[87] And to Socialist Marcel Ner, he said: "Every minute, hundreds of thousands of men die on earth. The lives and deaths of one hundred, one thousand, tens of thousands of human beings, be they our compatriots, represents little."[88] In 1969 in his interview with Oriana Fallaci, he was asked: "How long will the war go on? How long will the people be asked to sacrifice, to suffer and die?" Giap replied: "As long as necessary: ten, fifteen, twenty, fifty years. Until we achieve total victory, as our President Ho Chi Minh has said. Yes! Even twenty, even fifty years! We're not in a hurry, we're not afraid."[89] This is national "kamikaze," but it could be very effective in a war against a nation with little patience and with a high price put on the lives of its citizens.

Sacrificing innumerable Vietnamese lives and fighting very long wars were naturally not sufficient for the achievement of the revolutionary aims that the CPV leaders had set for themselves. Other conditions had to be met. Three external factors were considered by them to be essential.

The first condition was *thoi co,* a Vietnamese term that can be translated as "favorable circumstances," or "opportunity." The CPV leaders realized that determination to fight and readiness to endure hardships were not sufficient for the achievement of their revolutionary aims. Ho Chi Minh did not really find the opportunity for using his "wonderful weapon" until 1945, more than two decades after he had discovered it. And when this opportunity finally came, it came not from inside but from outside Vietnam.

The second essential condition was international support, especially the support from Communist countries. Vo Nguyen Giap, who has been credited with many impressive military victories, said that they were due essentially to internal causes, but, he added, at the same time they were "inseparable" from the support and aid given us by the revolutionary peoples of the world. The world revolutionary movement had created "very favorable objective conditions" for the Vietnamese revolution, and from the first very difficult moments of its struggle "our people has always had the benefit of the support and aid of the brother Socialist countries and of the peoples of the whole world, directly or indirectly, from the political as well as material points of view."[90]

Pham Van Dong was more emphatic and more specific. He said that "none of our victories could be dissociated from the very considerable and very valuable aid and support of the USSR, of China and the other Socialist countries. . . ."[91] As part of the strategy of "encircling" the enemy and defeating him, the CPV leaders advocated the setting up of a "Front of the Peoples of the World."[92] The Fatherland Front was created for that purpose.

The third essential condition was the unity of the international Communist movement. President Ho Chi Minh had always taught us that "international union is a determining factor of victory for the Vietnamese revolution," said Le Duan.[93] This international union, in particular the union between the Soviet Union and Communist China is "a sine qua non condition for uniting the revolutionary forces of the world against imperialism . . ."[94] This factor is important, if not even more so, than "thoi co"; it is a matter to which the CPV attached "special importance."[95] And this was a vital concern to Ho Chi Minh until his last day, as reflected in his will.

Let us now turn to the men responsible for applying strategy and tactics in the party's foreign politics. There is little doubt that in the field of foreign politics Ho Chi Minh reigned supreme in the CPV, and that as long as he lived his views were his party's views, and his politics were the party's politics. Ho held the post of foreign minister from 1945 to 1947, with an interruption of seven months, from March to October 1946, during which time it was held by Nguyen Tuong Tam, a member of the VNQDD. That interruption was only apparent, for Tam was just a figurehead, and real diplomacy, in particular negotiations with the French, were conducted secretly and single-handedly by Ho.

In March 1947, Ho relinquished the post to Hoang Minh Giam, who had been deputy foreign minister. But Giam, too, was only a figurehead. A Socialist, he was used only for window dressing, to hide the Communist face of the Ho Chi Minh government, and also to give more comfort to the French Socialists, who were participants in the French government at the time. Giam's socialism obviously was very useful in this respect. On the official level, Giam continued to play the role of "constant intermediary" between Ho and Sainteny.[96] But Ho also used Giam in his dealings with the Americans. Patti called him "the pragmatic socialist-diplomat."[97] Diplomat, he was perhaps, but never a policy maker, and he could never be one, not being a member of the politburo, central committee, or even of the party.

In April 1954, Pham Van Dong was appointed foreign minister and head of the DRV delegation to the Geneva Conference. Dong was better known as an administrator. But as a member of a small group trusted by Ho Chi Minh, he was often chosen for sensitive tasks. He was picked to head the DRV delegation in the negotiations with the French government in France in 1946. In 1959 he gave up the post, which went to Ung Van Khiem, "a man remarkable for the gaffes he has committed," and who, apparently, was chosen not so much for his outstanding abilities as because he was born a southerner.[98] In 1963 Khiem was relieved, and the post went to Xuan Thuy, who had headed the foreign affairs section of the central committee and who was to be named head of the Vietnamese delegation in the Vietnam-American talks in 1968, merely a formal position, for the real negotiations were conducted by Le Duc Tho.

In 1965 the ministry went to Nguyen Duy Trinh, who was considered pro-Chinese and who, for this reason, lost both his position as minister of foreign affairs and as member of the politburo in 1982, in the second purge of the party. His successor was Nguyen Co Thach, who had been vice foreign minister and who was the most urbane of the CPV leaders, the nearest to the usual Western view of a diplomat, thanks to many years spent in New Delhi as representative of the DRV.

Among the members who played an important role in foreign politics of the CPV, one should mention Hoang Van Hoan, a veteran highly trusted by Ho Chi Minh. His association with Ho dated back to the Canton days. Like Pham Van Dong, he was charged with sensitive tasks; he was considered "the party's foremost expert on external affairs and international organizations,"[99] and the party's "principal advisor" on the Sino-Soviet dispute and "in foreign policy in general."[100] He was a senior member of the DRV delegation to the Geneva Conference in 1954, the DRV's first ambassador to China, and representative of the CPV to the CPC, a post he kept for eight years. He was also head of the international liaison department of the party, vice-chairman of the standing committee of the national assembly, and, naturally, until his purge in 1976, a member of the politburo, a position he had held for twenty years.

Hoan defected to China via Pakistan in August 1979, and from Peking, he wrote virulent denunciations of the "Le Duan clique."[101] It was the first open rift of the CPV, and from Hoan's statements, one learns that there were serious differences in the CPV in regard to foreign policy going back as far as 1968. This, however, did not seem to threaten the position of Le Duan. After Ho's death in 1969, Le Duan obviously became the policymaker of the party in foreign affairs, and his views seemed respected by his comrades. Major pronouncements on strategy and tactics in foreign affairs were made by him.

Of the other senior members of the CPV leadership, Vo Nguyen Giap confined himself to military affairs and shunned diplomatic questions. Truong Chinh, although no longer secretary general of the party, continued to make important, although only occasional statements on foreign policy. Another member involved deeply in foreign politics was Le Duc Tho, Kissinger's opposite number in the Paris negotiations. But Le Duc Tho is known to be more interested in the party's internal affairs.

The question of personality is, however, not a decisive one in the determination of the party's foreign politics, as the party operates according to the principle of collective leadership. In any case, as Le Duan has pointed out in the political report to the Fifth National Congress, the foreign policy pursued by the party for over fifty years consistently followed the Leninist line laid down by Ho Chi Minh.

Let us now examine how this Leninist foreign policy was applied in the CPV's dealings with different countries.

4

The CPV and the United States: Putting Special Friendship to Good Use

The CPV had its first dealings with the United States in 1944, but its first U.S. contacts can be traced to three decades before that. These contacts were made by Ho Chi Minh at the end of 1913 when he was seafaring. They are important because of their influence on Ho's, and therefore on the CPV's, basic perception of the United States.

Ho had clearly studied American history and was obviously interested by the American Revolution. For this reason, some authors have linked him to Lincoln and Jefferson. Colotti-Pischel speaks of Ho's "Lincolnism,"[1] whereas Lacouture asserts that there are "evident indications of intellectual and political links" between him and the United States. They cited as evidence the facts that Ho had "placed the birth of "his" republic under the sign of Jefferson" and that his journalistic and polemic writings were "vaguely inspired by the ideas" of Lincoln.[2] Such linking of Ho to Jefferson and Lincoln has important implications for Americans, for it makes America's war against Ho absurd politically and unjustifiable morally. But we are not concerned with this aspect here.

What is clear from a careful examination of Ho's writings is that he was interested mostly in the darker and uglier side of American civilization, in particular in the treatment of black Americans. In 1927 in *Duong Cach Menh,* after analyzing the American Revolution, he told his students to reject it because it was a capitalist revolution, and a capitalist revolution could not be "a completed revolution," because "nominally it was republican and democratic, but in fact, it was spoliative."[3] In 1945 Ho talked about the United States in glowing terms, but only with Americans and in private conversations; this obviously formed part of his efforts to seduce Americans to win U.S. support and recognition at the same time for the Viet-Minh, his front organization.

From 1920 to the foundation of the party in 1930, the few references Ho made to the United States were in connection with the situation in the Far East, in particular to the Nippo-American rivalry as a source of inevitable war. They reflected the analyses of the Comintern leadership, in particular concerning the Washington conference on naval disarmament and the situation in the Pacific. Ho's main specific reference to the United States is to be found in an article he wrote in 1924 in *Correspondence Internationale,* under the significant title "Lynching, a little known aspect of American civilization." Ho said with irony: "Execution by lynching deserves to occupy a place of honor in a file on the crimes of American civilization."[4]

Specific references to the United States by the CPV were also rare in the period 1930–1940. In line with Comintern thinking then, Japan was considered the main concern, whereas the United States was simply viewed as one of the fierce contenders for supremacy in the Pacific in the coming war among imperialists for the division of spoils.[5] It was only in 1944 that the CPV, through Ho Chi Minh, had much to do with the United States.

HO'S HANDLING OF THE OSS

From 1944 to 1985, the CPV's politics in regard to the United States can be roughly divided into five periods: 1944–1946, 1946–1954, 1954–1965, 1965–1975, and 1975–1985. For the purpose of this book, we focus only on the period 1944–1946, which is decisive for the history of Vietnam since 1945. It is centered on Ho Chi Minh's handling of the Office of Strategic Services (OSS) team, and especially of its head, Major Archimedes Patti.

On the diplomacy of the period 1940–1945, in *Vietnamese Communism, 1925–1945,* speaking of the Viet-Minh's conduct of relations with the non-Vietnamese anti-Japanese forces (the Gaullists in Vietnam, the American OSS in southern China, and the Kuominmgtang), Huynh Kim Khanh said:

> These efforts were part of the Viet Minh application of the National United Front to widen its circle of support and at the same time isolate its principal enemies, the Japanese and the Decoux regime. Although from today's perspective these diplomatic efforts appear to be a historical curiosity and, in terms of concrete material assistance for the Viet Minh, deserve no more

than a few footnotes, they help illuminate both the conditions under which the Viet Minh Front labored to power and the Viet Minh strategy in dealing with the international forces that shaped the destiny of Vietnam.[6]

Khanh added, however, that the Viet Minh's diplomatic efforts during the Japanese interlude "proved almost as important as the Front's political and military preparations at home," for if the Viet-Minh had been unable to win the confidence and concrete support of the other groups until the coup, "they began to meet with success after the Japanese coup," and subsequent relations between the Viet-Minh and the Allied forces in southern China "eventually helped establish Viet Minh authority among the population."[7]

Although this is broadly correct, to dismiss the diplomacy of the Viet-Minh, that is, of Ho Chi Minh, from 1940 to the Japanese coup of March 9, 1945, as "only historical curiosity" and deserving "no more than a few footnotes" is a view that does not correspond to the facts. Indeed, Ho Chi Minh's diplomatic exertions during this period played an important part in the seizure of power and the establishment of a CPV-controlled government in Hanoi in August 1945 before the arrival of the French, Chinese, and Americans, and this was the most decisive fact of the post-war history of Vietnam.

In August 1945 and thereafter, the CPV was in control of *a* government of Vietnam. What remained for it to do was to transform this government into *the* government of Vietnam. Since it had possession, and possession is nine points of the law, the achievement of this aim, although not easy, was made considerably easier and would be half accomplished in 1954 and fully accomplished in 1975. Then, it would have both possession and law on its side. A study of the CPV's politics in this period thus deserves more attention that has been given to it so far.

Two remarks should be noted at this point. I am not concerned here essentially with American policy; my focus is on the CPV's politics. And in this regard, CPV publications have said very little, if anything, on its relations, or rather on Ho Chi Minh's relations, with Americans during this period. Fortunately, there are two very valuable sources on Ho's maneuverings at this time: K. C. Chen, and Colonel (then Major) Archimedes L. A. Patti.

Chen has given many important details concerning Ho Chi Minh's activities in China between 1938 and 1945 in a searching study, and Patti was the American who spent more time with Ho Chi Minh and was told more confidences—sincere or calculated, true or false—by him than any foreigner at that time, and Patti's memoirs, published in 1980, are very probably the most important source on the CPV's politics, in particular on Ho's politics toward the United States, at the time.[8] I draw heavily on these two books in the following pages.

It may be recalled that to Russia, czarist or Communist, the Far East has always been a sensitive area, and Japan, a potential enemy. For that reason, developments in the Pacific were watched closely by Moscow. This was very evident in the Comintern's analyses relating to the Washington Conference.

With the rise of German and Italian fascism in Europe and Japanese militarism in Asia in the early 1930s, and especially after the conclusion of the anti-Comintern Pact in November 1936, a clear threat to the Soviet Union arose in the East. In its expansionist policy, Japan could move either southward, against the European colonial possessions and against the United States, or westward, against the Soviet Union. It was known that these questions were hotly debated in Tokyo in the second half of the 1930s. Moscow had to be prepared for both contingencies.

It is against this background that one should view Ho Chi Minh's return to China on the orders of the Comintern and his efforts to impress the Americans he sought to contact from 1940 onward and to help the Allies in the fight against Japan. However, to Ho and to the CPV leaders, *Allies* meant the Soviet Union. In fighting Japan, they fought an enemy of the Soviet Union, as ordered by the Comintern. The Americans did not know this; they only knew that the Viet-Minh was a movement of Vietnamese nationalists who wanted national independence and who declared at the same time that they wanted to fight Japan. For good reason, Ho Chi Minh and his companions carefully avoided telling them the whole truth.

Since there was no Soviet presence, nor even a significant Chinese Communist presence, in southern China after 1940, it was through the Americans that Ho was to seek to implement his plan for the double purpose of helping the Soviet Union and seizing power in Vietnam. Ho's objectives were: (1) to seek recognition for the forces under his control as part of the Allied forces fighting Japan, (2) to get material aid, in particular weapons and training, for his forces, (3) to prevent the return of France to Vietnam, and (4) to have the organization under his control recognized as the official and exclusive representative of the Vietnamese nationalists. In his relations with the Americans in Southern China over the next five years, he was to put Leninist tactics to good use for the achievement of his objectives.

Ho Chi Minh came to the formal notice of the Americans for the first time in December 1942, four months after his arrest at Tsing Tsi by the Chinese. This resulted from his companions' request, in the name of the Vietnamese section of the International Anti-Invasion League, to the American ambassador in Chungking to secure his freedom.[9] Ho was then in a Chinese jail and was to remain there until September 1943. During that time, the OSS, at the suggestion of Mao Tse-tung's representative in Chungking, intervened with the Chinese authorities to have him released so that he could be used in gathering intelligence in Indochina, for which the American forces in southern China, in particular General Claire Chennault's Fourteenth Air Force, had a pressing need.

Ho had actively sought to attract the attention of the Americans. He was a frequent visitor at the U.S. Office of War Information (OWI) at Kunming, Kweilin, and Liuchow, and he did part-time work with OSS and OWI officials in conducting Allied propaganda. In January 1942, he had applied for a visa to go to the United States, but his application was turned down by the State Department on the ground that he could not obtain a Chinese passport as required.

For its part, the OSS had been seeking authorization to use Ho and his organization for gathering intelligence and rescuing downed American pilots in Indochina. In mid-July, it approached Ho through his men in Kunming. Discussions were started for his cooperation, and Ho made it clear to American officials conducting these discussions that he wanted for his organization "official recognition at the highest level." Since using Ho was objectionable to the Chinese and the French because of his communism or nationalism, OSS decided to do it "subrosa."[10]

However, as a result of an order from President Roosevelt on October 16, 1944 to "do nothing" in regard to the resistance groups in Indochina, no concrete arrangement was arrived at until after the Japanese coup of March 9, 1945 had shattered all Allied intelligence networks there. This called for urgent measures to restore the situation. It was then that the OSS obtained authorization to use "any and all resistance groups." This cleared the way for the use of Ho Chi Minh and his organization, and the OSS did not wait to recruit Ho for its service.

On March 17 an OSS representative, Lieutenant Charles Fenn, met with Ho for the first time. Three days later, they met again and worked out details for Ho to return to Vietnam to help set up listening posts with OSS radios and OSS-trained Vietnamese operators. The Japanese coup thus represented a big chance—a "thoi co"—for Ho.

A still bigger chance for Ho, although with retarded effect, had occurred in November 1944, when a Lieutenant Shaw, an American pilot downed in Vietnam, was rescued by Ho's men. When he learned about this, Ho ordered that the American be escorted, not only to the border, but all the way back to Kunming. Ho had his own plans. He would use this rescue as a key to unlock General Claire Chennault's doors, and many others.

In his dealing with Americans, Ho Chi Minh exploited several factors to the fullest: (1) the Americans' instinctive anticolonialism, (2) their antagonism toward the French and their opposition to the restoration of French rule in Indochina—and hence to the return of French forces there, (3) their pride in their country's history and institutions, (4) their inclination to trust their fellow men and to consider a man innocent unless proved otherwise, (5) their pragmatism, and (6) their lack of political sophistication.

Ho worked very hard to plant firmly in the minds of the Americans with whom he came into contact that he was not a Communist, but simply a nationalist seeking the independence of his country and the betterment of the lot of his people. He also sought to generate the image of himself as a frail and likeable man, "a sweet little guy," an ascetic who wanted nothing for himself, in particular no money, but was working only in the interest of his country and people, and, naturally also eager to help the Allies in winning the war against Japan. The Americans found nothing wrong in all that.

After the Japanese coup had wiped out all French as well as American intelligence networks existing in Indochina, only Ho Chi Minh's network remained immediately available, and it had proved reliable. The OSS was delighted with it and naturally wanted to expand it by providing material and training for Ho's men. This is precisely what Ho had been seeking since 1940.

But more than the material and the training, Ho now got what he wanted most: visible association with the Americans. This opened up for him two big advantages: (1) getting material support and some sort of recognition, or the possibility of future recognition, and (2) use of the American connection to secure for the CPV—always under cover of the apparently innocuous Viet-Minh—control of the Vietnamese nationalist movement, and for him, undisputed leadership of this movement, a basic condition for seizing and keeping power later.

After direct contact had been established between Ho and the OSS, plans were worked out for his cooperation, first with Lieutenant Fenn in March and then with Major Patti, head of OSS operations in northern Indochina, in April. The OSS dropped men into Ho's jungle base at Kim

Lung in the Tuyen Quang area in July. A team, coded name "Deer," headed by Major Allison Thomas was dropped on July 16. It had half a dozen men who were to stay with Ho's troops for seven weeks and march with them to Hanoi, which they entered on August 25. To the Vietnamese population, Ho's propaganda apparatus presented these men as "Lien Quan Viet-My" (Joint Vietnamese-American Forces).[11] The Deer team trained some 200 Viet-Minh guerillas, including future generals Chu Van Tan and Vo Nguyen Giap, the first two DRV ministers of defense. In addition to training, the OSS provided Ho's men with arms.

There have been divergent views as to how many weapons the OSS had supplied to Ho's army. According to R. Harris Smith, Colonel Paul L. E. Helliwell, chief of the OSS in southern China, has denied that he gave "any significant assistance" to the Viet-Minh. He said that "OSS-China was at all times consistent in its policy of giving no help to individuals such as Ho, who were known Communists and therefore obvious sources of troubles." Yet, at an important meeting of American military and diplomatic personnel in Chungking later in April concerning Ho and his men, to the objection that "the boys at the Embassy don't like to deal with them. They are supposed to be Communists and anti-French," the same Helliwell had retorted: "Bull. If they are any good we ought to use them."[12] "Good" had different meanings for him and for Ho.

Helliwell admitted that he had sent Ho six revolvers and 20,000 rounds of ammunitions, but only "as a token of appreciation" for the rescue of American flyers, that he had refused to send other arms shipments to the Viet-Minh unless they agreed not to use them against the French, "a condition that Ho would not accept." Smith added the comment that "Helliwell, however, did not speak for all divisions of OSS. The course of events soon forced other officers of Donovan's organization to take a more intense interest in the Viet-Minh movement."[13]

Other figures have been given. According to Halberstam there are indications that some 5,000 arms had been parachuted to the Viet-Minh during the summer of 1945.[14] Patti said that the Thomas team trained "about 200 handpicked future leaders of the armies of Chu Van Tan and Vo nguyen Giap in the use of the latest American weapons and guerilla tactics."[15] This means at least 200 individual weapons, and at least some crew-handled weapons. This is indeed what actually happened. As Smith revealed, "the Thomas team was able to secure small OSS supply shipments of rifles, mortars, machine-guns, grenades and bazookas."[16]

Whatever the quantity of weapons supplied to Ho, he made big political capital out of it. At Tan Trao on August 16, at the Viet-Minh national congress, said Patti, the participants were treated to "discreet glimpses of well-uniformed, well-armed, and well-disciplined troops" of the Liberation Army, and "the American arms and equipment were new, of identical make and caliber."[17] Fenn has recorded the following story by a Vietnamese witness about the effect Ho made on other Vietnamese at a meeting thanks to his American connections and weapons:

> Since Ho was away so long there were rumors he had died. Others said he had gone to America. Then suddenly we heard he had arrived in Ching Hsi in an American plane. We could hardly believe it. Then when he arrived at base he had with him this Chinese-American [Frankie Tan] as well as a radio operator and all sorts of weapons, better than anything the French or Japanese had. Uncle Ho arrived very ill after his long hard walk. . . . over two weeks, walking only at night, raining most of the time. When he got well enough, he invited all the top leaders to a conference, not his own people, but rivals working for other groups, who had used his absence to push themselves forward. Ho told them he had now secured the help of Americans including Chennault. At first nobody really believed him. Then he produced the photograph of Chennault signed "Yours sincerely." After this he sent for the automatic pistols and gave one to each leader as a present. The leaders considered Chennault had sent these presents personally. After this conference there was never any more talk about who was the top leader.[18]

Fenn added that, soon after, the OSS dropped a load of supplies; radio sets, medicines, gadgets, weapons. According to Frankie Tan, an OSS member who was then at Ho's base, "this drop caused a sensation and Ho's stock went up another ten points."[19]

When Ho ordered the rescued pilot, Shaw, escorted to Kunming in December, asked for only six pistols from Helliwell, and an autographed photo from General Chennault during his visit to Kunming in March, he already knew exactly what he was going to do with them: prove his connection with the Americans and ensure his undisputed leadership of the Vietnamese nationalist movement. Furthermore, Ho wanted American help to build a well-equipped army.

Ho also sought to achieve another objective: winning the OSS completely over to his side so that they would become his propaganda agents. For this he worked very hard. He spent hours talking to the Deer team about the aims of his movement, about French misrule, about his admiration for America. He made enquiries about the wording of the American Declaration of Independence. But he took great care not to say anything about his ulterior aims. When discussing the French, he insisted that his movement was "only anti-Jap."[20] The members of the Deer team were "thoroughly impressed," said Patti, "even to the point of accepting Ho's assertion that it [his movement] was not a Communist movement."[21] Even Captain Lucien Conein, who was to become a well-known CIA agent in Saigon in 1963, "soon came to believe that Ho was a great statesman whose nationalism transcends communism."[22]

There was in particular the interesting case of Lieutenant Phelan, assigned as liaision officer between the OSS and Ho's organization. He had been reluctant to go on this mission because he had heard that Ho was a Communist. But, said Fenn, within a week of his arrival, Phelan was sending back wires to prove that "Ho was not in the least Communist: we had it all wrong." One of his messages said: "*re* deal with French you are misunderstanding Viet-Minh attitude. They are not anti-French merely patriots deserving full trust and support." It was Phelan who later told journalist Robert Shaplen that Ho was "an awfully sweet guy."[23]

Another member of the OSS, a civilian named Roberts, later in Hanoi frequently met with Ho, who constantly expressed his "friendship" and "admiration" for America. Said Smith, Roberts "had long concluded that Ho was a great and charismatic leader, a nationalist who was "above communism." He wrote the final report "strongly recommending American support for Ho and his national movement."[24]

Above all, Ho Chi Minh was successful in winning completely over to his side the key man among the Americans, Major Patti, chief of OSS operations in northern Indochina and the first American representative to land in Hanoi and to be present there during the crucial months of August and September 1945. Ho made a strong impression on Patti that was to remain even thirty-five years later, as is clear from Patti's memoirs. From their first meeting in the small village of Chiu Chou Chieh, at Tsing Tsi, on the Chinese border, on April 27, 1945, until many years after Ho's death, Patti was to remain a strong and steady defensor of Ho Chi Minh, whereas Sainteny, also favorably impressed in 1945, developed doubts about Ho afterwards.

Patti's reactions to his first meeting with Ho were very favorable. Despite the American's studied objectivity and purposeful awareness of not allowing himself to become involved politically in the Indochina question, he said, "Ho's sincerity, pragmatism, and eloquence" made an "indelible impression" on him. Ho did not strike him as "a starry-eyed revolutionary or a flaming radical" given to cliches, mouthing a party line, or bent on destroying without plans for rebuilding. Patti thought that "this wisp of a man was intelligent, well versed in the problems of his country, rational and dedicated," and he felt that Ho could also be trusted as an ally against the Japanese. As Patti saw it, Ho's "ultimate goal" was to obtain American support for the cause of a free Vietnam, and he felt that "this desire presented no conflict with American policy." From the practical viewpoint, Ho and the Viet-Minh "seemed to be the answer" to Patti's immediate problem of establishing operations in Indochina.[25]

At that meeting, as at later meetings with Patti, Ho retained the American until late into the night. He wanted to take all the time he needed to present his views and case to a man who, Ho felt, "after some probing," was sympathetic to his cause. Ho continued to "delve with gentle, tactful probing" to find out Patti's attitude toward the Vietnamese people and on the anticolonial issue. Patti wanted to "gain Ho's confidence" and "willingly participated in his dielectical jousting."[26] "Willing" is a term Patti seemed to favor to describe his attitude toward Ho. He was to use it again on another important occasion.

What impressed Patti most was that Ho did not ask for funds. He merely exposed the potential value of his politico-military organization, bided his time, asked no commitments. This was unlike the previous experience of the OSS, which was accustomed to pay for intelligence. Patti did not realize that Ho was playing for different and higher stakes. And indeed he won, for Patti concluded that "much good would come from that night's meeting."[27] For Ho, too, good would come; being associated with the Americans was the main thing he wanted. With the Chinese, he would play a quite different game, and accept, or even ask for, funds.

The Tsing Tsi meeting between Ho and Patti was followed by more elaborate arrangements for the dropping of arms, equipment, and instructors at Ho's jungle headquarters at Kim Lung in Tuyen Quang province. But Ho was to use the channels of communication provided to him by the Americans to play another game: diplomatic maneuvers against the French.

Only one day after Major Thomas's arrival at Ho's jungle base (on July 17), Ho asked the Americans to forward a message to the French to propose talks on the basis of a set of reforms. The proposal was repeated on July 25. Considering that the requested reforms were quite mild compared to what Ho was to demand later, or even to the Declaration of the French Provisional Government on March 24, one could wonder whether the messages were intended for American or French eyes, whether Ho was really sincere, or whether he was trying to give the Americans the impression that he was a reasonable man, and that intransigence came from the French side.

Whatever Ho's intentions, the outcome was in his favor: there was no response from the French. Sainteny had an explanation for this (see chapter 5). But, in the meantime, the Americans put the blame on the French. As Patti recorded his reactions:

> In so far as I could determine Ho's messages went unanswered and unacknowledged. . . . It is interesting to reflect. . . . that the modest demands of the Viet Minh, although obviously not acceptable to the French might have served as a convenient basis for negotiation. . . . The overwhelming evidence is that the French intransigence made attempts at negotiation quite vain.[28]

Ho had achieved his purpose, or reaped the advantageous result, of alienating the Americans, and in particular Patti, from the French or, since such incitation was not needed in Patti's case, in hardening his attitude toward the French.

Patti was apparently not aware that the reforms requested by Ho were obviously milder than the offers made by de Gaulle in the French declaration, or that in conversations with the members of the CPV from 1940 onward, Ho had spoken a different language and prepared them for "a struggle to the death." Later, at his first meeting with the French representatives in Hanoi, Ho would feign total ignorance of his July proposals (see chapter 5).

After his entry into Hanoi, Ho continued to work hard at winning Patti's allegiance, calling him "a special friend" with whom he could "confide" and showing him "personal regard" to which Patti was obviously sensitive, for it "moved" him.[29] Ho bestowed on Patti the special privilege, offered to no other foreigner and reserved to only a few very trusted members of the CPV, of revealing his secret presence in Hanoi after arriving there in August. He invited Patti to his residence for long *tête à tête*, made him privy to his plans, and consulted him on many matters, including Vietnamese national policy.

Through Patti, Ho sought to have the American authorities pursue their anticolonial policy in regard to Indochina. For this he must make them believe that he was not a Communist. Thus in several intimate conversations lasting well into the night, he sought, through Patti, who was willing to listen, to dispel the "misconception" that he was "an agent of the Comintern" or that he was a Communist. My willing attention provided him with the only channel to Washington available, and he took full advantage of it. He admitted quite candidly that he was a socialist, that he had associated and worked with French, Chinese, and Vietnamese communists, but added, "Who else was there to work with?" He labelled himself a "progressive-socialist-nationalist" with an ardent desire to rid his country of foreign domination. He spoke eloquently, not making a speech, but with sincerity, determination, and optimism.[30]

The above conversation took place on August 26 at Ho's secret hideout in Hanoi. On August 30, on the eve of his public appearance for the proclamation of Vietnam's independence, Ho had a second long heart-to-heart talk with Patti. And again, he brought up the question of the many "allegations" concerning his political affiliations. As Patti recorded:

Ho said he was aware of French, British, and Chinese charges that he was a "Soviet agent" and the Viet Minh was an extension of the "Moscow apparatus in Southeast Asia"; but the United States. . . . should not be concerned about the communist label given to his movement. He took the position that at that particular moment the Viet Minh was a "nationalist movement, democratically embracing all revolutionary parties." Of course, he admitted, the Indochinese Communist party was a leading element in the movement for national independence, but its members were "nationalist first and party members second.[31]

At a third and farewell dinner, on September 30, Ho brought up the question again. He told Patti that he still "did not consider himself a Communist but a national Socialist," and reflected aloud "how wrong he had been ever to believe that the French, British, or Russians would concern themselves with the Vietnamese problem." And Ho added what must certainly move not just Patti, but any American: "I place more reliance on the United States to support Vietnam's independence before I could expect help from the USSR."[32]

Ho said that the Americans considered him a "Moscow puppet," an "international Communist" because he had been to Moscow and had spent many years abroad. But, in fact, he was "not a Communist in the American sense"; he owed only his training to Moscow and, for that, he had "repaid" Moscow with fifteen years of party work. He had "no other commitment." He considered himself "a free agent." The Americans had given him "more material and spiritual support than the USSR." Why should he feel indebted to Moscow? However, with events coming to a head, he would have to find allies "if any were to be found," otherwise Vietnam would have to "go it alone."[33]

In order to attach Patti more securely to him, Ho played on the latter's sentiments as an American and as an individual. He told Patti that his people aspired to go outside Vietnam, "particularly to America" as he did long ago, that he looked forward to the day when Vietnamese students could study not only in France, "but also in the United States." He said he wanted American technical experts.[34] He asked Patti to carry back to the United States a message of "warm friendship and admiration" for the American people. He wanted the Americans to know that the people of Vietnam would "long remember the United States as a friend and ally" and that they would "always be grateful" for the material help received, "but most of all for the example the history of the United States had set for Vietnam" in its struggle for independence.[35]

The really big piece in Ho's scheme aimed at winning American goodwill and support, however, was his insertion into Vietnam's declaration of independence the famous sentence from the American Declaration of Independence; he showed it to Patti on the eve of its proclamation. Nothing was more convincing that Ho Chi Minh was not with Moscow, and nothing more flattering, even overwhelming to Patti, than the tangible, spectacular gesture of worship of American ideals. Ho began his declaration by reproducing the famous words from the second paragraph of the American Declaration of Independence of 1776: " . . . that all Men are created equal, that they are endowed by their Creator with certain inalienable Rights, that among these are Life, Liberty, and the Pursuit of Happiness . . . " Naturally, Patti was more than pleased. As the translator read the text to him, he said:

> I stopped him and turned to Ho in amazement and asked if he really intended to use it in his declaration. I don't know why it nettled me—perhaps a sense of proprietary right, or something equally inane. Nonetheless, I asked. Ho sat back in his chair, his palms together with fingertips touching his lips ever so tightly, as though meditating. Then, with a gentle smile he asked softly, "Should I not use it?" I felt sheepish and embarrassed. Of course, I answered, why should he not? . . . I was becoming uncomfortably aware that I was participating—however slightly—in the formulation of a political entity and did not want to create an impression of participation.[36]

Ho and his close associates, in particular Hoang Minh Giam, naturally on orders from Ho, sought to win over Americans in other ways, by dangling before them the prospects of economic, political, and even military advantages to the United States.

In the days following the news of Japan's surrender, recalled Patti, Koreans, Burmese, Thais, and Vietnamese waded into OSS offices in Kunming with reports, schemes, and proposals for various causes. Most prominent were the Vietnamese, all clamoring for preferential treatment and Allied support, especially American. The Viet-Minh spokesmen "seriously proposed making Indochina an American protectorate."

The Viet-Minh's central committee of Hanoi sent a note stating that it "wishes to make known to the United States government" that the Indochinese people desire "first of all the independence of Indochina" and were hoping that "the United States, as a champion of democracy, will assist her in securing their independence." It listed four requests aimed at preventing the French from re-entering Indochina by force, preventing the Chinese from looting and pillaging, sending technical experts to Indochina, developing industries that Indochina could support. It concluded by saying that the Indochinese would like to be placed "on the same status as the Philippines for an undetermined period."[37]

The four requests reflected what Ho would say he felt concerned about in his conversations with the Americans in Hanoi in the coming months. The Philippines was a theme that Ho had frequently discussed at his jungle headquarters with the men of the Deer team. He said then what he was going to say later to Patti, that he had "always been impressed" with U.S. treatment of the Philippines. "You kicked the Spanish out and let the Philippinos develop their own country. You were not looking for real estate, and I admire you for that," he said.[38]

The question of American technical experts, capital, and commerce had been raised by Ho, and especially by Hoang Minh Giam at their meeting with Patti on August 30. Giam was to raise it again at a meeting with Abbot Low Moffat, chief of the State Department Southeast Asian Affairs Division, in December 1946. It was the height of Franco-Vietnamese tensions, and this had certainly to do with Giam's remarkable proposal to Moffat. In addition to technical experts and capital, Giam dangled a really big carrot, the placing of Cam Ranh Bay at the disposal of the United States.

Moffat reported to the State Department on the mission undertaken on orders of Dean Acheson. He had a meeting with Ho Chi Minh, at which

Hoang Minh Giam was present. Ho said that his aim was "not communism" and if he could secure independence, "that would be enough for his lifetime." Tea was offered. Then Giam asked to talk privately with Moffat. They met at the U.S. consulate in the presence of Vice Consul James O'Sullivan. Giam presented Moffat with an autographed photo and a piece of embroidered brocade on Ho's behalf.

> Then he started to explain how Vietnam wanted free ports, and the right to trade freely; to get foreign capital where they would; they wanted American capital, commerce; they hoped an American airline would use Hanoi; an American shipping line would use Haiphong regularly etc.. . . . In short, he kept reiterating they did not always want to be "compressed" by the French. . . . He then stated that Vietnam had no navy and had no intention to be warlike, but would be glad to cooperate with the U.S. in developing Cam Ranh as a naval base, that it was a very important location between Singapore and Hongkong and opposite the Philippine Islands. . . .[39]

According to Harris Smith, Ho told a totally different story to the French. Sainteny sent a report to Paris in which he said he had obtained a piece of startling intelligence. He had learned that Patti had proposed to Ho that economic interests connected with the Donovan group would help reconstruct Vietnam's roads, highways, and airfields in exchange for economic privileges in Vietnam. Ho, however, had rejected the American offer. According to Sainteny, his source for this information was Ho himself.[40] This was obviously a continuation of Ho's tactics of pitting French against Americans, and vice versa.

So far we have seen how Ho had used the help of certain Americans, the OSS, and especially Patti, to achieve some of his major objectives. That help was conscious, deliberate, and dictated by deep personal convictions regarding both Ho as an individual and regarding the Vietnamese people's aspirations, which Ho was believed to represent. But there is another aspect of the American presence in Vietnam in 1945 that was also used by Ho. Certain acts, gestures, and attitudes of the Americans were unplanned, but had perhaps at least as many, if not more, momentous consequences in so far as helping Ho acquire more prestige, hence more influence, hence more power, and enabling him and the CPV to gain an early, big, and firm lead in the competition for control of the Vietnamese nationalist movement. Ho knew it and used it deliberately for the achievement of his own ends and those of his party in the coming crucial months.

THE CHENNAULT PHOTO

We have noted the case of General Chennault's autographed photo given to Ho. We must now examine this in greater in detail for two main reasons. The first is that it shows how Ho planned and executed his schemes, in particular how he exploited the innocence of certain Americans; the second is that it had a tremendous influence on the lining up of large numbers of Vietnamese behind Ho, thus enabling him to gain control of the nationalist movement at a crucial period in 1945. It is to Fenn that we owe the very illuminating story of Ho's encounter with General Chennault.[41]

Fenn said that when Ho ordered Lieutenant Shaw escorted to Kunming, he "could hardly guess that this action would prove the magic key to open doors otherwise impregnable."[42] Fenn was seriously mistaken, for Ho had a very clear plan in mind. He intended to use this rescue operation as a means to approach Chennault.

Thus, as soon as Ho arrived in Kunming in February, he "at once" endeavored to contact the Americans. He "particularly wanted" to meet General Chennault. But when he applied, Ho was politely shown the door. Nobody would credit his story about having engineered the escape of Shaw, and the latter had by then gone home. So Ho had to wait for another "thoi co." It came with the Japanese coup of March 9. The OSS, now authorized to use Ho's services, assigned Fenn to make contact with him.

When Fenn discussed concrete plans of cooperation on March 20, Ho insisted on meeting Chennault. Fenn agreed to arrange it on condition that Ho would "agree not to ask him for anything: neither supplies nor promises about support." Fenn arranged for Ho to meet Chennault "as the native who had helped rescue Shaw."

The meeting took place on the morning of March 29. Fenn took Ho to Chennault's office, together with Bernard, another member of the OSS. In Fenn's words:

> Chennault told Ho how grateful he was about the saved pilot. Ho said he would always be glad to help the Americans and particularly to help General Chennault for whom he had the greatest admiration. They exchanged talk about the Flying Tigers. Chennault was pleased the old man knew about this. We talked about saving more pilots. Nothing was said about the French, about politics. I heaved a sigh of relief as we started to leave. Then Ho said he had a small favor to ask the general. "Here we go boys,

hold your hats," was written all over Bernard's face. But all Ho wanted was the general's photograph. So he presses the bell and in comes Doreen [the secretary] again. In due course, it's some other girl who produces a folder of eight-by-ten glossies. "Take your pick," says Chennault. Ho takes one and asks would the general be so kind as to sign it? Doreen produces a Parker 51 and Chennault writes accross the bottom, "Yours Sincerely. Claire L. Chennault." And out we all troop into Kunming's sparkling air.

Fenn also says that before leaving for Tsing Tsi, Ho asked for "six new Colt 45 automatic pistols in their original wrappings" (Helliwell's six pistols referred to earlier). Fenn also points out that it was by waving Chennault's photograph "like a magic wand that Ho was later to produce a magnificent rabbit. But Chennault never heard about it."[43]

Chennault did not have the political sophistication of Stalin, who also gave Ho an autograph, but, suspicious of what Ho might do with it, had it stolen back from Ho's hotel room (see chapter 10). Fenn did not have the political sophistication, either, for imagining what could be in the mind of a clever Communist when he asked for an American Air Force general's autographed photo, or for six new pistols in their original wrappings.

Commenting on the Ho-Chennault meeting, Patti said that to be received by Chennault was very important in Ho's mind as "official American notice," but the inscribed photograph turned out to be of vital importance "only a few months later when he was badly in need of tangible evidence to convince skeptical Vietnamese nationalists that he had American support. It was a ruse which lacked foundation, but it worked."[44] The American view was again wrong, for Ho's use of the Chennault photograph, as well as the new pistols in their original wrappings, was thought out carefully and long before the event, and was not just a ruse resorted to in desperation at the last minute.

By the end of June, Ho's position had become very strong. To cite Fenn's testimony again:

> Thus it will be seen that these three months since the Jap coup in March 1945 were perhaps the most significant in Ho's career. At the beginning he had been the leader of a party that was but one amongst many: unrecognized by the Americans, opposed by the French, shunned by the Chinese; with no weapons and no equipment. He was also, at the time, cut off from his group by a formidable 600 miles and no chance of flying any part of it. By the end of June, he was, largely thanks to GBT, the unquestioned leader of an overwhelmingly strong revolutionary party.[45]

Ho's position was further strengthened at the key national congress at Tan Trao on August 13–16, at which it was decided to launch the general uprising that was to carry the Viet-Minh—and the CPV behind it—to power, and Ho Chi Minh to the position of undislodgeable leader of the nationalist movement. At this congress, Ho was "modestly silent but pleased at the delegates' curiosity and interest." said Patti. What with Chennault's autographed photograph in Ho's hut and those well-equipped guerillas "rumors were rampant that the Viet-Minh, and Uncle Ho in particular had secret Allied support."[46]

But there was more. The members of the Deer team assuaged their displeasure at not being allowed to disarm the Japanese by accompanying the Viet-Minh troops all the way to Hanoi. They thought they did so "only as observers," and they "probably were totally oblivious to the impression they gave of Ho's secret Allied support." When the congress concluded, the delegates went back to their homes all over Vietnam, carrying their impressions with them.[47]

The CPV deliberately made use of the Chennault autographed photo and the other American connections in a big way in their nationwide propaganda, stretching all the way to southern Vietnam. Madame Le Thi Anh, who joined the resistance movement in southern Vietnam in 1945, recalled the events of that time as follows:

> At that time we believed that Ho Chi Minh had the support of the Allies, especially the United States. . . . Ho had a photograph of the American general Chennault, with the general's autograph addressed to him, which Ho reproduced to show everyone. And even more important, Ho had several photographs of an American OSS team providing weapons and training to Ho's guerrillas in North Vietnam. We had been shown those photographs by Ho's communist guerilas in the south. . . . In the South we had heard that Ho had formed a government of national union in Hanoi and called upon all of the other nationalist parties to join him. We all believed that he had the support of the U.S. because of the photos. . . . Ho had sent these pictures south and his agent told us: "Do you want independence? We have to go with the victorious Allies. And Ho is the person who has the Allies' blessing.[48]

SEIZING LEADERSHIP

By using the same kind of tactics, the CPV was able also to seize the leadership of the nationalist movement in southern Vietnam. On August

14 the various pro-Japanese nationalist organizations and groups had formed a Unified National Front. But on August 22 Tran Van Giau, the Communist leader in the South, persuaded them to give up the direction in favor of the Viet-Minh. He argued that the Viet-Minh, which had the recognition of the Allies, would be in a better position for preserving independence in the negotiations with the Allied representatives who were due to arrive soon in Saigon. "Yielding to that subtle argument, the leaders of the nationalist parties decided to step aside and have their parties and groups adhere to the Viet-Minh which became a kind of broadened National Front." A provisional executive committee of South Vietnam was set up, of which Tran Van Giau was president. Of the nine members composing the committee, seven were Communists.[49] When they realized that they had made a mistake, it would be too late: the Communists' control of the nationalist movement would be too strong to be shaken. The same applied to Bao Dai.

In his memoirs, Bao Dai explained why he abdicated without a fight and without hesitation. He said that upon receiving a message from the Viet-Minh calling for his abdication, his reaction was:

> What is it, that Viet Nam Independence League, which has been able to mobilise crowds, give concrete form to their aspirations, and dictates my conduct? I do not know any of its leaders. And yet . . . .. They have contacts with the Chinese, American, French Allies, whereas my appeals to President Truman, to Generalissimo Chiang Kai-shek, to the King of England, to General de Gaulle have drawn no response. . . . They have arms, means; I cannot even rally my faithful, and people around me are hiding or intriguing against me. . . . [50]

Patti summarized the situation appropriately when he said that, in terms of August 1945, "Ho parleyed his narrow resources into a legendary success story," but it is certainly true, however, that Ho could not have succeeded if his CPI had not been well organized and prepared for seizing power. "Nevertheless, without the aura of American backing, the Viet-Minh might very well have failed to achieve national leadership at any step of their progression from obscurity to preeminence."[51] In all that, the OSS, and particularly Patti personally, had played a big part.

One may wonder whether Patti had acted in full conformity with the letter, and especially with the spirit, of the American government's policy, or whether he had taken advantage of the confusion prevailing in Washington, or the vagueness of the instructions sent to the men in the field to carry out a highly personal policy.

Even more than three decades after he had left Vietnam, and in spite of what had happened since the Communists took full control of Vietnam, Patti continued to maintain his position and to defend Ho Chi Minh vigorously. In his memoirs published in 1980, he shows how deeply he had been influenced by Ho. He wrote:

> "Whether Ho was a nationalist or communist should not have been the issue. The fact was that he was a nationalist first, a communist second. Ho was more concerned with Vietnam's independence and sovereign viability than with following the interests and dictates of Moscow and Peking. With American support Ho might have adopted some form of neutrality in the East-West conflict and maintained the DRV as a neutral and durable bulwark against Chinese expansion southwards. . . . Were it not for our "communist blinders," Ho could well have served the larger purpose of American policy in Asia. . . . Ho was forced into dependence upon Peking and Moscow by American opposition or indifference.[52]

As far as Ho Chi Minh and the CPV were concerned, the OSS had been an extremely useful instrument in the building up of their influence and subsequent seizure of power, and they exploited it to the fullest. But this instrument became blunted by mid-September, when, as Smith pointed out, the OSS officers were no longer "free agents" and "the days of influence of OSS" were drawing to a close. The American command in China was becoming "increasingly leery of the intelligence team's political associations." On September 27, Colonels Heppner and Helliwell, Patti's OSS superiors, made a visit to Hanoi and "quickly reached the decision" that Patti was "too closely identified with the past days of ill feeling" (with the French) and had to be replaced. Patti was relieved of his post and recalled to China.[53] He left Hanoi on October 1 after spending the previous evening, his last and a long one, with Ho Chi Minh.

The professions of admiration, friendship, and gratitude for America, so profusely expressed by Ho and his closest associates to Americans, and so easily believed by the latter prior to September 1945, now, in retrospect and in the light of what was said after that time, appear in a different aspect. Vo Nguyen Giap, who on September 2, 1945 had publicly spoken of "particularly intimate relations with the Americans," which "it was a pleasant duty to dwell on,"[54] expressed surprise in 1975 at Patti's attitude, saying: "Major Patti, for unknown reasons, showed his sympathy for the anti-Japanese struggle of the Viet-Minh."[55] The history of the party published in 1980 speaks of Chiang Kai-shek being commanded from a distance by "American imperialism."[56]

In particular, Ho's confidence to Bao Dai shows his true opinions of America when not talking to Americans who could be useful to him. As Bao Dai reveals in his memoirs, Ho told him one evening, in connection with his negotiations with the French:

> You see, Sir, I have been very disappointed by the attitude of the Allies. . . . The Americans, you have seen them with me. When I left China, their representatives made me promises, gave me assurances. To be pleasant to them, I have introduced into the Preamble of our Declaration of Independence the exact terms of Jefferson's Declaration of 1776. But what have we got from it? Nothing. . . . Their only concern is to replace the French, and that is the reason why they are in competition with the Chinese. Gallagher had accepted to serve as intermediary between us and the State Department and to present our demands. But, in return, he wanted freedom to organize our economy, in fact, to place us under their thumb. They are capitalists, they have it in their blood. To them, the only thing that counts is business.[57]

The thoughts expressed here are more like Ho Chi Minh's. Like an old horse returning instinctively and unerringly to the old road, here, Ho shows that, instinctively and unerringly also, an old Communist always goes back to his Leninist road. The first Americans who came into contact with Ho in 1944–1945 did not know this, because Ho Chi Minh did not want them to know, and the Americans who were far away could not know because the reports of their intelligence in the field pointed the other way.

There was something else the Americans did not know at that time. Apart from the objectives mentioned earlier, why did Ho Chi Minh give so much play to his American connections and to the anti-Japanese character of his organization?

The answer is rather simple: because Ho knew that the Americans were very popular in Vietnam at that time. The overwhelming majority of the Vietnamese had their eyes and their minds turned toward the United States. They felt that their hope for freedom and for a better life lay in that direction. With the exception of the members of the CPV, few, if any, Vietnamese looked to the Soviet Union, or even thought of the Soviet Union.

The Vietnamese, not just among the political groups and organizations, but among the population at large, were not anti-American. If they had accepted Japanese support, they did so as nationalists seeking aid—any aid, from any source—for the overthrow of French rule. It was a patriotic act, and they saw no contradiction between association with the Japanese and being on friendly terms with America and expecting American support. Their acceptance of Japanese support was in no way directed against America.

In spite of Japanese propaganda to the contrary, no Vietnamese in his or her right mind would think of Americans as enemies and would want to wage war against America. On the contrary, they looked to America as a liberator, but from the French, not from the Japanese, who were not their enemies. But being associated with Japan was, of course, impolitic after 1943, and especially after 1944 when the victory of the Allies was becoming obvious.

For their part, basically, Ho Chi Minh and the CPV had adopted an anti-Japanese position in support of the Soviet Union, not of the United States. The history of the party and the writings of the CPV leaders refer to the victory over Japan in the Pacific in 1945 primarily as a victory of the Soviet Union, and if they mention the Allies, they do not mention the United States by name.[58] And they exploited the political position of the other nationalist groups and organizations to the fullest, by denouncing them as "collaborators" and "puppets" of the Japanese Fascists, to stir up American ill will toward them.

On the other hand, they exploited to the fullest also their participation in the fight against Japan, although, in fact, there was little active participation on their part. "Rather than using his newly-acquired weapons to fight the Japanese, Ho Chi Minh saved them for future action against the French," says Turner.[59] And their action against the Japanese was limited to a raid against the post of Tam Dao on July 17. According to Devillers, "it was merely an attack carried out with difficulty by 500 assailants against a Japanese post of 40 men, eight of whom were massacred after 24 hours of fighting."[60] Indeed, the history of the party tells us that the CPV leadership was extremely cautious in regard to engaging the Japanese. An order from the politburo dated March 12, 1945 told the members:

The moment when the Allies land in Indochina to attack the Japanese will not be the moment for us to start the general insurrection immediately. We must wait for the moment when the Allied forces are able not only to hold their ground, but also to advance on our land. At the same time, we must wait for the moment when the Japanese move to the front to stop the Allies, leaving their rear unprotected; only then will it be to our advantage to start the general insurrection.[61]

This, just as the CPV's ulterior motives, the Americans did not know. They were hostile to the other nationalist groups and organizations, thinking that the latter were pro-Japanese, and therefore anti-American, and supported Ho Chi Minh and his organization, thinking that they were anti-Japanese, and therefore pro-American. This was a big error.

But the error enabled Ho Chi Minh and the CPV to accomplish more easily in 1945 two feats of which they were very proud, and which they frequently cited: the establishment of "the first workers' and peasants' state in Southeast Asia,"[62] and "the first victory of Marxism-Leninism in a colony."[63] By inventing a special friendship and putting it to good use, Ho Chi Minh served the cause of Marxism-Leninism well.

5

The CPV and France: Dealing with Bandits

Pham Van Dong has said: "we can have socialism only if we first have independence and freedom."[1] If the CPV wanted to follow the Communist road, it would have to try hard to recover Vietnam's national independence first; otherwise it could not freely practice communism and take Vietnam into the international Communist camp. That is why the Vietnamese Communists had to be fierce nationalists and stand visibly in the forefront of the fight against France for their country's independence.

This reasoning seems to be elementary logic, but a logic that, for many years, most people, Vietnamese as well as foreigners, failed to grasp because it is a two-step logic and, as a result of skillful Communist propaganda, they focused attention primarily on the first step—the independence aspect—and overlooked the second—the Socialist aspect—of the Vietnamese question. But a full understanding of this question requires that attention be paid to both aspects, especially in the light of what has happened in Vietnam and in Southeast Asia since 1975.

The CPV's politics toward France from 1920 to 1985 can be divided broadly into four phases and seven periods. Phase one covers 1920–1930; phase two, 1930–1939, and 1940–1945; phase three, 1945–1947, 1947–1954; and phase four, 1954–1975 and 1975–1985. For our purpose, the most relevant period is 1945–1947 because it is the most illuminating. We therefore focus attention here on this period and, to a lesser extent, on 1954–1975.

As in the case of the United States during this period, it centered on one man, this time a Frenchman, Jean Sainteny, the French representative who had most to do with the CPV, first in southern China and then in northern Vietnam. In particular, Sainteny would be responsible on the French side for negotiating with Ho Chi Minh the Franco-Vietnamese

Preliminary Agreement of March 6, 1946. Since Sainteny was the key French official, Ho would make a special effort to win him over by applying the special friendship tactics, just as he had done with the key American, Major Archimedes Patti.

CPV POLITICS, 1930–1945

Before examining Ho's efforts to win over Sainteny, it is appropriate to review briefly the main features of the CPV's politics toward France from 1930 to 1945. This policy obediently followed the twists and turns of the Comintern line, that is, of Stalin's policies.

In 1928, two years before the CPV (CPI) was founded, the Comintern, under Stalin's control, adopted a militant "class versus class" line. Accordingly, the program adopted by the CPI at its First National Congress in October 1930 advocated the overthrow of French imperialism, feudalism, and land owners, the confiscation of "all land belonging to the landowners and foreigners," the confiscation of "all large scale enterprises belonging to foreign capitalists," and complete independence of Indochina.[2]

The years of 1930 and 1931 were marked by the CPI's attempt to set up soviets on the Russian model, following Moscow's belief that the revolutionary situation in Indochina, as elsewhere in Asia, was mature.[3] The attempt resulted in bloody and devastating repressions by the French colonial authorities.

When, with the help of the Comintern, the CPF, the CPC, and the CPS (Communist party of Siam), the CPI had recovered sufficiently to become operational again in 1934, the Soviet Union was engaged in a westward shift, which was marked, in the case of France, by the signing of a non-aggression treaty in 1932, and the conclusion of a defense pact in 1935. In parallel, the Comintern had been moving toward the adoption of the united front line (the "Dimitrov line"), which was formally proclaimed at the Seventh Congress in 1935.

In France, a Popular Front government emerged in 1936. Its main concern was not fighting against imperialism, but against fascism. In Vietnam after some demurring, which was firmly smothered by the leadership, especially by Ho Chi Minh, the watchful eye of the Comintern, and Le Hong Phong, who had attended the Fifth Comintern Congress and learned first hand about the new line, the party dutifully operated a painful switch. This meant shelving the struggle against French imperialism.

Accordingly, the plenum of the central committee in July 1936 decided that

> If anti-imperialism and anti-feudalism, the tasks set for the Party since its foundation, remain unchanged, the direct and immediate objective, however, is not the overthrow of French imperialist power and the implementation of the agrarian revolution, but the struggle against French colonial reactionaries, the servants of the imperialists, and the demand for democratic freedoms and the improvement of living conditions.[4]

Until 1940, and, indeed, until 1947, the struggle for the overthrow of French colonialism, as essential and immediate task, was shelved, or at least soft-pedaled, to make way for tasks considered more urgent by the Comintern. The plenum of the central committee resolved on March 30, 1938 that "our task at present is to do everything in our power to establish a democratic front."[5] On October 29, 1938, the party issued a declaration calling for "the strengthening of the defenses of Indochina against fascism."[6] Ho Chi Minh urged the party to adopt a moderate line and shelve the issue of independence. He said: "At present, the party should not make excessive demands (national independence, assembly etc . . .) because that would play into the hands of Japanese fascism."[7]

After the signing of the German-Soviet treaty in August 1939, the line switched again. The war that had broken out on September 3 became an imperialist war. Good Communists must therefore not only refuse to participate in the national war effort, but they must also fight their own governments. For the CPI, it was therefore perfectly legitimate to agitate against the French authorities.

Accordingly, a resolution of the central committee on November 9, 1939 stated that "now the situation has changed completely," as "French imperialism at present is a criminal who is starting the world imperialist war." In Indochina, the current French policy was considered clearly "militarist Fascist"; and in regard to Japan it was capitulatory. For the peoples of Indochina, there was "no choice other than the overthrow of French imperialism and all foreign invaders," whether their skin was white or yellow (a reference to the Japanese). The resolution called for the setting up of an Indochinese National United Front against Imperialism and Fascism, whose aims would be to overthrow French imperialism and win total independence for Indochina.[8]

On November 9, 1940, after the French colonial authorities in Indochina had capitulated to Japanese demands, the central committee passed a resolution stating that "the principal enemy of the Indochinese peoples at this moment is French-Japanese imperialism," and called for the establishment of a Anti-Imperialist National United Front, whose aim would be to overthrow French-Japanese imperialism by armed violence, to win total independence for Indochina, and to set up an Indochinese Democratic Republican Federation.[9]

After the Soviet Union became involved in the war in June 1941, for the CPV the struggle again became a fight against fascism. The position adopted by the party at its important eighth plenum in May 1941 was, however, not modified, as it suited the new situation very well. It said that "the Indochinese revolution is a component of the world revolution, and in the present phase, it is a component of democracy fighting fascism."[10]

From the moment the Soviet Union was involved in the war and became automatically an ally of France, or more exactly of the Gaullist forces whose Free French National Committee was recognized by Stalin on September 26, 1941, the United Front line and World Democratic Front were applicable again. For the CPV, the war had become a war of democracy against fascism. But it faced a dilemma regarding France. Since the latter was an ally of the Soviet Union and a member of the World Democratic Front against fascism, fighting France would be going against the United Front line.

The dilemma was fortunately solved for the CPV by the Vichy government when it ordered the French authorities in Indochina to yield to Japanese demands. In Indochina the fight against the French authorities became perfectly legitimate, as the French there had become, in fact, allies of Japan and part of the Fascist camp; on the other hand, by occupying Indochina Japan became the real colonial master of Indochina. So, for the CPV, it was a matter of killing two birds with one stone: their struggle was a fight against both French and Japanese fascism for both the independence of Indochina and the implementation of Comintern policy, the latter being the primary aim.

The CPV continued to apply the anti-French-Japanese fascism line until March 9, 1945, when Japan became the sovereign power in Indochina after its coup against the French authorities. As a result of this new situation, on March 12, the politburo issued directives telling members to consider that from then on "the principal, concrete, and only enemy of the peoples of Indochina is Japanese imperialism and fascism." The Frenchmen who fought the Japanese became "objective allies."[11] The slogan "Kick the French and the Japanese out" was replaced by "Kick the

Japanese Fascists out."[12] From then on began a new phase, during which the CPV, and particularly Ho Chi Minh, displayed their manipulative skill in dealing with the French.

Until Ho was contacted in March by the OSS and his men began to receive arms and training in July 1945, he had only two possible sources of aid: Chinese and French. The politburo declared its readiness to "join hands" with the French fighting Japan and called on them to provide the party with arms.[13] On July 2, two weeks before the Deer team dropped into Ho's headquarters, the Viet-Minh (i.e., CPV) representative at Soc Giang on the Chinese border met with a French officer, Major Revol, to discuss common action against the Japanese. The Viet-Minh representative asked for two months to state his party's position, but, in the meantime, he asked for French weapons and instructors for their organization.[14]

It was on this occasion that the question of a meeting between the chief of the Viet-Minh and the chief of the French military mission was raised. On July 17, two weeks before this meeting, Ho Chi Minh had asked the Deer team to transmit a message to the French authorities in southern China suggesting discussions on the basis of five requests. The message said:

> We the V.M.L. request the following points be made public by the French and incorporated into the future policy of French-Indochina:
> 1. That there be universal suffrage to elect a parliament for the governing of the country, that there be a governor general as president until such time as independence be granted us; that he choose a cabinet or group of advisers acceptable to that parliament. Exact powers of all these officers may be discussed in the future.
> 2. That independence be given this country in not less than five years and not more than ten.
> 3. That natural resources of the country be returned to the people of the country by just payment to the present owners, and that France be granted economic concessions.
> 4. That all freedoms granted by the United Nations will be granted to the Indochinese.
> 5. That the sale of opium be prohibited. We hope that these conditions will be acceptable to the French.[15]

The demands transmitted through the OSS were very mild compared to the objectives set by the CPV in the various resolutions mentioned earlier. They were certainly milder than Bao Dai's declaration of complete independence on March 11, and also milder than what the VNDDD leader Nguyen Tuong Tam had told Sainteny in Kunming at about the same time; that he and his nationalist friends "required a radical revision of the French position in Indochina, supposing that it had one."[16]

The demands were also very mild compared to the terms of the declaration of March 24, 1945 of the French Provisional Government headed by General de Gaulle.[17] This declaration contained certain provisions that would, in the long run, allow the Indochinese people to exercise decisive powers and, eventually, independence, or a very strong dominion status: an elected assembly with the powers of voting taxes of all kinds, as well as the federal budget, debating all bills, examining treaties of commerce and good neighborhood of Indochina; access to all positions in the civil service; the development of education; economic autonomy and freedom to develop commercial relations with all countries; freedom of thought and religion, of the press, of association, and all other democratic freedoms.

The rub in the French proposal was that it envisaged an Indochinese federation composed of five countries—Cambodia, Laos, Cochinchina (southern Vietnam), Annam (central Vietnam), and Tonkin (northern Vietnam), and the retention of supreme powers in external affairs and defense by France (see map 1). But considering that a Vietnamese could live wherever he or she pleased in the five "countries" and be among compatriots, the deferred formal unity of Vietnam was not a disaster, especially as in time the matter would surely be settled in favor of the Vietnamese. With regard to defense and external affairs, again, for a time it would be to the advantage of the Vietnamese to do without these expensive items and concentrate on educational and economic development, as the experience of postwar Japan had shown, unless they wanted to dissociate completely from France in order to associate with another power. This was a crucial question. The Viet-Minh message, however, was silent on this, as on the unity question.

One may ask: why did Ho Chi Minh put forward such modest demands in his message of July 17 (which was repeated on July 25)? Apart from the explanation given in chapter 4—to impress the Americans that intransigence came from the French side—two other motives were possible. One is that Ho knew through his intelligence network that Sainteny had met Nguyen Tuong Tam of the VNQDD,[18] and he wanted to block all further French approaches to the other nationalist parties by offering a lower price for France's continued presence in Vietnam. Another reason, and a much more important one, is that at that time and until 1947, Stalin's policy was to leave it to the French and the Americans.

According to Stephane Solosieff, the Soviet representative in Hanoi, the Vietnamese were "not quite ready for independence," the French were "the best equipped" of the Western powers to reconstruct the country and guide it toward self-government, the Indochinese would have to assume a role of "responsible nationalism," and "with enlightened French help and American technical assistance" they could achieve independence "in a few years." Finally, the Soviet Union would not be able to "interpose itself in Southeast Asia," as such interference would conflict with traditional French and British interests, "which would not be in the best interests of the Soviet Union."[19]

As Sainteny was to learn later from the Americans who had been at Ho's jungle headquarters, at that time "a French delegate was highly desired by the leaders of the Viet-Minh League" who, for the occasion, "had prepared tricolor flags and welcome streamers wishing welcome to the French delegates." Sainteny added that the Viet-Minh leaders "seemed to have wanted to enter Hanoi at the side of a French delegate charged by the provisional government with retaking possession of the Tonkinese capital after the Japanese surrender."[20] Indeed, on August 14–16 at Tan Trao, the CPV had envisaged the possibility of "the Allies (Chinese, French, British, Americans) landing in force in Vietnam and establishing a French Gaullist government or some other puppet government against the wishes of the people."[21]

Contrary to the CPV leaders' fears, however, events took another turn. The Viet-Minh received crucial American aid; the Japanese surrendered unexpectedly; the French troops and representatives were prevented from entering Vietnam by the Americans and the Chinese, and those detained by the Japanese remained detained; the Japanese offered no opposition to the Viet-Minh; Ho Chi Minh's troops and agitprop agents entered Hanoi first; and when Sainteny could finally fly in with Patti, he had no troops, no means, and even no official status.

As a result of the decisions of the Potsdam conference, not only Sainteny but the French government also had no status in Indochina in August. Neither did Ho. But Ho did have possession of the place, and an army and a political organization at his disposal, not to say anything about an "objective ally"—the United States—at least for a few crucial weeks. These were extraordinary assets, and Ho was going to exploit them to the fullest in his dealings with the French when the time came for it.

DEALING WITH SAINTENY

The time for Ho to decide that it was necessary to talk to the French was the end of September, when the idyll between the Americans and him was coming to an end, and Patti, his American "special friend," was about to be relieved and ordered back to China. By early October the American officials in Hanoi were ordered to distance themselves from Ho's government and to collaborate with the French. By late September also, it was confirmed that the French were negotiating with the Chinese government for the replacement of Chinese occupation troops by French troops. At the same time, General Lu Han and his team had arrived in Hanoi and begun to apply pressure on Ho in favor of the other nationalist leaders who had arrived from China with them.

In a conversation with Bao Dai in the second half of September, Ho Chi Minh, reviewing the international situation, said that the Russians were totally indifferent to what was happening in Indochina, the English had taken the side of the French, the Americans were interested only in business and in taking the place of the French, and the Kuomintang was a gang of vultures. "Yes, all things considered, there remain only the French," he concluded.[22] This was a new attitude, for earlier Ho had rejected Patti's suggestion that he talk to the French representative Sainteny.

At his first meeting with Patti in Hanoi on August 26, Ho said that he had been "disappointed and offended" by French "haughtiness." He was "particularly irritated" with Sainteny, de Gaulle's representative, and saw his mission as hostile to the Vietnamese and therefore bound to create problems for his government. At a suggestion by Patti that the Sainteny group, which had arrived with him on August 22, could be useful in establishing contacts with the French to induce them to tentatively accept that the Viet-Minh was in power, Ho disagreed. He said that for the time being he was not disposed to make any further overtures after the ones he had made in July had been ignored.

At a repeated suggestion of dialogue with Sainteny, Ho remained unconvinced that it would produce any constructive results. But he left it to Patti to use his best judgement in the matter.[23] Ho would let his lieutenants meet with Sainteny in the next few weeks. He himself would not meet personally with Sainteny until October 15, after it had become clear that he had no choice in the matter.

The first meeting of Ho's lieutenants with Sainteny took place on August 27, one day after Ho had rejected Patti's suggestion that he meet with the French group in Hanoi. The meeting was requested by Sainteny and arranged by Patti. Vo Nguyen Giap, the interior minister, and Duong Duc Hien, the education minister, represented the provisional government.

According to Sainteny, the meeting was "courteous"; Giap expressed the desire to maintain close contacts. They talked about various aspects of the problem of French-Vietnamese relations until Giap was told by Sainteny that the Potsdam conference had charged the Chinese with the task of disarming the Japanese north of the 16th parallel. Giap seemed "extremely upset" by that news, which he claimed to have ignored until then, and insisted on knowing whether Sainteny was certain of what he was affirming. The meeting ended as courteously as it had begun; Giap declared that he was "delighted" and expressed the wish that such conversations be renewed "as often as possible."[24]

Patti, who was present at the meeting, has given more details and a rather different report. He said that Sainteny's diplomatic dexterity was "at its lowest ebb," and that the Frenchman took a lecturing tone. But Giap restrained himself and said he had come not to listen to lectures, but for an "exchange of views" and asked for "specifics" on what Sainteny said regarding French policy.

Concerning the revelation about China's occupation of northern Vietnam, Giap "appeared momentarily crushed" when the information was confirmed to him by Patti.[25] Obviously, Giap was on an information-fishing trip. As he himself has revealed, the appearance of a delegation of some ten French officers in Hanoi "was a matter of concern for Uncle Ho and his companions," and they wanted to know why these officers had arrived even before the arrival of the Chinese.[26]

The next meeting took place the following month, again at the initiative of the French. On September 3 a French officer on Sainteny's staff, Lieutenant Misoffe, managed to leave the governor general's palace and deliver a message from Sainteny to Vice Foreign Minister Hoang Minh Giam requesting a meeting with an official representative of the provisional government. According to Vo Nguyen Giap, Giam went to see Sainteny, who wished to explain the position of the French government on the Indochinese question. "Some time after that," Giap was designated to meet Sainteny. It was decided at this meeting that a liaison would be established between the French mission and Ho's government.

Thereafter, said Giap, talks were held "from time to time" between the two parties. At one of these meetings, the French informed the provisional government representative that a treaty would be signed soon

between China and France, that they wanted to negotiate a political solution, and warned that a refusal on Vietnam's part would harm future
French-Vietnamese relations. Giap said that "it was clear that our enemies
began to agree among them" and that the French government and the
French mission in Hanoi wanted to use the treaty, which was not yet
signed, "to bring pressure to bear on us."[27]

On September 19 General Marcel Alessandri arrived in Hanoi as the
representative of General de Gaulle. His request for air passage to Vietnam was promptly met by the American command this time—a clear sign
of American change of heart. Nine days later, accompanied by Leon Pignon, a senior official, Alessandri succeeded in being received by Ho Chi
Minh, but not without difficulty.

Soon after his arrival, Alessandri authorized Sainteny to send word to
Ho that a conference between him and a French representative in India
would be welcomed. Ho replied that he would not meet with an intermediary, but only with de Gaulle. Then Alessandri persuaded Admiral
d'Argenlieu, who was in Calcutta, to meet with a representative of Ho.
But Alessandri had not given prior notice to Ho. So, when he informed
Ho that d'Argenlieu would meet with him, Ho designated Bao Dai to
represent him. All these details, strangely enough, come from Patti,[28] and
not from Sainteny, who said nothing about them in his memoirs.

At this point, the Americans intervened. Patti said that on September
22 he took General Gallagher to meet Ho, "who had asked for our advice
on the French proposed meeting." Patti and Gallagher suggested that it
would be useful to open a direct dialogue. They felt that a meeting could
do no harm and that Ho should accept, that if the French went through
with their invitation, that would indicate an intention to recognize Ho's
government. Ho seized on that idea and said that instead of sending a
representative, he himself would go, but he would do so only if the French
would meet him in China and in the presence of an American observer.

At that point, Lieutenant Colonel Peter Dewey, chief of the OSS in
Saigon, was murdered, and the French had second thoughts. Alessandri's
memorandum relating to the invitation mentioned only "the French and
the Vietnamese people represented by the National Revolutionary party,"
and all reference to a Ho-d'Argenlieu meeting was omitted. Thus Alessandri's overtures came to nothing and left Ho still more skeptical about
French intentions.[29]

A week later, on September 28, however, Ho received Alessandri and
Pignon. He would receive them again on October 6. Nine days after that,
on October 15, he received Sainteny, now appointed French commis-
sioner for northern Vietnam. And from then on, Sainteny and Ho would

conduct secret negotiations until the conclusion of the French-Vietnamese preliminary agreement on March 6.

The Chinese unwittingly had accelerated the rapprochement between Ho and the French. September 28 was the day of the formal Japanese surrender ceremony, to which neither Ho nor Alessandri were invited as official representatives of their governments and countries, but only as individual guests of General Lu Han. In the eyes of the Chinese authorities, Ho's government had no official status, and the Chinese carefully avoided any gesture that could imply an official recognition of it. As regards the French, pending the signing of an agreement between the French and the Chinese governments, they had no formal status in Hanoi either. Roosevelt's ghost was still haunting them in Indochina.

A rather paradoxical situation developed in North Vietnam: those who claimed to be its actual masters—the Vietnamese—or its legal masters— the French—were completely ignored. Symbolic of this paradox was the "conspicuous absence" of French and Vietnamese guests at the surrender ceremony, and the absence of Vietnamese and French flags inside or outside the building where the ceremony took place.[30] It was therefore natural for French and Vietnamese to think of working together, or using each other, to put an end to that situation by getting rid of the insolent and unwelcomed intruder.

It was no accident that Ho, as a "special guest" of General Lu Han and not as president of the provisional government of Vietnam, could not attend the surrender ceremony "for reasons of health," but found enough strength that same day to receive General Alessandri, whom he had refused to see until then in spite of the latter's insistence. As Ho had told Bao Dai in a conversation noted earlier, "all things considered, there remain only the French."

Ho would now negotiate with the French. These negotiations illustrate the typical way in which the CPV, and Ho in particular, dealt with enemies: (1) determination of the principal and immediate enemy, (2) isolate and concentrate one's fire on him, (3) divide his ranks, (4) use one enemy to eliminate another, and (5) compromise to gain time.

For the CPV, there was a possibility of coming to some agreement with France, but the main enemy was still "the French colonialists aggressors," and it was on them that they would concentrate their fire. The directives, issued by the politburo on November 11, 1945, analyzed the situation as follows:

> France's attitude now is different from her attitude in the past. The reason for it is: the internal situation in France has undergone some change, es-

pecially after the election. The French Communist Party is the strongest party in the National Assembly, and in the French Government at present there are five members of the French Communist Party. Another reason is that our whole people is united in a heroic struggle; consequently if earlier France was prepared to accord autonomy to Indochina (Declaration of de Gaulle's government of March 25, 1945), now it is quite possible that it will recognize Indochina's independence and sign a treaty of friendship in order to save France's face internationally and salvage French economic interests in Indochina.[31]

But the same directives said that "our main enemy is the French colonialist aggressors and it is on them that we must concentrate our fire."[32] The same directives enjoined the party propagandists to isolate the French colonialist aggressors and concentrate their attacks on them while "avoiding putting France, England and India in the same bag and considering them enemies in the same degree."

One of Ho's great assets was his ability to detect divergences, even slight ones, among the members of the enemy camp. Thus he immediately saw that Sainteny's attitude differed from that of Admiral d'Argenlieu and others, and he concentrated his efforts on winning Sainteny over to his side by treating him as a "special friend," a tactic that would pay big dividends, even two decades afterward. In his conversations with Patti only two weeks before his first meeting with Sainteny, Ho had rejected Patti's suggestion that he met with the French, noting "with irony" that Sainteny was the son-in-law of Albert Sarraut (a former minister of colonies), and that not only had Sainteny refused to talk with him in July, but even a month later in Hanoi, he had shown "absolutely no sympathy for the Vietnamese cause" when he spoke with Giap.[33] Now he would be a sincere friend of Sainteny's. As d'Argenlieu has said, Ho's great source of strength was his "successive sincerity."[34]

Ho was fully successful in his enterprise. When one reads Sainteny's memoirs and other writings on Ho, one cannot help feeling the warmth that permeates everything Sainteny remarked about him, and his great efforts in putting the best interpretation possible on Ho's deeds and intents. Indeed, Sainteny became Ho's best champion among the French officials.

Ho thoroughly convinced Sainteny that he had "great value" and "tremendous power," that he "abhorred violence" and "aspired to be the Gandhi of Indochina," that his "only real and final aim" was the independence of Vietnam. Above all, he somehow convinced Sainteny that he was prepared to concede to France "what it cherishes most: its economic and cultural interests," that he "envisaged with satisfaction the idea of being the first to set the cornerstone of the French union," that if he wanted independence, he wished it to be given "by France itself," and that he wanted an "entente and rapprochement" with France.[35]

The beliefs entertained by Sainteny seem mere wishful thinking or surprising naivety now, in the light of what Ho and his companions said and did afterward, especially after the first big military successes of Ho's forces against the French in 1950. Until 1954, however, they surely raised doubts in the minds of many French people about the wisdom of their government's policy of confrontation with Ho.

Sainteny also said some unflattering things about Ho, but, whether deliberately or not, he never said them publicly, only in his secret telegrams to Admiral d'Argenlieu. For example, in a wire dated February 27, at an apparently difficult point in the negotiations, an exasperated Sainteny told the admiral: "Ho has proved more and more demanding. . . . he uses every and all pretexts to stall and does not hesitate to go back on his word. . . . [his bargaining] is based on systematic bad faith. . . . " In noting these passages, the admiral stressed that they were Sainteny's comments on the morality of Ho "for whom he was rather sympathetic."[36]

MOTIVATIONS AND TACTICS

At this point let us consider some very revealing details concerning Ho's motivations and tactics in conducting negotiations with the French, especially from December 1945 onward. Sainteny has said little about them in his memoirs, but he had discussed them in great detail in his secret telegrams to Admiral d'Argenlieu, and it is thanks to the admiral, who reproduced the telegrams in his memoirs, that we know about them (see chapter 4).

According to Admiral d'Argenlieu, the first official move was made on December 1, "at the initiative and on the insistence" of Hoang Minh Giam, acting on behalf of Ho. A meeting was held that evening between Ho, Vo Nguyen Giap, and Giam representing the Provisional Government of Vietnam (PGV), or Annamite Revolutionary Government (ARG), as the admiral called it, and Sainteny, Pignon, and Louis Caput (chief of the French Socialist section in northern Vietnam who served as adviser to the French mission). And it was "at the request of Giam" that other meetings took place in the following days.

On December 4 Giam insisted on "the necessity of moving fast" because the Chinese danger was becoming clearer. Also at the request of Giam, Pignon submitted a first draft agreement. On December 8 it was Giam again who requested a meeting for the following day, and he was "insistent." He clearly revealed his fears of a Chinese coup against the PGV before the elections set for December 23. The PGV intended to resist by force. Giam said that to avoid such confrontation, the PGV had already made many concessions to the Chinese and would be making more, but he wanted to know whether they "could count on the support of France."

Pignon, who was not unaware of that mixture of truth and ruse, replied that he could only report the request to his superiors, for Giam did not bring anything new regarding the crucial question of independence. At the meeting the next day, Giam told Pignon that it was the last time that he would try to negotiate with the French government.[37]

At this point, Caput, in a letter to the admiral, pleaded for the inclusion of the recognition of independence in an agreement with the PGV; otherwise the agreement would be "null and void"; in his opinion, the PGV was "the only ones morally deserving to talk with the representatives of France" and "the most capable of getting support for a French-Annamite agreement." Furthermore, Caput urged that "loyally, we, French, should assist the PGV and raise its credit" to enable it to "react more vigorously" against the "nationalists" and the Chinese whom they considered as "our common enemies." And quoting the PGV: "If we obtain independence from France, we shall be gratified, but if this is impossible, we shall accept it from the Chinese, and shall deal as best as we can with them afterwards."[38] Obviously Caput was acting as a spokesman for his comrade Giam, who had militated in the ranks of the French Socialist party.

In mid-January Sainteny reported that "certain behaviors" of the PGV, "and especially of Ho Chi Minh," indicated "a conciliatory attitude towards France,"[39] and after a crucial meeting on Februay 16, he reported that Ho concurred with the main lines of an agreement in which he renounced the use of the word "independence" and accepted Vietnam's inclusion in the Indochinese Federation and the French Union. This was the agreement that was going to be formalized on March 6, 1946.

It should be noted that on January 27 the Chinese had suggested a joint French-Chinese action to replace Ho's government by another that would be anti-Communist or non-Communist,[40] and this certainly had something to do with Ho's decision. Indeed, until the signing of the agreement, and especially in December and January, and PGV was in a really critical situation, as it was subjected to intense pressure from the Chinese and still had no international status. By the agreement with France, it now had one. This agreement was a sort of international guarantee of its existence.

VIETNAMESE-FRENCH AGREEMENT

Sainteny believed that the signing of the agreement was evidence of Ho's desire for an entente with France and his acceptance of the French Union. He made a distinction between Ho's position and that of the "irreducible" of the "Tong Bo" (the politburo).[41] But Sainteny was only deluding himself as Ho was the undisputed leader and strategist of the party. Ho himself explained to the party members afterward, in 1951, when, with the victory of Mao Tse-tung in China and the availability of massive Chinese Communist aid, he no longer feared defeat, that the agreement

> caused concern among many people who considered it a too rightist policy. But our comrades and compatriots in the South considered it a correct policy. And correct it was, for our comrades and compatriots in the South skillfully used that opportunity to rebuild and expand their forces.
>
> Lenin has said: if it serves the Revolution, we must not shrink from concluding agreements with bandits.
>
> We needed peace to build up our country. So, we had to make concessions to maintain peace. Even if the French had violated the agreement and provoked war, almost a year of temporary peace has given us time to build up our basic forces.[42]

Concerning acceptance of the French Union, Ho told the sixth plenum of the central committee in 1953 that "in the last eight or nine years, the position of our party has remained unchanged: Vietnam, Cambodia, Laos must be completely independent; we refuse to recognize the French Union; we want to push the French troops out of Indochina. . . . "[43]

On March 9 the politburo, in a directive called "Making peace in order to advance," explained to the party members:

> We made peace with France for the following reasons:
>
> 1. Avoid an unfortunate situation in which we would be isolated and have to fight several reactionary forces at the same time (the French colonialists, the white Chinese, and the domestic reactionaries) which would form a single bloc, and the English and American imperialists would help

them fight us at a time when the world peace forces (like the Soviet Union, the communist movements in China and France, the revolutionary movements in the colonies) cannot yet help us directly.

2. Conserve our forces, secure a breathing spell and consolidate the positions we have just seized, perfect the organization of our revolutionary troops, fill up the ranks of our cadres, reinforce and consolidate our movement, in a word, make full preparations so as to be in a position to seize the good opportunity that will permit us to move to a new revolutionary phase. . . . the Preliminary Agreement is only the first step.

The directive concluded by saying that "we make peace with France in order to gain time, conserve our forces, maintain our position, and move quickly to complete independence"[44]

General Giap, speaking of the preliminary agreements (in the plural), stressed that "they are the first international agreements signed by the DRV," that in spite of his large forces equipped with planes, ships, armored cars, the enemy "was compelled to negotiate with us as equals," that the DRV had accepted the entry and the presence of 15,000 French troops "for a fixed period of time" in order to "eject from our soil 180,000 Chiang Kai-shek troops." He added that "the fight was only postponed" and "the enemy has only made one fundamental step backward, and that was for us one first success," and "final victory is still far away," but "Uncle Ho has warned the opponent that our fight will be pursued until final victory."[45]

Last, the history of the party explained that in signing the agreement, the Vietnamese revolution had been able to eliminate "a ferocious enemy telecommanded by American imperialism" to concentrate its fire on "the French colonialists, the principal immediate and the most dangerous enemy," to gain time to rebuild and develop the bases of resistance in the South and "prepare them for a long resistance." Likewise, the signing of the modus vivendi by Ho Chi Minh in France in September was described as a move "to gain still more time."[46]

General Giap spoke about the agreements in the plural. This was indeed a very fine point. Whereas most people have talked about the agreement of March 6, 1946 in the singular, there were in fact two agreements, a principal and a supplemental. The latter dealt with military arrangements for the presence of French troops in northern Vietnam.[47] But Giap was right in viewing the agreements as an integrated whole, and for good reason.

Under the military agreement, 10,000 Vietnamese troops were to form part of the Allied forces replacing the Chinese troops; the French units charged with maintaining public order on Vietnamese territory were to be replaced by Vietnamese troops by slices of one-fifth each year, and thus "the replacement will be completed within a period of five years"; the progression, installation, and utilization of the French forces were to be defined by a conference of the general staffs of the French and Vietnamese commands. Thus, by a detour, the DRV had obtained some control over the French forces, and especially their evacuation within five years.

Admiral d'Argenlieu was very upset by the military provisions and complained that Sainteny had gone *ultra vires* without consulting or informing his superiors. The Paris government, through Marius Moutet, minister for Overseas France, also expressed strong displeasure for the *fait accompli* about which it stressed that it had never been consulted. Moutet registered his displeasure in a telegram to the admiral on March 14. In another telegram dated March 17, he told the admiral that the minister for foreign affairs (Georges Bidault) had "vigorously protested" against the acceptance of the military clauses.[48]

But there was more. The political agreement contained a promise by France that the future complementary negotiations were to take place in Hanoi, Saigon, or Paris. This, in the view of the admiral, was "a serious error from all points of view,"[49] and he bemoaned the fact that his representatives "have made virtual commitments on matters which were not within their jurisdiction" and that "Sainteny has gone too far,"[50] and they did so "to please Ho Chi Minh."[51] When he questioned Sainteny about such "imprudence" and on "the unbelievable circumstances" in which the commitment had been made, Sainteny explained these circumstances as follows:

> In the exhilaration to have thus terminated. . . . and happily. . . . with the exhausting discussions, I had not thought of it. As we were talking, in the same place, in the same atmosphere amidst signatories and witnesses, Mr Ho Chi Minh, graciously turned towards me, declared to me: "My dear Commissioner, I choose Paris." To that, without any further reflexion, I answered: "Mr. President, I see no inconvenience to that."[52]

D'Argenlieu added that General Leclerc had also gone too far in the matter, even further than Sainteny.

Sainteny also explained his decision mainly as a move "to take Ho Chi Minh and the Vietnamese delegates away from the influence and the pressures of the irreducible nationals" as well as from the maneuvers of "those who were not pleased to see French and Vietnamese prepared to reach a mutual agreement." He said that he knew that "certain Allied intelligence services" had not given up and sought to sow confusion, and that Leclerc, who had been aware of that "insidious undermining process," shared his view and supported him with all his authority.[53] By "certain Allied intelligence services" Sainteny meant the Chinese services.[54]

Sainteny further believed that by accepting to hold the complementary conference in Paris, Ho did France an honor. He said many years later that he wondered "whether France has ever understood properly the true value of the homage which Ho Chi Minh rendered to its loyalty in accepting to go" to what was still at the time the protecting power, a power that had hunted him for more than thirty years and condemned him to death.[55]

Ho had different aims than paying homage to France when he insisted on going to Paris. He wanted to use the French capital as a platform for propaganda aimed, on the one hand, at dividing French opinion and isolating the colonialists in France as well as in Vietnam, to bypass Admiral d'Argenlieu and circumvent the constraints imposed on his government by the March 6 agreement, and, on the other hand, reaching out to international public opinion.

As Ho himself explained in an address to the nation on his return from France on October 23:

> 1. We [the Vietnamese delegation and Ho Chi Minh] have brought our national flag to France. Our national flag was honored by the French Government and people, as well as by peoples of other nations.
> 2. We made the French Government and people pay attention to the Vietnamese problem and understand it better. The world, too, paid attention to the Vietnamese problem and understood it better than previously.
> 3. The majority of the French people became the friends of the Vietnamese people, very strongly supported the independence of Vietnam and the frank cooperation between Vietnam and France on a basis of equality.
> 4. We raised the status of the Vietnamese youth, women, and labor organizations, because international organizations recognized us as members.
> 5. The French-Vietnamese conference has not ended, and will resume next January. The *modus vivendi* of September 14 has made the work of France and Vietnam easier, and cleared the way for the future conference to progress in a friendly atmosphere.[56]

During the three and a half months of his stay in France, Ho tried to convey, and did so quite successfully, the image of the "sweet old man," the "nice Uncle Ho," the fatherly figure so full of goodwill and friendliness, and incapable of harming anyone. Jean d'Arcy, the principal personal secretary of Edmond Michelet, minister of the armed forces, who accompanied Ho during his flight to France, and Michelet himself, who was put in charge of receiving Ho during his stay in France, were both conquered by his charm.[57] From the moment he landed at Biarritz in early June until his final departure from Toulon in mid-September, Ho put on a masterly show. "If the Fountainebleau Conference ended in failure, Ho's sojourn in France was a great success," said Sainteny in his memoirs. "His personage broke down many reservations, rallied many hesitants, even adversaries. The persuasion and seduction operation which he performed single-handedly, the one man show succeeded beyond his hopes."[58]

In Paris Ho saw as many people as possible, appearing to the press as "a small man, thin, looking intelligent, kindly, and extremely likeable," said Azau.[59] Through arrangements made by Sainteny, Ho met a number of important French people representing industry and commercial interests in Indochina. According to a summary account of this meeting, he told them that his main concern was to avoid seeing his country fall under Chinese domination. It was this fear that had made him adopt a "pro-French attitude." He gave assurances that the interests of French nationals would be protected and his government would not tolerate spoilation or expropriation of French property. "We are imbued with French culture and want to prosper with France," he concluded. This was very different from what he had told the Chinese a month earlier.

However, Ho warned, pointedly, that either France and Vietnam came to an agreement, or they would fight, and if there was a war, "you can kill ten of my men, but I will kill one of yours."[60] While Ho was trying to lull Frenchmen with promises of economic and cultural protection in Paris, at Fountainebleau, out of sight of the public, Pham Van Dong, head of the Vietnamese delegation, was making diametrically opposite demands and holding a diametrically opposite kind of speech.

Among the Frenchmen who did not succumb to Ho's charm, two stood out: General Leclerc and General de Gaulle. Leclerc had been taken in by Ho in the first days of his arrival in Vietnam in March a year earlier. He had pushed hard for the use of the word "independence" and had been strongly in favor of Ho's visit to France. But when Ho was in Paris, Leclerc refused to see him. Leclerc did not tell Sainteny why, but the latter believed that Leclerc had changed his attitude toward Ho because he had proof of Ho's duplicity.[61]

Ho could not see General de Gaulle either, although he made the request several times through Sainteny. De Gaulle was no longer in the government. That was an understandable reason. But it becomes less understandable if one is told that Sihanouk was received warmly by de Gaulle at his private home at Colombey during the same period. Ho was deeply disappointed as, according to Sainteny, being received by de Gaulle was "without any doubt one of his most sought after objectives."[62]

Ho's objective was not de Gaulle, but the propaganda gain he could make among large sections of the French, as well as Vietnamese, public by being linked to the general. As in the case of Chennault and the OSS in 1945, Ho could use with devastating effect a picture of him standing by the great Frenchman known to be opposed to the Viet-Minh. But Ho would persist, and in the end succeed, after de Gaulle's return to power, through and thanks to Sainteny.

As Edmond Michelet tells it:

> Every year I received the good wishes of Ho Chi Minh which it was my mission to convey to General de Gaulle. Ho persisted in maintaining contact. And so, until one day the General said: "All the same, he sent me good wishes; he'd better send them to me one day through official channels; that would have more weight." That was how Ho's good wishes were conveyed through official channels to General de Gaulle, although France had not yet recognized the Hanoi government.[63]

Sainteny said that "Ho admired de Gaulle so much that he was obsessed with the idea of meeting him" when he was in Paris. And this is where Ho's investment in Sainteny paid off: Sainteny often talked to de Gaulle about it.[64] Ho surely knew that Sainteny was close to de Gaulle and was his natural informer on Indochina. In July 1966 de Gaulle finally responded, and Sainteny was naturally the man chosen to carry "a very warm letter" to Ho. As Sainteny recalled, the letter from General de Gaulle gave Ho "extreme delight." It attenuated the frustration he had felt in Paris in 1946 at not being received by the leader of Free France. And his satisfaction "appeared clearly" in his answer, which he entrusted to Sainteny's care.[65]

Sainteny was not aware that Ho Chi Minh played for bigger stakes than just a warm personal letter from the general. At the time when de Gaulle sent the letter through Sainteny, North Vietnam was not recognized by France. In Paris in 1956, it was represented only by a commercial attaché, which was replaced in May 1961 by a "commercial delegation," whereas South Vietnam had been represented since 1955 by a full embassy. Following de Gaulle's letter to Ho, the commercial delegation was raised to general delegation on August 1, 1966, but it was still headed by a delegate ad interim. That was considerable progress. But Ho was aiming for something much bigger.

The big thing came at the end of August when de Gaulle made an official visit to Cambodia. From Phnom Penh, in a resounding speech de Gaulle declared that "only a political agreement could restore peace" in Vietnam, and this agreement should "restore and guarantee the neutrality of the peoples of Indochina and their right of self determination," leaving to each of them "full responsibility for their internal affairs."[66] That was a slap in the face of the United States.

As Mourad Bourboune has pointed out, de Gaulle's speech was "the harshest condemnation of the Asian policy of the United States" and "the slap in the face was colossal: it was the greatest diplomatic success scored by Hanoi since the beginning of the war."[67] And Ho Chi Minh knew then that his chances of winning the war had vastly improved because his enemies were divided: the Western alliance was broken. This was what Ho had been using Sainteny for.

Ironically, France now played the role that America had played in Indochina in 1945: the French were now the liberals who wanted to keep the American colonialists out; de Gaulle replaced Roosevelt as the protector of the downtrodden Indochinese, and Sainteny replaced Patti as Ho's "special friend." Only Ho Chi Minh had not changed. In 1945 he used the Americans against the French; now he used the French against the Americans. Admiral d'Argenlieu has said that Ho's sincerity was successive. So was his friendship or enmity. In 1966 the friends of 1945 had become bandits, and the bandits of 1945 had become friends.

6

The CPV and China: Facing Troublesome Fellow Asian and Communist Neighbors

In dealing with the United States and France, two distant Western democratic nations, Ho Chi Minh and the CPV were able to manipulate people and exploit situations to their advantage by applying Leninist strategy and tactics. With the Chinese, the situation was different.

China was Vietnam's nextdoor neighbor. The Chinese were fellow Asians. Their leaders ruled over a country that was not subject to the constraints of parliamentary democracy. Many of them were fellow Communists equally versed in Leninist strategy and tactics. With China, therefore, the CPV faced a number of problems that were absent in its dealings with the Western powers. As between 1925 and 1985 China had been under two regimes—Kuomintang and Communist—one would have to study the CPV's politics toward both of these. With each, the CPV would face a different set of problems.

With the Kuomintang, the CPV involvement was rather short. Although the CPV had begun its existence in China in 1925, it became directly involved with the Chinese authorities only between 1940 and 1946, mainly between September 1945 and March 1946. With the Chinese Communists, the involvement lasted much longer: starting in 1924, it went through several phases. The most important of these were 1950–1954 and 1975–1985. There was inevitably some overlapping, as until 1949 both Kuomintang and Communists were active in China. We focus here on those aspects that bear directly on the CPV's politics, first regarding the Kuomintang, then the Communists.

THE KUOMINTANG

Until 1950 the Vietnamese Communists never operated overtly as Communists, but always under the cover of various Vietnamese nationalist, or anti-imperialist, or anti-Japanese organizations: the Vietnamese Revolutionary Youth Association (VRYA), Vietnam Anti-Imperialist League, Vietnam Association for Support of China against Japan, International Anti-Invasion Association (Vietnamese Section), Vietnam National Liberation League (Dong Minh Hoi), Vietnam Independence League (Viet-Minh), and so on.

During a large part of this period, Moscow strongly supported China against Japan. In conformity with Comintern policy, the CPV made support for China one of its major tasks, especially after 1936. Party members were constantly reminded of the obligation to assist China in its fight against Japan. A resolution of the central committee dated September 4, 1937 urged party members to give maximum propaganda to the successes of China and to expose the misdeeds committed by Japan against the Chinese people.[1] Another resolution dated November 11, 1940 called for the establishment of a United Front against Imperialism, aid to China, an alliance between this front and the Chinese Front against Japan, and contact with the Chinese anti-Japanese government.[2] This government, although headed by Chiang Kai-shek, had the support of Moscow, and the Chinese Communists were participating in it.

The CPV became more actively involved with the Kuomintang in 1940, after Japan's de facto occupation of Indochina. The Japanese move was viewed as a threat to China. In this, it agreed with the Chinese view. The emergence of such a threat naturally led the Chinese military commanders in southern China to think of eliminating it by an invasion of Indochina at some point. To this end plans had to be drawn up. For this, they needed the cooperation and help of the Vietnamese. General Li Tsi-chen, chief of staff of the Fourth Corps Area, accordingly searched for such cooperation and help.

Vo Nguyen Giap, who was at Kweilin at the time, was one of those approached by General Li Tsi-chen. But Ho Chi Minh firmly cautioned Giap against cooperation with the Kuomintang. "In this matter, we must have clear ideas," said Ho. "We have only two real allies in whose successes we can rejoice: the Soviet Red Army, and the Chinese Red Army."[3]

The Chinese military commanders' need for Vietnamese cooperation and help in their invasion project opened up a big opportunity for the Vietnamese nationalists of all colors, as in return for services rendered, they were certain to get Chinese support and aid in their struggle for independence. However, what the Chinese needed—accurate intelligence, propaganda, agitation, and eventually a popular uprising in support of the invading forces—required a solid organization inside Vietnam, as well as an effective leadership working with the Chinese in China. These were the services that General Chang Fa-kwei, commander of the Fourth Corps Area, wanted to secure.

Chang Fa-kwei had more than a military plan for defeating the Japanese. He also had definite political ideas about the future of Indochina. He wanted a Vietnam liberated from French colonial control, but ruled by a government under the influence of China. For the implementation of his "grand plan," Chang Fa-kwei created a special training class for the military training of Vietnamese recruited by him, and sponsored the formation of a political organization, the Dong Minh Hoi, from whose ranks the future pro-Chinese government of an independent Vietnam was expected to emerge.

On the Vietnamese side, the objectives for all the Vietnamese nationalist groups militating in China were: (1) to be included in the Chinese-supported Dong Minh Hoi, (2) to gain control of this organization, (3) to secure from the Chinese authorities exclusive recognition, and with such recognition, exclusive material aid and political support.

In 1943 it had become clear to Chang Fa-kwei that for the execution of his "grand plan" the various groups in the Dong Minh Hoi, divided and ineffective, could not provide the kind of services he needed. At this point, by chance, Ho came into the picture.

Ho had been arrested in July 1942 at the Sino-Vietnamese border, and was to spend 13 months in Chang Fa-kwei's jails. During this period, turning bad fortune into good opportunity, he won the favors of Chang Fa-kwei, as well as that of General Hsiao-Wen, who was Chang's deputy chief of staff for foreign affairs, and who was to be in charge of political affairs of the Chinese occupation forces in northern Indochina in 1945. These two men were to play a key role in helping Ho gain power in Vietnam.

While in jail Ho put his extensive knowledge of Chinese and of international affairs to good use. In his contacts with Chang Fa-kwei and Hsiao Wen, he carefully concealed his real identity and especially his real aims, and sought to impress the two men that he was a great admirer of Sun Yat-sen and was well versed in world affairs, and capable of helping them achieve their objectives in Vietnam. He translated Sun's *Three Principles* into Vietnamese to prove that not only did he know about the Chinese great leader and his ideas, but he admired him to the point of wanting to spread those ideas among his followers, just as, later, he would show "admiration" for Jefferson when dealing with Patti, and for de Gaulle when dealing with Sainteny.

To impress the two Chinese generals about his knowledge of world affairs, Ho wrote a long essay analyzing the international situation and discussing the future of China's resistance war. It came to the attention of Hsiao Wen, whom K.C. Chen described as "a Communist sympathizer." Hsiao asked permission to talk with Ho. As Chen tells it:

> Their talks were so congenial that they covered such subjects a the ICP [Indochinese Communist Party] and its popular leader Hoang (Vuong) Quoc Tuan, whom they had not seen (sic!). Hsiao and Ho became good friends. Hsiao asked Chang to write a petition to Wu Tieh-ch'eng (Secretary General of the Kuomintang) and Ho Ch'en-chun (Executive Director of the Military Laws Department) in Chungking, suggesting that "Ho Chi Minh, a man of fine qualities, and honest and sincere, should regain his freedom." Chungking approved the request and ordered that Ho be "treated well." Ho was released and worked in the Dong Minh Hoi while maintaining "legal" contacts with home under the protection of Hsiao Wen.[4]

By now, Chungking had received a reliable report that Ho was a member of the Comintern. The report was forwarded to Chang, who ignored it and continued to let Ho work for the reorganization of the Dong Minh Hoi. According to Hou Chi-ming, who was director of the Dong Minh Hoi from May to October 1943, "Chang was "surrounded" by Communists and pro-Communists such as his confidential secretary, Tso Hung-tao, his chief of staff General Wu Shi, and Hsiao Wen. These men had "influenced" Chang to protect and help Ho. But Chang, in defense of himself, invoked the cooperation among the central government of China, the Chinese Communists, and the Soviet Union. He also viewed Ho as a man who had "a better knowledge" of world affairs than other Vietnamese, who could speak Chinese, English, and French, and who was "energetic and hard-working."[5]

Ho put his Chinese connections to good use. For his work for Chang Fa-kwei he asked for travel papers, medicine, a large amount of weapons (1,000 guns, 4,000 grenades, 6 machine guns). Furthermore, unlike his later approach to the OSS, Ho asked for 50,000 Chinese dollars, 25,900 Indochinese piastres "without specific explanations," and some money for traveling expenses. Last, but obviously not least, using the same technique as he was to apply later in his dealings with the Americans, he asked for a letter from Chang Fa-kwei to all patriotic parties and groups, and a certificate of appointment of his mission.[6]

As in the case of the Chennault photograph and Helliwell pistols, Ho was thinking of the months ahead. When he returned home, in a letter addressed to all compatriots on October 10, 1944 (choosing the Chinese National Day celebration for issuing his message), he said that in August 1942, obeying orders of the community (he did not say which), he went in search of foreign aid. Now he had brought back to the compatriots "an extremely precious present, the warm solidarity of 450 million Chinese compatriots for the 25 million of Vietnamese compatriots. . . . the news that China will do its utmost to help us in our national liberation."[7] Chinese aid was precious at this time, as it was the only one available before Ho had access to the Americans.

From early September 1945 to early March 1946, Ho and the CPV were to face the Chinese again, this time under very different circumstances. On August 27, contrary to expectations, it was announced that General Lu Han instead of General Chang Fa-kwei had been designated by the Chungking government to head the Chinese occupation forces in northern Indochina. According to Hsiao Wen, that was "the worst possible choice:"[8] But Ho, who knew Chinese politics well, immediately understood the reasons for this apparently strange choice, and how to exploit it to his advantage.

On the day of the arrival of Lu Han's troops in Hanoi, September 5, Ho said: "It is a tactic of Chiang Kai-shek to draw the tigers away from their den. All is not for the best in their camp and we can profit from it."[9] But if Ho could take advantage of the internal divisions among the Chinese, he would also face serious material and political problems arising from the presence of Lu Han and his troops in Vietnam.

On August 24, the Chungking government had made public its intentions concerning Indochina. It said that apart from sending troops to accept Japan's surrender north of the 17th parallel in accordance with the decision of the Allied powers, China "definitely does not have any territorial ambitions in Vietnam."[10] The emphasis here is on "territorial." The Chinese government did not have those ambitions, but it definitely had others, among them using Vietnam to obtain economic advantages in Indochina, and political advantages in China in its bargaining with France. China's relations with France do not concern us here, except in one respect: in recognizing France's sovereignty over Indochina, the Chungking government posed two big problems for Ho Chi Minh and the CPV, one external and one internal.

The external problem besetting Ho was that his government had no international status and faced a return of the French who were now juridically in a very strong position. How Ho coped with this problem has been examined in chapter 5. The internal problem concerned the return of the other nationalist parties and groups that had accompanied the Chinese troops, in particular the VNQDD and the Dong Minh Hoi. These groups vigorously challenged the CPV's claim that the Viet-Minh represented the whole nationalist movement, and actively sought the support of the Chinese authorities to challenge and eliminate the CPV. How Ho and the CPV dealt with the Chinese authorities during the period of occupation of Vietnam by the Chinese forces is one of the most interesting aspects of the foreign politics of the CPV.

Following Marshall Chiang Kai-shek's statement of August 24, the Chinese government formulated a 14-point policy for the occupation forces. The two most significant of these points were: (1) to confer and maintain close contact with the delegations of the American military and the French mission, and (2) to maintain a strictly neutral attitude toward the Franco-Vietnamese relations.[11] The Chinese authorities were instructed to avoid formal government communication with the local government.[12] Lu Han, however, had ideas of his own on how to deal with Ho's government, and Ho was aware of it.

Vo Nguyen Giap has recorded that it was evident from Lu Han's attitude that "the Chiang Kai-shekists had not come only to disarm the Japanese troops,"[13] and "Uncle perfectly understood the class nature of the Kuomintang . . . [they] very obviously wanted to overthrow our revolutionary power and annex our country."[14] Ho himself explained to party members in 1951 that the Chinese "used the disarming of the Japanese troops as a pretext, but in fact, they had three wicked aims: (1) annihilate our party, (2) destroy the Viet-Minh, and (3) help the reactionary overthrow the people's government authorities to set up a reactionary government serving as their henchmen."[15]

The first move by the CPV to forestall the establishment of a pro-Chinese government—a government of "traitors" in their eyes—was to seize power and have a government functioning in Hanoi before the arrival of the Chinese troops. The CPV accomplished this by taking a number of measures: it set off a general insurrection on August 16, negotiated with the Japanese to secure their neutrality, made maximum propagandistic use of their OSS connection, set up a provisional government, and maneuvered for Bao Dai's abdication. All that was accomplished by August 30. At the same time, Ho had given orders to the CPV cadres to delay the entry of Chinese troops as much as possible by the use of all kinds of pretexts and stratagems, the major one being the destruction of the bridges leading toward Hanoi.

The first Chinese troops did not reach Hanoi until September 5, and General Lu Han did not arrive there until September 11, whereas on September 2, Ho Chi Minh had already proclaimed the independence of Vietnam and set up a democratic republic, with a provisional government exercising effective control. Yet, the position of this government was precarious. It was only a de facto government and had no status in the eyes of the Chinese government. As Vo Nguyen Giap recalled, Lu Han addressed Ho as "Mr. President," but in their official correspondence, the Chinese generals addressed him simply as "Monsieur Ho Chi Minh" and "considered us as a *de facto* government and not as a *de jure* government."[16]

The worst fear of Ho and his party was that Lu Han would order the disbandment of their armed forces and the dissolution of their government. What General Gracey did in the south was a clear indication that this was a distinct possibility. Lu Han was to betray Chiang Kai-shek later by going over to the Communists, but at this time he represented a Chinese government that was conducting a bitter struggle against the Communists in China, and that naturally did not want to have a Communist government at its rear in Vietnam.

Ho's tactic was to convince the Chinese that (1) there would be no danger from the establishment of a Communist government in Vietnam, (2) his government would cause no trouble at all to the Chinese occupation forces, and (3) that, on the contrary, it would cooperate fully with the Chinese occupation authorities to help them achieve their objectives.

To avoid giving Lu Han any pretext for disarming his army and suppressing his government, Ho changed the name of Liberation Army to Ve Quoc Doan (National Defense Brigade), the word "doan" evoking in the Chinese mind the idea of a small regional armed organization and attracting less attention. The Military and Political School was renamed School of Cadres. This decision followed a demand by General Lu Han that a report be submitted to him on the size and organizational structure of the Vietnamese armed forces.[17] Moreover, to avoid possible armed confrontation with the Chinese forces, Ho ordered his troops moved out of Hanoi and of the main cities.

To win the Chinese generals' confidence, Ho assured them that he would carry out their orders. On September 16, two days after General Hsiao Wen arrived in Hanoi, Ho went to see him to emphasize that he would "obey" Chinese orders and accept their direction, and he "offered his life" as guarantee to assure him that there would be no anti-Chinese actions or words from the Vietnamese, and that his government would be willing to accept the participation of other parties.[18]

Earlier, already in 1944, Ho had impressed Chang Fa-kwei for being "always cooperative" and "always accepting Chinese demands and advice."[19] Concerning his communism, Ho told Chang Fa-kwei in August 1944: "I am a Communist, but my present concern is for Vietnam's freedom and independence, not for communism. I give you a special assurance that communism will not work in Vietnam in fifty years."[20]

Later, in May 1946, Ho was to repeat to General Hsiao Wen what he had told General Chang. He told Hsiao that he also had "three principles of national policy," which were: (1) to adopt a pro-Chinese line, (2) not to surrender to France, (3) not to carry out the Communist program for 50 years. He explained to Hsiao that communism was "unsuitable" for industrially backward Vietnam, that his government was "not a Communist government," and that the main policy of his government was "the same as China's as announced by Generalissimo Chiang—"People first, nation first."[21] This is not what Ho told the French in Paris a month later, (he told the French he wanted an agreement with them and had adopted a "pro-French" attitude because he feared the Chinese; see chapter 5).

General Lu Han was, however, not satisfied with words of assurances from Ho. He wanted to make sure that the Chinese government would not find a Communist Vietnam on its southern borders and that pro-Chinese, non-Communist Vietnamese nationalists would dominate, or at least have a strong voice in the government of Vietnam. In October, through Hsiao Wen, he applied strong pressure at a moment when Ho could no longer rely on American support and when it had become clear that the French would return to Vietnam as the sovereign power. Ho had no choice but to take unpleasant steps to reduce Chinese pressure. The first was to dissolve the Communist party of Indochina; the second was to open the doors of his government to the members of the VNQDD and the Dong Minh Hoi.

On November 11, the party's central committee announced that it had decided to "voluntarily" dissolve the CPI "to destroy all misunderstandings, domestic and foreign, which can hinder the liberation of our country."[22] Six years later, explaining the real motives of this spectacular act, Ho said that the party then faced a "very difficult and pressing situation," and for that reason it had to "resort to all means in order to survive, to act and to develop," to continue to lead "less conspicuously and more effectively," to gain time in order "to consolidate the forces of the people's government power" and the United Front. At that moment, the party had to resort to "even the most painful means" to save the situation. However, "although the party had declared its dissolution, in fact it continued to lead the government and the people."[23]

The dissolution of the CPI came more than a month after the visit to Hanoi of General Ho Ying-ch'in, chief of staff of the Chinese armed forces. According to Giap, the men of Ho Ying-ch'in disclosed that the latter had come to Hanoi with the intent of "annihilating the communists and arresting Ho Chi Minh on instructions from Chungking," but once on the spot, he saw that this was impossible."[24] General Ho arrived on October 1 and departed on October 4. On leaving, he instructed the Chinese occupation forces "to be careful in dealing with the provisional government of Vietnam while maintaining a friendly position. Formal government communication with it should be avoided."[25]

General Ho Ying-ch'in's instructions were rather neutral. But Lu Han had different ideas. From October onward, he increased the pressure on Ho's government. These pressures were to grow in intensity in December–January. This led Ho to postpone until January 6 the elections originally set for December 23, to reserve 80 seats in the future national assembly for VNQDD and Dong Minh Hoi members, and to eliminate the Communists from his government and replace them with neutrals or people from the opposition. But the Chinese were not quite satisfied. On January 27 they proposed to the French joint action to replace Ho's government with an anti-Communist or non-Communist government.

Admiral d'Argenlieu was advised against accepting the Chinese proposal by Pignon, who considered it "imprudent" for France to "contribute to the hastening of the disintegration of the Viet-Minh," and desirable to maintain contact with it. The admiral would tell de Gaulle a month later that, after several months of studies and reflexions, he could find "valid listeners. . . . only in the ranks of the Viet-Minh."[26] Ironically, later, both d'Argenlieu and Pignon worked very hard to get rid of the same Viet-Minh "valid listeners."

Ho would thus find unexpected allies in the French in January. But, in the meantime, he would have to maneuver extremely carefully to avoid possible disaster. As usual, he would seek to exploit the contradictions in the enemy camp and, in addition, resort to corruption to achieve his ends. Ho told Vo Nguyen Giap that while seeking at all costs a compromise with the enemy, they must also seek to discover the contradictions and the cracks within his ranks that they could exploit.

The Kuomintang generals coming to North Vietnam were not all from the same side, Ho said. Some were from the Yunnan ruling junta, others from Kwangsi and Kwantung, still others from the central government in Chungking. Their common denominator was anticommunism. But because of the contradictions prevailing among them, their reactionary attitudes toward the Vietnamese revolution were not the same . . . "Although all Chiang-kaishekists are reactionary, we must treat the ones differently from the others," Ho advised.[27] With "surprising perspicacity," said Giap, Ho seemed to have "pierced through" the mental makeup of the adversary, as well as his deepest feelings. "He applied with great finesse different tactics in dealing with different categories of enemies, and even with each man."[28]

Giap said that in the Chinese army, it happened that some junior officers had great influence. Some, thanks to the beauty and the fine savoir-vivre of their wives, to their expertness in preparing an opium pipe, had become useful intermediaries. "Very soon, one does not know how, Uncle had discovered men of that kind and recommended to our diplomatic cadres to apply an approach which was suitable to each of them." Thanks to their intervention, many conflicts were avoided afterward.[29]

Ho used corruption to secure the Chinese generals' support or their neutrality. The Gold Week was part of this scheme. Officially, the week was organized to collect funds for the purchase of arms to oppose a return of the French. Strong appeal was made to the patriotism of the people. The government collected 20 million piastres and 30 kilos of gold. But two-thirds of it went to the purchase of political favor and of arms from the Chinese. "I felt like a traitor in allowing the farce to take place . . . every sou went to the Chinese," he told Patti.[30] When Ho talked to Bao Dai about the Chinese, he had few kind words for them, including Hsiao Wen, to whom he had always spoken with visible consideration. He said:

> China is a hungry stomach, the Kuomintang a gang of rogues, war lords, vultures. All that means an unsatiable appetite. . . . Only one man is usable; he is Hsiao Wen. But he is a rascal, and he is very costly, but I think he has understood what we wanted and his schemes can serve our purposes.[31]

Eventually, however, Ho would have to get rid of the Chinese presence, especially as from October onward it had become quite clear that, willy nilly, he would have to deal with the French, either by reaching some kind of agreement with them, or by fighting them. Thus the moment of the most intense Chinese pressure, early December, was also the moment of the start of serious negotiations involving him, Vo Nguyen Giap, and Hoang Minh Giam with Sainteny, while the French were also negotiating hard with the Chinese government in Chungking.

On February 28, 1946 the French and Chinese governments finally reached an agreement on the replacement of Chinese troops by French troops, and on March 6, Kuomintang China ceased to be a major factor and an immediate problem for Ho and the CPV. But it would not completely cease to be a problem until, defeated by the Chinese Communists, it had to evacuate the mainland, including the Sino-Vietnamese border area, in 1949.

Until the total communist victory in October 1949, Ho still maintained an attitude of caution, and just like Stalin, he avoided a complete break with Kuomintang China. In March 1946 he sent a goodwill mission to Chungking. In May, even after he had concluded an agreement with France, he still continued to assure Hsiao Wen that his government took inspiration from Sun Yat-sen and Chiang Kai-shek. In August 1947 he sought agreement from the Chinese government for the sending of a similar mission to Nanking.

Until August 1949, two months before the total Communist victory, he abstained from making any unfriendly statement against the Kuomintang. The establishment of a Communist government in Peking in October and the arrival of the Chinese Communist troops on the Sino-Vietnamese border soon thereafter freed him from the necessity of observing caution. From now on, he could count on a friendly and reliable government in China. At least until it turned out otherwise.

The departure of the last Kuomintang troops from Vietnam in September 1946 marked the end of one phase of the CPV's politics regarding China. But it also marked the beginning of a second, apparently simple but in fact very complex, phase. If the Kuomintang generals from Yunnan had extensively plundered North Vietnam and threatened the existence of the CPV, their presence in Vietnam was short, and the CPV could, by applying Leninist tactics, keep some control of the situation.

THE COMMUNISTS

With the Chinese Communists, Vietnam would be subjected to bigger and more difficult problems, and the CPV would no longer be able to play its own game. So long as the Chinese Communist party (CPC) pursued the same objectives as the CPV, the latter could find in China a valuable source of aid, support, and protection; but the moment the CPC changed course, the CPV would be faced with very big problems, especially if the course of the CPC was in collision with its own.

From 1924 to 1945 most of the CPV's really significant activities against the French and Japanese were conducted on and from Chinese soil. There, the CPV could draw on the CPC's vast reservoir of comradeship and goodwill. Ho Chi Minh and other CPV leaders have acknowledged their great debt to the CPC. On the occasion of the resurfacing of the party in February 1951, and especially on the occasion of the fortieth anniversary of the CPC in July 1961, Ho stressed that the Chinese revolution had "very great influence" on the Vietnamese revolution, that it was through China that the influence of the Russian October revolution and Marxism-Leninism were introduced to Vietnam. He told party members that the Chinese comrades had always given their "wholehearted aid" and they should "remember with gratitude" the role played by the Chinese revolution in the Vietnamese revolution, and "to learn from the experience of the Chinese revolution" of "the great Communist party of China" headed by "beloved comrade Mao-Tse-tung."[32]

Vo Nguyen Giap has recalled how, when he was at Kweiyang and Kweilin in 1940, he was received "with warmth and friendliness" by the Chinese comrades, who gave him "devoted aid in the spirit of warmest brotherhood";[33] and Nguyen Luong Bang has acknowledged that while he was militating in Shanghai in 1930 the Chinese comrades "helped us wholeheartedly."[34]

After Ho returned from Moscow to China in 1938, then to Vietnam in 1941, he maintained close contact with the central committee of the CPC. Obviously, he obtained vital information from the CPC and coordinated his plans of action with it. Indeed, according to K.C. Chen, in August 1940 the CPC and the CPV concluded a secret agreement to coordinate their actions during the war, in particular by establishing a United Front of the Sino-Vietnamese Peoples against Japan. Under this agreement the CPI was to send cadres to the Resist-Japan University in Yenan for training, and the CPC served as representative of the Asian Information Bureau of the Comintern to guide the CPV, and offered the latter 50,000 Chinese dollars per month for its activities in China. Moreover, the CPC gave secret assistance to the CPV in Chungking, Kweiyang, Kweilin, and Kunming.[35]

When Ho was arrested in 1942 during a trip to Chunking to contact the CPC, Mao Tse-tung's representative in Chungking intervened with the Kuomintang for his release. This representative was very probably Chou En-lai, as Ho was known to have visited him frequently in Chungking.[36]

During the period 1945–1949, when both the CPC and the CPV were struggling to seize power and hold on to it in their respective countries, contact between the two parties was unavoidably difficult, as they were physically separated by the Kuomintang armies in southern China. This was a period during which Ho was very careful to avoid antagonizing, or even offending, the Kuomintang. Obviously, any aroused hostility on the part of the latter would confront Ho with a hostile rear.

At this time, Ho, in line with Stalin's thinking, did not expect a Communist government to emerge in China in the near future. He had therefore to move extremely cautiously, keeping the CPV contacts with the CPC strictly secret, and the activities of the Chinese Communists in Vietnam restrained.

Until the autumn of 1949, Ho and his men fought a waiting battle, isolated and cooped up in a corner of northwest Vietnam. The unexpected sweeping victory of the CPC and the arrival of the Chinese Communist troops on the Sino-Vietnamese borders completely changed the strategic situation. As General Giap put it:

> The great historical event, which changed the face of Asia and the world, had a considerable influence on the war of liberation of the Vietnamese people. Vietnam broke out of the isolation imposed by the enemy and found itself from then on linked to the socialist camp. This fact, combined with others, among which the recognition of the DRV by China and the Soviet Union, contributed to changing the face of the war to our advantage[37]

From now on, the DRV had a safe and friendly rear, a sanctuary, and a base, as well as unlimited aid from the Chinese to embark on the next two phases of revolutionary war: equilibrium of forces and counteroffensive, which would lead to victory over the French. In this the Chinese undeniably played an important role.

The CPV leaders and the CPV propaganda have emphasized the "count on our own forces" theme, and presented the DRV's victory as a victory of the Vietnamese people under the "genial" leadership of the party. It is true that such a victory would have been impossible without the heroism of the Vietnamese people and the skilled leadership of the CPV, especially in the field of psychological action. But is is also true that without the massive aid from the Chinese Communists, it would have been impossible for the CPV to lead the DRV to a decisive victory over the French.

The CPV leaders admitted in a white paper in 1979 that China was "an important source of arms supplies for Vietnam in the last year of the war" against the French, and that China had supplied Vietnam with "the most important military aid" (arms, equipment) in the last years of the resistance against the French.[38] Hanoi speaks of "an important source," and "the most important source," but Peking has given a different story, which, to this date, has not been challenged by the CPV:

> In 1950, the Military Advisers' Mission, dispatched to Vietnam by China at the request of President Ho Chi Minh, helped the Vietnamese win a series of battles including the boundary battle. Between December 1953 and May 1954, the Mission helped the Vietnamese army and people to organize and carry out the world-famous Dien Bien Phu campaign. All the arms and ammunitions, communication equipment, food and medicine used and expended during this campaign were supplied by China. . . . The Vietnamese authorities in the White Book do not mention at all the role of China's assistance in this campaign. Nor do they mention how they made up their mind and how the campaign was won.[39]

At the Geneva Conference (May–July 1954), which followed the victory of Dien Bien Phu, the CPV leaders were to make a painful discovery: their objectives and those of the CPC leaders were not the same, and it was those of the CPC that would prevail. In other words, they had sacrificed Vietnamese lives and property and made the Vietnamese people fight a nine-year war to serve the interests of China rather than those of Vietnam. In 1954 they kept quiet, but 25 years later, they would strongly denounce China's "betrayal."

The white paper published in October 1979 accused the Chinese Communist leaders of having reached a compromise with imperialism "on the back of the Vietnamese people,"[40] of posing as "principal negotiator" with the French imperialists, "colluding" with them in order to reach "a compromise leading to a settlement of the conflict advantageous to China and France," and disadvantageous to the peoples of Cambodia, Laos, and Vietnam. "They sacrificed the interests of the three Indochinese peoples to ensure the security of China, realized their aims of seizing Vietnam and Indochina," and, at the same time, "play the role of a great power" in the settlement of international problems, in particular those of Asia."[41]

The white paper accused the Chinese leaders of preventing the three Indochinese peoples from achieving "total victory," which was "an entirely realist eventuality," and of using the threat of extension of the war by the United States to put pressure on Vietnam."[42] At a joint Soviet-

Chinese-Vietnamese policy coordination meeting in April prior to the conference, the Chinese delegate stated that China "will not be in a position to help Vietnam openly in case of an extension of the conflict in the region."[43]

In a remarkable study of the position of China in the Geneva negotiations in 1954, François Joyaux has noted the following significant occurrences: at the first secret meeting between the French and the Chinese delegates on May 16, the latter told the French: (1) We are not here to support the Viet-Minh point of view, but to make every effort to restore peace, (2) China does not necessarily encourage the Viet-Minh to move toward the delta,[44] (3) at a meeting with Eden on June 15, at a very critical point in the conference, Chou En-lai told the British foreign secretary that he believed he could "persuade" the Viet-Minh to withdraw from Laos and Cambodia.[45]

As the conference proceeded, China would further agree to the separation of the military from the political questions and to the settlement of the military questions first, to the partition of Vietnam at the 17th parallel, to a two-year delay for the elections that were to reunify Vietnam, and to rather loose conditions regarding the holding of these elections, and to an international armistice supervisory commission composed of Canada, India, and Poland.[46]

All the above provisions were distasteful to the CPV, but the latter accepted them because it had no choice: it was accepting or going it alone, and the CPV knew very well that the latter course was unthinkable. Thus the CPV had to renounce what it considered to be the achievement of its most cherished aims because these aims did not coincide with those of the Chinese leaders. But there was nothing the CPV leaders could do; the Chinese leaders could not be manipulated or bribed like the Kuomintang generals from Yunnan.

Ho Chi Minh, with his high sensitivity to the complexities of world politics, seemed to have understood the situation well, for in his address to the party on July 15, 1954, he chided party members who saw "the trees but not the forests, the French but not the Americans," who insisted on "too high conditions which were not acceptable to the enemy," who wanted "to move too fast in everything," who did not see the dangers of Left deviation, which were "isolation, separation of our people from the peoples of the world, and failure."[47] Ho's admonitions surely reflected what had been said to him by Chou En-lai at his meeting with the latter on the Sino-Vietnamese border on June 5.

Obviously, many in the party did not share Ho's views then, but they had to wait until after his death and for a good opportunity to give full and unrestrained expression to their pent-up resentment against the CPC leaders. The open Sino-Vietnamese conflict in 1979 would be the occasion for and the white paper the expression of this resentment.

To the CPV leaders, mentally conditioned by Ho since 1927 always to seek total victory whatever the costs, and to strongly believe in pure proletarian internationalism, the refusal of the Chinese leaders to give them all-out help to crush the French colonialists was incomprehensible. They failed to understand that China, just emerging from a costly war in Korea, did not want to be dragged into another that would get more Chinese young men killed, Chinese territory devastated, and China's economic development retarded, for the defense of what the CPV leaders might consider to be overriding objectives, but which did not represent vital Chinese interests or a Chinese priority at that time. And China's priority was peace and avoidance of an extension of the war, which carried with it the risks of a direct military confrontation with the United States.

At the same time, in denouncing the Chinese leaders for "having sacrificed the interests of the Vietnamese people" and for "having put pressure on the Vietnamese to force them to yield,"[48] the CPV admitted by implication that in the name of proletarian internationalism, they had served as instruments of Chinese policy. But as the 1979 white paper shows clearly, carried by the same dynamics of their obsession with revolution, the CPV leaders continued to pursue the same course, in the same spirit, and run into the same problems with the Chinese leadership.

Thus from 1954 to 1969, the CPV leaders found the Chinese "blocking the Vietnamese's struggle for reunification," resorting to "tortuous allegations" to hide their real intentions of "maintaining the political status quo in Vietnam," and recognizing the "parallel existence" of the DRV government and "the Saigon administration." The paper says that the "irrefutable evidence" of this was Chou En-lai's suggestion to Ngo Dinh Luyen, Ngo Dinh Diem's brother, only 24 hours after the conclusion of the Geneva Conference, that South Vietnam open a legation in Peking.[49]

According to the paper, Mao Tse-tung himself was a great culprit, for in July 1956, expiring time for the period fixed by the Geneva agreement for elections, he told the CPV that the problem of reunification of Vietnam "could not be solved in a short time," that it would take long, and "if ten years are not enough, one will have to take 100 years"; in July 1957, he would again tell the CPV: "The question is to preserve the existing frontier. Preserve the 17th parallel. . . . It could last long."[50]

When the CPV decided to resort to military action in 1957 and started their tactic of "chain uprisings," that is, partial insurrections, the Chinese leaders did not approve. They advised the CPV to "abstain from all aid," refused to help the Vietnamese set up a regular army, and supplied only light weapons and logistic equipment. What Peking wanted was "a long struggle," for even if Diem were overthrown, "reunification would still not be achieved immediately because the Americans would not tolerate it."[51]

Again, there was little the CPV could do. They would have to wait until 1960, when the open break between China and the Soviet Union would provide them with room for maneuvering and opportunities for exploiting contradictions. But this time it would be contradictions not among enemies but among allies, and this was possible because they were competing allies. However, the costs of using this tactic would turn out to be extremely high for the CPV, and still higher for the Vietnamese people.

In its competition with the Soviet Union for the role of head of the world revolutionary movement, China had to give support and aid to the Vietnamese Communists. But the Chinese leaders were in favor of a long drawn out, low key war. The 1979 white paper says that the Chinese leaders considered that "the appropriate form of struggle in South Vietnam is guerrilla warfare with small scale fights at the platoon or company level." And during the Laotian crisis in 1961, they advised the CPV to "abstain absolutely from interfering directly in the war." The white paper also reveals that in the early part of the 1960s, Peking sought to draw Vietnam into a new Communist International directed by Peking, and in 1963 Deng Xiao-ping promised Hanoi one billion yuan if it refused Soviet aid.[52]

From 1960 to 1965 the situation in South Vietnam developed in favor of the CPV, especially after the American-instigated coup against Diem in 1963. But in January 1965, when President Johnson decided not only to send combat troops to South Vietnam, but also to bomb North Vietnam, the CPV faced a new war. Obviously, it could not hope to cope with it without the help of its allies. It had to call on the Soviet Union as well as China to give it support and aid. But, the CPV leaders charged, the Chinese leaders were interested in "helping the United States rather than the Vietnamese revolutionaries," and from 1965 to 1969, in "weakening and prolonging the resistance of the Vietnamese people."[53]

According to the white paper, the United States attacked North Vietnam because "it had received assurances from the Chinese leaders." Mao Tse-tung, through Edgar Snow, had told Washington that Chinese troops would not cross their frontiers, and if China was not attacked, it would not fight the United States. Thus the Chinese had revealed their "perfidious aims." They encouraged the United States to "get mired" in the war of aggression against Vietnam, so that they could in all tranquility carry out their cultural revolution "while weakening both the United States and Vietnam."[54]

In Hanoi's view, the Chinese wanted the United States to send as many troops as possible, because in this way they would have a hold on the country. In support of this view, it cited a statement made to that effect by Chou En-lai to an Egyptian close to Nasser.[55]

To keep Vietnam weak, said the white paper, the Chinese leaders did not want the war to end early. On the other hand, they advised Vietnam to conduct only a protracted war and stage only guerrilla operations instead of large-scale battles. To the same end, they supplied Vietnam only with light weapons, ammunitions, and logistical support.[56]

It is pertinent to mention in this connection that, in September 1965, Marshall Lin Piao published a booklet, *Long Live the Victory of the People's War,* in which he re-emphasized the principles of protracted people's war, the importance of guerrilla warfare, and self-reliance. One of the main audiences obviously aimed at by Lin Piao was the Vietnamese military strategists. But the latter rejected Lin Piao's ideas and, instead, favored a war of quick decision through the staging of big battles and inflicting of heavy casualties on the enemy—at the cost of still heavier Vietnamese casualties, naturally.

The CPV leaders further accused the Chinese leaders of engaging in "sabotage of all international action" in favor of Vietnam, by hindering the transport of war supplies to Vietnam from the Soviet Union, to "restrict the possibilities for the Vietnamese people to organize big battles, in particular during the dry seasons."[57] The Chinese leaders were also accused of plotting to sabotage the Indochinese Anti-Imperialist Front (Laos, Cambodia, North Vietnam, South Vietnam Liberation Front) established by the Conference of Indochinese Peoples at Phnom Penh in March 1965.

Last, the CPV accused the Chinese leaders of seeking to prolong the war by opposing Vietnam's negotiations with the United States, and, instead, of encouraging the United States to bomb North Vietnam more intensively, of "fighting the Americans to the last Vietnamese," thereby weakening Vietnam in order better to implement their expansionist policy.[58] In the eyes of the CPV leaders, however, the worst act of betrayal on the part of the Chinese leaders was to change camp and "negotiate

with the United States on the back of the Vietnamese people" in 1969–
1973.[59]

Before considering the CPV's reactions to China's reversal of policy,
it is appropriate to briefly recall the triangular relations between Hanoi,
Moscow, and Peking.[60]

Until 1957 there were no serious differences between Moscow and Peking, and therefore Hanoi had no problem in dealing with its big allies.
But with the announcement of a new general line—peaceful coexistence
and pacific passage to socialism—by Khrushchev at the Twentieth Congress of the Communist party of the Soviet Union (CPSU), and the CPC's
strong objection to the position adopted unilaterally by Khrushchev, a
new situation arose.

Until 1961 an open break was avoided because Moscow accepted at
the congresses of world Communist parties in November of 1957 and
1960 a Chinese formulation of peaceful coexistence which left open the
possibility of violent struggle and nonpacific passage to socialism in particular circumstances.[61]

In 1961, with Chou En-lai's spectacular walk out of the Twenty-Second
Congress of the CPSU, the break between Moscow and Peking became
open, and in 1963 it was total. In the meantime, Khrushchev pursued his
policy of detente with the United States with vigor, and disapproved of
small wars—including the war in Vietnam—as they carried the risks of
escalation and extension into a general nuclear war. For the Chinese leaders, however, the United States was just a "paper tiger."

From 1957 to 1961 the CPV pursued a course of fine balancing, carefully avoiding antagonizing one or the other of the two big parties and
trying to work for the preservation of the unity of the Socialist camp on
the basis of proletarian internationalism and Marxism-Leninism. Ho Chi
Minh was very active in this respect at the 1960 congress, as Le Duan
stressed in his report to the central committee that December 1960.[62]

Ideologically, as well as practically, the CPV's position was closer to
that of the CPC than to Khrushchev, as the Khrushchevian interpretation
of peaceful coexistence would make it impossible for the CPV to embark
on a forward policy in South Vietnam by war.

There was a strong temptation for the CPV to follow the CPC in its
break with Moscow, and it took the full weight of Ho Chi Minh's authority and a dramatic action on his part to prevent the party from adopting such a course of action.[63] The CPV leadership's preference for a more
revolutionary stance against imperialism, with a very sharp criticism of
"revisionism"—that is, Khrushchev—was made quite clear by Le Duan
in a lecture given in March 1963.[64] Although the CPV's public statements

had nothing of the violent anti-Soviet rhetoric of the CPC, its position regarding the substance of the matter was the same as the CPC's.

After the intensification of the Sino-Soviet dispute following the Laotian crisis (1960–1962), the Cuban crisis (October 1962), and the Sino-Indian border war (1961–1962), the CPV moved closer to China; Khrushchev had made it clear that he did not approve of Hanoi's resort to armed struggle, and did not give it the support Hanoi expected. This situation lasted until the fall of Khrushchev in October 1964. With Brezhnev at the helm in Moscow, Soviet support to Vietnam was resumed.

A Vietnamese proverb says that when buffaloes and oxen fight, flies and mosquitoes get hurt. This was the situation in which the CPV found itself after 1961, for Vietnam was caught in the middle of China's ideological war with the Soviet Union. Continuation of the war there and support for Hanoi became part of China's competition with Moscow for influence in the Third World by providing visible evidence that China was a true supporter of revolution. In addition, from 1969 onward, the Vietnam war became an important element in China's diplomatic maneuverings aimed at a rapprochement with the United States.

Thus, from 1969 onward, some of the CPV's objectives coincided with those of the CPV, but some did not. Like the CPC, the CPV wanted to maintain the offensive against the United States and put it on the defensive. But it preferred a strategy of quick decision through big battles and heavy casualties. Such a strategy carried with it the risks of American escalation of the war and its extension to North Vietnam, which might require Chinese intervention. This was what the Chinese wanted to avoid, and this is where CPC and CPV objectives diverged. What the CPV wanted was a decisive victory over the United States. What the CPC wanted was to force the Americans to turn to it for help in disengaging honorably from Vietnam, and to accept normalization of Sino-American relations, which would enable China to face the Soviet Union from a stronger position.

The Chinese objectives coincided with those of President Nixon. Thus, while pursuing the peace negotiations with the DRV and the Liberation Front of South Vietnam (LFSVN) in Paris after his inauguration in January 1968, Nixon announced a series of steps to convince American opinion, but also the Chinese leaders, that he seriously wanted to disengage from Vietnam and adopt a new policy toward China.[65] These steps, taken together, constituted the "Nixon doctrine." They included recognition of China, dialogue, and the lifting of certain restrictions on American trade and travel to China.[66]

To the overtures made by Nixon, China responded positively, especially after the armed incidents with Soviet troops on the Sino-Soviet borders in 1969 and the American failure to penetrate into Laos to rescue the South Vietnamese forces there in 1971. In December 1970, through Edgar Snow, Mao Tse-tung in effect invited Nixon to visit China by saying that he would be welcomed. Secret negotiations between the two sides led to Henry Kissinger's dramatic trip to Peking in July 1971, then to Nixon's visit and the warm welcome extended by the Chinese leaders in February 1972. By that time, the Soviet Union had become "the most dangerous and most important enemy" of China.[67]

The turnaround of China instilled indignation and anger in Hanoi. By their attitude, it said, the Chinese leaders had uncovered their "odious faces of traitors." It was an "open betrayal of the Vietnamese revolution, of those of the other countries of Indochina, and of the world." The CPV accused the Chinese leaders of having "secretly worked to weaken the resistance of the Vietnamese people" during the period 1969–1973, and especially after 1971, of "openly entering into collusion with the aggressive American imperialists," of giving help to them "when they were confronted with new strategic offensives of the Vietnamese people, and of "playing the Vietnamese card in their bargaining with them."[68]

The white paper accused the Chinese leaders of "exerting continuous pressure on Vietnam to accept the American solution," in particular withdrawing North Vietnamese troops and leaving General Thieu in office. It quoted in this connection Mao's statement to a Vietnamese party in November 1971 that the overthrow of the Saigon administration was "a long-term problem" and "where the broom cannot reach, the dust stays."[69]

In another area closer to home, the CPV accused the Chinese leaders of preparing the ground during this period for "turning Kampuchea into a jumping board for attacking Vietnam." In its view, as early as the mid-1960s the Chinese leaders were already scheming about Kampuchea and sought to use the two Indochinese summit conferences, in 1970 and 1971, "to undermine the solidarity of the peoples of Indochina, deviate their struggle from their objective" and, at the same time, "bring together all the forces under the direction of Peking in order to negotiate with Washington from a strong position."[70] The CPV's concern about Cambodia, in particular its disapproval of China's desire to exercise influence over the Indochinese peoples (Cambodia and Laos), is an indication of its claim to Indochina as its sphere of exclusive influence nine years later.

During the next three years, from 1973 to 1975, relations between the DRV and China continued to deteriorate, and the signs of conflict began to surface. But the war had not yet ended, and the CPV still needed

Chinese aid, or at least it could not afford an open conflict with China and have a hostile country at its rear. To the CPV leaders, the Chinese were "traitors in the ranks of the Communist and worker's movement" who wanted "a Vietnam that is weak and dependent on China." Thus the CPV viewed its victory in 1975 not only as "a big defeat for the aggressive American imperialists," but also as "a big defeat for the Peking expansionists."[71]

In 1975, with the war finally ended, total victory achieved, and all of Vietnam under their control, the CPV leaders felt that Chinese aid and goodwill was no longer imperative. On the other hand, now that the screen of American danger had been removed, the Chinese danger appeared more clearly.

The danger signals were already visible before 1975. The momentous realignment of China's foreign policy, dramatized in 1972 by its redefinition of the Soviet Union as the most dangerous enemy, by the warm reception extended to Nixon, and by the normalization of Sino-Japanese relations, had made it clear that China no longer belonged to the same camp as the DRV. Clearer and more direct signals came in 1973: the cessation of military aid to Vietnam; incidents on the Sino-Vietnamese border resulting from conflicting claims; military occupation of the Paracel Islands by Chinese forces; support for the Pol Pot-Ieng Sary faction in its actions to liquidate pro-Vietnamese elements in the Cambodian Communist party.

From 1975 onward, China and Vietnam were increasingly on a collision course. The causes for conflict were a frontier dispute growing in intensity; China's indignation at what it considered to be mistreatment of the Hoa (Vietnamese of Chinese origin) by Vietnamese authorities, and its stopping of all aid to Vietnam as a result; Vietnam's strong determination to bring Cambodia under its control and China's equally strong determination to prevent it. The last dispute, more than anything, was to lead to armed conflict between the two countries in 1979. Ho Chi Minh used to compare China and Vietnam to "lips and teeth." After 1975 the teeth were going to feel very cold.

The CPV's policies toward China after 1975 were bound up with its policies toward Cambodia and Southeast Asia, which are examined further in the next two chapters.

7

The CPV and Laos and Cambodia: A Special Kind of Special Relationship

Being a militant Leninist party that firmly believed it had "sacred internationalist obligations" and had to play the role of "outpost of socialism in Southest Asia," the CPV was bound to be expansionist and to view Vietnam as a convenient and strong base for the spreading of communism into neighboring countries.

Geographically, from Hanoi, today as in the past, a ruler seeking to expand Vietnam's borders or power has nowhere to look but south, starting with Laos and Cambodia. In the north there is China, and in other directions, the way is blocked by great obstacles to mass movement of personnel and material.

Historically, from its home base adjoining China, Vietnam continuously expanded toward the south. This "southward march" has been one of the major themes of its history. Begun in the thirteenth century, it progressively pushed the borders of Vietnam southward, totally destroying the southern kingdom of Champa by the sixteenth century, reaching the eastern half of the Mekong delta by the middle of the nineteenth century, and absorbing a large chunk of Cambodian territory in the process. Without the arrival of the French in 1840, the march southward would have swallowed all of Cambodia, or at least that part east of the Mekong River.

THE LAOTION NEIGHBOR

With regard to Laos, the penetration and annexation process accelerted in the early part of the the nineteenth century, and by the end of the reign of Emperor Minh Mang (1820–1840), who had pointedly named the country

Dai Nam (Greater Southern Empire), all of the Laotian principalities adjoining Vietnam from Thanh Hoa down to Quang Tri—Sam Neua, Tran Ninh, Vientiane, Cam Mon, Savannakhet—had practically been integrated into Vietnam (see map 3).

The "southward march" spirit was reasserted from 1945 onward, first without much fanfare from 1945 to 1954, then clearly at the Geneva Conference in 1954, then discreetly again from 1954 to 1975, and finally dramatically since 1975. Considering the history of the CPV and the ideological background of its leaders, one can take the view that Communist militancy rather than the traditional expansionist tendency was the predominant motivation. This view would be strengthened by a study of the CPV politics regarding Laos and Cambodia since 1945, and especially since 1975.

The Vietnamese Communist party first took the name of Communist party of Vietnam, then changed it to Communist party of Indochina. The first decision was logical: there was no known non-Vietnamese Communist at the time. The change of name was also logical: the various parts of Indochina had been welded into one single political unit, and a Communist movement in Indochina should operate as a unified unit and under unified direction. Besides, that was the order of the Comintern.

From the start, the direction was Vietnamese, and it has always remained Vietnamese. If separate Laotian and Cambodian Communist parties were created in later years, these parties were only front organizations operating in fact as units of a single movement, whose direction remained under the control of the CPV. As a Pathet Lao cadre commented on the foundation of the Lao Workers' party in 1952 following the appearance of the Vietnamese Workers' party: "The Tonkinese dragon has taken the form of a snake with three heads."[1]

The CPV's policy toward Laos and Cambodia changed with changes in the situation. We can distinguish five broad periods: 1930 to 1941, 1941 to 1945, 1945 to 1954, 1954 to 1975, and after 1975.

According to the history of the party, the first Communist cells in Laos were organized at Vientiane, Thakhet, and Boneng in April 1930. At the beginning of that year, the first cells in Cambodia were organized at Phnom Penh and Kompong Cham.[2] Between 1930 and 1939, the party was busy with problems of building itself, and especially rebuilding after the disastrous failures of the "Nghe Tinh Soviets" and the merciless repressions of the French colonial authorities. It thus had little time for Laos and Cambodia. By 1939 the party was firmly back on its feet and began to look seriously at these two countries. A plenum of the central committee

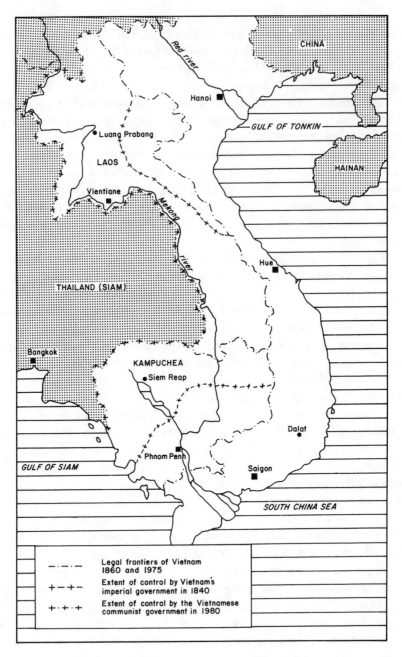

CHINA

Red river

Hanoi ■

GULF OF TONKIN

HAINAN

Luang Prabang

LAOS

Vientiane ■

Mekong river

Hue ■

THAILAND (SIAM)

Bangkok ■

KAMPUCHEA

Siem Reap

Dalat

GULF OF SIAM

Phnom Penh ■

Saigon ■

SOUTH CHINA SEA

— ·· — Legal frontiers of Vietnam
1860 and 1975

+ — + — Extent of control by Vietnam's
imperial government in 1840

+ ·· + ·· + Extent of control by the Vietnamese
communist government in 1980

Map 3. Vietnam and Indochina in 1840 and in 1980.

in November 1939 decided to "strengthen the bases of the party in Laos and Cambodia."[3] Two years later at the important plenum of May 1941, it as decided to assign to the Viet-Minh "the task of supporting the Laotian and Cambodian peoples to set up the Ai Lao Doc Lap Dong Minh (Lao Independence League) and the Cao Mien Doc Lap Dong Minh (Cambodian Independence League) as steps toward the creation of an Indochinese front against the Japanese and for the reconquest of independence in each country."[4] These Laotian and Cambodian fronts were exact replicas of the Viet Nam Doc Lap Dong Minh (Vietnam Independence League—Viet-Minh). Basically, these three fronts, with appropriate changes of names at different periods to fit new circumstances, were to be the instruments used by the CPV for carrying out its policy regarding Indochina and Southeast Asia after 1975.

Until 1940 the only member of the CPI known to be non-Vietnamese was a Laotian, Kaysone Phomvihane, and the latter was not even a full Laotian: his father was Vietnamese. Phomvihane grew up entirely in a Vietnamese milieu. He studied law in Hanoi and was a member of the central committee of the CPI.

From 1940 to 1945, Ho Chi Minh and his close associats operated from Chinese territory or from Vietnamese jungle bases on the Sino-Vietnamese borders. Geography and the still weak state of the party did not permit them to extend their activities or control as far as Laos, and still less as far as Cambodia. But once in Hanoi in August 1945, and free from the hindrance of the French colonial authorities, they could intensify their work in those two countries.

In Laos from August onward, control and direction of the Laotian nationalist revolutionary movement was exercised by a "committee of the CPI." Party history recorded that "the Lao committee of the Communist party of Indochina timely led the uprising of the Lao people, eliminating the puppet apparatus, founded the people's power in Vientiane and in the cities and provincial towns, and set up an independent government."[5]

At this time, two men emerged who would play a key role in the expansion of communism in Laos in subsequent years. One was Nouhak Phomsavan, who joined the CPI in 1945, the other was Souphanouvong, "the Red Prince." Souphanouvong first joined his half-brothers, Prince Souvanna Phouma and Prince Phetsarath, who founded the Lao Issara to oppose the return of French rule. But unlike his brothers, he avocated armed struggle to the end and the merging of the Lao Issara with the Viet-Minh. In this he was no doubt influenced by his wife, a Vietnamese

Communist. His proposal was strongly opposed by his brothers; so he went his own way and linked his fate to that of the CPV.

The "History of the Party" recorded that from January 1949 to August 1950, "the committee of the Party in Laos will lead the people" in its struggle crowned with successes of great significance, "namely the birth of the Liberation army of Laos, of the Front of Free Laos [Pathet Lao], and the Lao Government of Resistance."[6] The date used is significant as the party had proclaimed its official dissolution in Hanoi in November 1945 to convince foreigners and Vietnamese alike that it had no Communist designs in Vietnam, let alone in the rest of Indochina.

In Cambodia a Communist group associated with the Viet-Minh was active in the anti-French movement in 1945–1947. It was led by Son Ngoc Minh. Speaking of this movement, the "History of the Party" said that "the committee of the Communist Party of Indochina, set up in the early years of the resistance, led the Cambodian people" in its heroic struggle, liberating many regions and "enlarging the revolutionary bases." In April 1950 at the behest of the leadership of the party's committee, which now took the name of "national directorate," a National Congress of Free Cambodia founded the Committee of the United Front (Khmer Issarak Front) and the National Committee of Liberation "with Son Ngoc Minh as its leader."[7] Again, the date given in this connection is interesting.

From 1950 onward, with massive help from the Chinese Communists, the CPV was in a position to take the offensive. The tempo of military operations was stepped up not only in Vietnam but throughout Indochina. In the eyes of the Hanoi military strategists, Indochina was a single war theatre, in which they could resort to the strategy of dispersion of the French forces. Steps had to be taken to prepare the legal ground for the use of Laotian and Cambodian territories by Vietnamese "volunteers" and the coordination of the military operations of the Vietnamese, Laotian, and Cambodian revolutionary forces.

At the Second National Party Congress in February 1951, the party resolved that because of "the new conditions in Indochina and in the world," Vietnam would establish a party with a political program and a constitution suited to Vietnam's conditions. Laos and Cambodia would do likewise. "As a result, said a Vietnamese foreign ministry document, the Vietnam Workers' party, the Cambodian Revolutionary party (the Communist party of Kampuchea), and the Lao People's Revolutionary party came into being."[8]

On March 11, 1951, a very important conference was held. It brought together representatives of three united fronts: the Lien Viet Front of Vietnam, the Itsala Front of Laos, and the Itsarak Front of Kampuchea. The conference decided to form a "Viet-Khmer-Lao Peoples' Alliance" to "oppose all devisive schemes of the enemy" and to "wholeheartedly help each other."[9] This organization was the forerunner of the "Indochinese bloc" set up after 1975.

The creation of the Viet-Khmer-Lao alliance set the stage for the overt presence of Vietnamese "volunteers" in Laos and Cambodia in the next few years, and indeed down to 1985. For the present, it prepared the ground for the military moves of General Vo Nguyen Giap, which were to lead to the battle of Dien Bien Phu and the Geneva Conference.

At the conference, the DRV delegation did what was in fact a reassertion of the spirit of the "southward march" when it took the position of official spokesman for the Lao and Cambodian revolutionaries and demanded that the representatives of the latter be permitted to participate in the conference. It thereby posed as protector of Laos and Cambodia and as leader of Indochina. In the course of the conference, it defended the right of the Pathet Lao and Khmer Issarak to the control of a portion of territory in each respective country, which, in fact, would mean the possibility that the CPV could maintain footholds in those countries and exert an influence on their internal politics. In the next five years, the CPV will have to operate within the terms of the Geneva agreements. Its efforts would be directed at finding ways of circumventing the provisions of those agreements, which put very severe constraints on the extension of its power and influence into South Vietnam, Laos, an Cambodia.

The Geneva agreement on Vietnam presented the CPV with a major problem. Giving the DRV full control over its territory would mean reducing it to the portion of Vietnam north of the 17th parallel, instead of the 16th parallel as in 1945 under the Potsdam agreement (see map 2). It lost all control over the territory south of the 17th parallel, as it had to evacuate its troops as well as its cadres from the south, and was confronted by a staunch anti-Communist government strongly backed by the United States there. Restoring its control in the south could be done only through general elections, and with Ngo Dinh Diem at the head of the government of South Vietnam, this became more and more a remote possiblity.

The alternative course would be a resort to force. But in the international climate of the post-Geneva period, this was not possible, as until 1959 both the Soviet Union and China were anxious to avoid a major confrontation with the United States. An open military action by the DRV would certainly provoke strong reaction by the United States and activate the Southeast Asia Treaty Organization (SEATO). If the CPV chose to resort to force, it would have to go it alone, and this was unthinkable.

There remained only a third, intermediate option: subversion while waiting for a more favorable international situation permitting military action. For effective subversion, as well as military action in the future, men and material had to be moved to the south. Passage through the 17th parallel was politically impossible and physically extremely difficult. The narrow stretch of land on which ran the 17th parallel was the only area that could be watched effectively by the International Control Commission, and the latter watched it carefully. The Annamese Range, which ran north-south along the western border of Vietnam, was a formidable barrier; there was no north-south through road, and the few easy passage points were blocked by South Vietnamese troops.

To circumvent these obstacles, the CPV would need the free use of Laotian and Cambodian territory, and this naturally required the agreement of the Laotian and Cambodian governments, or of organizations within Laos and Cambodia, which would make such free use possible. To obtain these conditions would be a major concern of the CPV in the post-Geneva years. The situations in Laos and Cambodia being different, the CPV would apply different politics to each, with different degrees of success.

In Laos the CPV enjoyed favorable conditions. The Geneva agreement on Laos had allowed the Pathet Lao to retain temporary control of the provinces of Sam Neua and Phong Saly, which adjoined North Vietnam. The Pathet Lao was also left in temporary control of its armed forces. But the Pathet Lao itself was under the control of the CPV, through two men, Prince Souphanouvong and Kaysone Phomvihane. Both were reliable. Through them, the CPV had a firm grip on the Pathet Lao and the Lao revolutionary forces, and could achieve its purposes in Laos and through Laos with relative ease. It had secure bases, reliable allies, an effective political organization, and an army. All it needed now was a favorable international situation. This would come in 1960.

THE CAMBODIAN SITUATION

In Cambodia the CPV faced a more complex and not so favorable, situation. There, it had created a Khmer Issarak movement, a liberation army, and, in the last days of the war, a government of resistance, but

it encountered two major obstacles: the personality of Sihanouk, and geography. Sihanouk was a popular figure in his country. In November
1949 he had secured a relatively satisfactory agreement with France, which
recognized Cambodia's formal independence, which became real in 1953,
and enabled him to keep all opposition in check.[10]

At the Geneva Conference, the Cambodian government could prove its
independence by signing a separate armistice agreement in its own name,
whereas the agreements on Laos and Vietnam were signed by the French
government. Cambodia was also successful in forcing the evacuation of
its territory by Viet-Minh troops and cadres, and in refusing to the Communists the right to have a base or a sanctuary on Cambodian territory.
This, combined with the obligation for the Viet-Minh troops and cadres
to evacuate South Vietnam, deprived the CPV of the possibility of according protection to its Cambodian protégés.

Accordingly, Ho Chi Minh, always mindful of the necessity to ensure
absolute physical security for his men, ordered the Communist troops and
cadres to move to North Vietnam for safety. Different estimates put this
number at 2,000–4000 or 5,000.[11] Not all Cambodian Communists followed Ho's orders; a few hundred remained in Cambodia to carry on the
struggle. This would be a source of much trouble for the CPV later.

Among those who remained behind were Saloth Sar (the future ill-
famed Pol Pot), Khieu Samphan, Ieng Sary, Son Sen, Hu Nim, and Hou
Youn. They created the Pracheachon party to carry out the struggle, first
through open legal activities. Then, on September 30, 1960, they created
the Communist party of Kampuchea (CPK), a clear sign of their disso-
ciation from the CPI and especially of their refusal to accept the CPV's
leadership. In 1963 Saloth Sar, Ieng Sary, and Hu Nim abandoned the
legal struggle and went underground after a revolt they staged against
Sihanouk failed.

The CPK's open opposition to the Phnom Penh government was contrary to the CPV line, which at this time was to court Sihanouk in order
to obtain his authorization to use Cambodian territory for its operations
against South Vietnam. The action of the Cambodian Communists obviously complicated the CPV's diplomatic maneuvers. Thus, in Cambodia the CPV did not have a safe base, sure allies, a reliable and pliable
political organization, or an army under its contol. This was going to
make a big difference with Laos when the time came for it to seek domination over Indochina.

To return to Laos, in 1960 the international situation changed to the
CPV's advantage. In spite of the Geneva agreement, attempts by Prince

Souvanna Phouma, prime minister of the Lao royal government, to re-store peace, political stability, national unity, and to pursue a policy of neutrality, failed because of the refusal of the Pathet Lao to be integrated territorially, military, and politically into the royal Lao government. This exasperated the Rightist elements.

In May 1959 Phoui Sannanikone, a Rightist who had become prime minister in July of the previous year, arrested and jailed Souphanouvong and a number of other Pathet Lao leaders after a Pathet Lao battalion took to the jungles instead of accepting integration into the national army. From this moment onward, the Pathet Lao was in open rebellion against the royal government. A new civil war had started, which opened the way for the DRV's armed intervention in Laos by sending in "volunteers" to support the antigovernment revolutionary forces, and by strengthening the position of Kaysone Phomvihane, who took control of the Pathet while Souphanouvong was in jail. From then on, under Phomvihane's influ-ence, that is, under the CPV's influence, the Lao party practiced increas-ingly a communism "à la vietnamienne" (Vietnamese style).[12] Souphan-ouvong would play a more and more nominal role after his escape from jail ten months later.[13]

In August 1960 a young captain, Kong Le, commander of a battalion of parachutists, staged a coup d'etat against the Phoumi government. The coup started a chain of events that led to an international crisis, to the convening of an international conference at Geneva in May 1961, and the conclusion of a second agreement on Laos in July 1962. This agree-ment contained two major provisions: establishment of a three-party co-alition government for Laos, and formal prohibition of SEATO interven-tion in that country. Under the first, the position of the Pathet Lao was strengthened: Government decisions must now have its approval. Under the second, the position of the other parties was weakened: it made it impossible for legalistic and democratic America to intervene in support of the non-Communist elements in Laos.

From 1962 onward, the non-Communist elements were therefore no longer protected from a military action of the Pathet Lao "in coordina-tion" with DRV "volunteers" and could no longer undertake any military action against the Pathet Lao forces without facing direct confrontation with the DRV "volunteers." Government forces could no longer penetrate into the areas controlled by the Pathet Lao. This left the CPV free to build a highway—the so-called Ho Chi Minh trail—through Pathet Lao-controlled territory for the massive and rapid dispatch of men and material to the south. This made the defense of both Laos and South Vietnam against a Communist conquest impossible.

In a highly illuminating article in the *Vietnam Courier* in 1984 entitled "The legendary Ho Chi Minh trail," Colonel Vo Bam told how, ordered by the party central military committee in May 1959 to open a quick supply route to the revolution in the south, he had to grapple with formidable difficulties until, in anticipation of the Zurich agreement of April 1961 (as part of the Geneva negotiations), "at the request of the Lao revolutionary forces," the Vietnamese army cleared "the Rightist troops" out of the Lao-Viet border area and opened a fifty-kilometer wide corridor, later widened to 80 kilometers, across route 9 (see map 4).

Through this corridor would run the "Ho Chi Minh trail" on which men and supplies could be sent quickly by trucks to the Vietnamese as well as Lao revolutionary forces in the south.[14] General Van Tien Dung, who commanded the troops that took South Vietnam in 1975, referred to the Ho Chi Minh trail as "our road eight meters wide" on which "large trucks, and armored vehicles drove at high speed in both directions, day and night, all year round."[15]

There is little doubt that the agreement on Laos in 1962 opened the way to the conquest and control of both South Vietnam and Laos by the CPV in 1975, through the Paris agreement of January 27, 1973 on Vietnam, and the Vientiane agreement of February 21, 1973 on Laos.

Like the 1962 agreement, the 1973 agreement did not lead to peace and stability in Laos, and for the same reasons. A Provisional Government of National Union was set up on September 14, 1973, but it did not lead to any union. The Pathet Lao, free from the risks of SEATO intervention, continued to extend progressively the territory under their control with the help of the North Vietnamese *dac cong* (special commandos). Using the same tactics of "popular" demonstration and intimidation learned from the Viet-Minh, they eliminated all opposition within a relatively short time.

In April 1974 Souphanouvong was back in Vientiane. A year later without opposition the Pathet Lao took control of the capital. Through a series of political maneuvers, it isolated the king and forced him to abdicate, and on December 3 it proclaimed the Lao People's Democratic Republic. Souphanouvong was elected president. He immediately appointed Kaysone Phomvihane as prime minister. This was followed by an accelerated and ruthless communization of Laos, about which Amphay Doré and Mangkra Phouma, who were close witnesses of those momentous events, have left vivid and revealing accounts.[16]

The CPV's intent to strengthen its control over Laos had been made plain in a resolution of the plenum of the CPV central committee in April 1973 more than two years earlier, and just two months after the signing

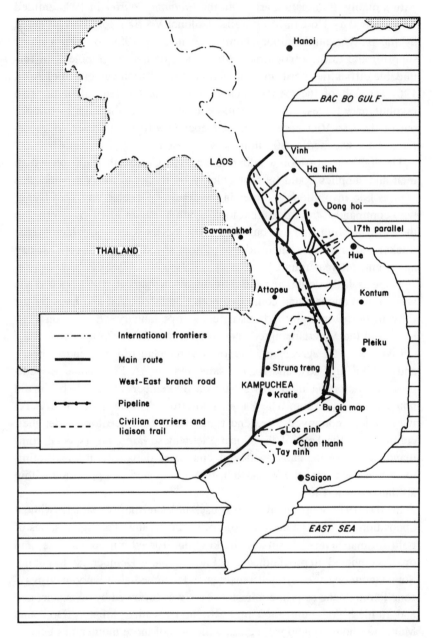

Map 4. Ho Chi Minh Trail. (*Source:* Vietnam Courier, Hanoi, no.5, 1984)

of the Vientiane agreement. The resolution said that the party had decided "to carry out its internationalist obligations toward the Laotian and Cambodian revolutions."[17] Thus, by the end of 1975, the lever had been firmly put in place. All that remained for the CPV was to activate this lever to bring Laos under its total control. This would be accomplished by July 1977. It was not difficult with the presence of three PAVN divisions deployed on Laotian territory.[18]

Meanwhile, in Cambodia the CPV followed a different tactic. Their main lever there was not the Cambodian Communists, but Sihanouk, who cooperated with the CPV partly out of Indochinese solidarity and "to deserve the gratitude of the Viet-Minh," and partly because the Chinese "encouraged" him to do so.[19] Sihanouk had no illusions about Vietnam, but he counted on China to protect his country from being "Hanoi-ized." To him, compared to Vietnam, Cambodia was just a "kitten" compared to a "lion," but "over the head of the lion, the Cambodian kitten will have its eyes fixed on the Chinese dragon."[20]

For ten years after the Geneva Conference, Sihanouk pursued a policy of neutrality in the Vietnam conflict. This policy was inaugurated at the Bandung Conference in April 1955. There, he accepted the "pipe of peace" offered by Pham Van Dong, who became "his best friend and most powerful support in the coming years." There, he was also "charmed" by Chou En-lai.[21] His neutrality was rather formal, as he made no secret of his hostility toward Ngo Dinh Diem and the Amerians, but it kept his country from dangerous involvement in the war.

In 1965, however, Sihanouk took the momentous decision of abandoning neutrality. In February of that year, he hosted a Conference of the Peoples of Indochina to set up a common front in support of the "Vietnamese patriots," i.e., the Liberation Front of South Vietnam, and North Vietnam, against the United States. In 1967 he established diplomatic relations with North Vietnam. A year earlier, he had already formally allowed the Vietnamese Communists the free use of Cambodian territory as a sanctuary. In 1969 he made a number of decisions that were to have far-reaching consequences for his country and for himself.

One was to allow North Vietnam to send the Khmer-Vietminh back to Cambodia. These were the Cambodian Communists who had regrouped in North Vietnam in 1954 after the Geneva Conference. This decision would lead to the internal fight among pro-Vietnamese and anti-Vietnamese Cambodian Communists, which was but a prelude to the Cambodian-Vietnam conflict after 1975. Another was to raise the status of the representation of the provisional revolutionary government of the Republic of South Vietnam (South Vietnam Liberation Front) to that of embassy.

This followed a similar decision he made two years earlier in favor of the representation of the DRV. Cambodia was now completely, in fact as well as in law, on Hanoi's side.

Sihanouk has explained that his decision to allow the Vietnamese revolutionary forces to use Cambodia was made at the request of Chou En-lai in 1966, but he was also motivated by the desire to "generate as much as possible the gratitude of the Vietnamese" toward Cambodia and to "exorcise the Vietnamese threat" against his country.[22] He was particularly concerned about the territorial integrity of Cambodia after the end of the Vietnam war, which, in his view, the Vietnamese Communists would surely win, and he sought advance assurances from them that they would respect Cambodia's frontiers. He was given all the assurances he sought and more, although, as it turned out after the Vietnam war had ended, these assurances were only empty pledges made by the CPV leaders essentially for the purpose of securing his political support and, with it, the free use of Cambodian territory.

On May 31, 1967, the central committee of the National Liberation Front of South Vietnam (NFLSVN) issued a declaration recognizing "the present frontiers" of Cambodia and the existing frontiers between South Vietnam and Cambodia, and pledging to respect those frontiers. On June 8, 1967, the DRV government made a similar declaration, which was accompanied by a personal letter from Pham Van Dong to Sihanouk.[23] These assurances were to be repeated again in the joint communique of the Indochinese summit in Canton in April 1970.[24] But the CPV was to tell the Cambodians in May 1976 that Vietnam had to give the above assurances in 1966 "simply because of the pressure of the needs of the war against U.S. aggression."[25]

The CPV leaders also missed no opportunity of endearing themselves to the latter and to his favourite wife, Princess Monique. Sihanouk has told with irony how, on the occasion of his presence in Hanoi for Ho Chi Minh's funerals in September 1969, Truong Chinh clumsily flattered Monique by telling her: "Your beauty is moving"—a compliment that only a revolutionary like Truong Chinh would make to a French woman— whereas Vo Nguyen Giap, in spite of his obvious short size, turned himself into a constant "knight servant" to Monique.[26] In 1970, while in exile after being deposed by General Lon Nol, he had "friendly, trustful, even affectionate relations" with Pham Van Dong.[27] Again, this turned out to be illusory. The Pham Van Dong he thought was his "best friend next to Chou En-lai and Kim Il-sung", who had personally assumed the role of escort to him and had hugged him very warmly on his visit to Hanoi in

1969, would say coldly in a televised interview in 1980 that Sihanouk was "finished" and would prove himself "a ferocious enemy of an independent Cambodia."[28] Naturally, Dong had no more use for Sihanouk then.

But, by a twist of fate, Sihanouk was also the source of much trouble for the CPV. By denying the Communists control over any portion of Cambodian territory and by insisting on the evacuation of Cambodia by DRV troops at Geneva in 1954, and then by allowing the Khmer-Vietminh to return to Cambodia in 1969, he unwittingly sowed the seed of what was to plague the CPV from 1970 onward, especially after 1975.

In September 1978 the ministry of foreign affairs of the Democratic Kampuchea (Pol Pot) published a black paper to give the "facts and evidence of the acts of aggression and annexation of Vietnam against Kampucchea."[29] This book is very much like the white paper published by Vietnam in 1979 on Sino-Vietnamese relations. It reveals that from 1946 to 1978, unlike the situation existing between Laotian and Vietnamese Communists, relations between Cambodian and Vietnamese Communists were marred by mutual suspicions, tensions, and conflicts.

The Cambodian Communists accused the Vietnamese (CPV) of wanting to create in Indochina "a powerful military base from which they can realize their ambitions in Southeast Asia." In Kampuchea from 1946 to 1954, they had "several times" created a separate army composed of Khmers paid by them to be used as an "instrument of their policy of annexation"; when they came back in 1964 they resumed their activities "to the same end."[30] The paper described the various attempts of the CPV to force the Communist party of Kampuchea (CPK) to accept the policy laid down by it, in particular, to give up armed struggle and wait for Vietnam to liberate Kampuchea until after Vietnam had liberated itself. From 1965 onward the struggle was very "difficult and bitter," and tensions reached a peak in 1969 when words such as "friendship" and "solidarity" were "nothing more than empty formulas."[31]

In 1965 a meeting took place in Hanoi between the CPK and the CPV. At this meeting, which the black paper described as very "bitter," the CPK delegation, led by Pol Pot, resisted very strong pressure from the CPV delegation, led by Le Duan, to change its policy, which Le Duan called "adventurist and Leftist," and insisted on pursuing its own independent line. On this occasion, the paper recorded, the Cambodian delegates refused to address Ho Chi Minh as "Uncle Ho" and called him simply "Comrade Ho Chi Minh." This made Ho and his entourage furious because the appellation "Uncle Ho" implied that the Vietnamese were "the father of Indochina," and by rejecting this appellation the CPK leaders expressed "the national position of independence and equality of the Communist party of Kampuchea" in the relations between parties. "All the Vietnamese leaders, among them Le Duan, Pham Van Dong, and Vo Nguyen Giap, were irritated, for never a "younger brother" or a "son" has dared used such language in speaking to an "elder brother" or a "father."

At another meeting in Hanoi at the end of 1969, again the CPK delegation refused to bow to Le Duan, whom the paper described as "deceitful and treacherous." The CPV wanted the CPK to "give up their armed struggle and lay down their weapons." Le Duan told the Cambodians not to resort to armed struggle, but instead to wait for Vietnam to win victory, then liberate Phnom Penh.

The CPK delegation, again led by Pol Pot, refused to yield. The contradictions between the positions of the two delegations were therefore "irreconcilable," and Le Duan "could not contain his fury." The Vietnamese resorted to "open threats against the CPK delegation," and the members of the CPK unanimously thought that the Vietnamese were furious and capable of liquidating them "by resorting even to assassination." The atmosphere was so tense that certain members of the CPK, who were not used to such ordeals, were "badly shaken."

Contrary to what it advocated for Laos, the CPV did not want the Cambodian Communists to resort to armed struggle because it had in Sihanouk's government an ally willing to put Cambodian territory at the CPV's disposal, and to give it full political and diplomatic support. It was therefore in the CPV's interest not only to see to it that this government remained in power in Phnom Penh, but also that it should rule over a Cambodia enjoying maximum peace and quiet so that the Vietnamese revolutionary forces could have a perfectly safe rear for their assault on South Vietnam. Revolutionary activities in Cambodia, whether Communist or not, must therefore be shelved. That is why in a document carefully drafted by Le Duan and given to the CPK leaders in 1965, there was "no reference either to class struggle or struggle against the American imperialists." To add insult to injury, the document handed to the CPK leaders was written in Vietnamese.

On the other hand, if Cambodia was liberated by Vietnamese forces, then the CPV could claim that the Vietnamese, and not the Cambodian revolutionaries, were the liberators of Cambodia, and the CPK would be relegated to an insignificant position. In any case, if the Vietnamese Communists entered Phnom Penh first, they would be in a position to put in place a Cambodian government of their choice owing them a debt and obedience.

The CPK leaders were well aware of the dangers facing them if they adopted the line recommended by the CPV. As the CPK saw it, the CPV's aims were:

> 1. Induce the Kampuchean Communist party to put their trust in the Vietnamese forces, and to rely on them and depend on them.
>
> 2. Obtain from the Communist party of Kampucheaa that it abandon armed struggle. And if the Communist party of Kampuchea abandoned armed struggle, the revolutionary forces of Kampuchea would be destroyed. The Vietnamese would then have a clear path before them. . . . The Vietnamese could then reproach the Communist party of Kampuchea of being incapable of providing leadership and should let them lead and organize the revolutionary forces.[32]

The bitter feud between the CPK and the CPV temporarirly ended in 1970 following the coup staged by General Lon Nol against Sihanouk. The policy pursued by Lon Nol was the reverse of that followed by Sihanouk: he wanted the Vietnamese revolutionaries out of Cambodia, and he became an ally of South Vietnam and the United States. From Peking on March 23, Sihanouk, with encouragement and support from the Chinese government, proclaimed the dissolution of the Lon Nol government and the Cambodian national assembly, the creation of a National United Front and a National Liberation Army, and the building of socialism, "and even communism" in Cambodia. This put him on the same side as the CPK. The latter thus accepted to join his National United Front and to participate in the royal government of National Union of Cambodia, and also in the summit conference of the Indochinese peoples convened by him at Canton in April to establish an Indochinese front against the United States.

After the conference, during a stop in Hanoi on their way back to Cambodia, the CPK leaders were received by all "with overwhelming joy and by extremely warm embraces." At the banquet in its honor, the CPK delegation was "covered with praises from beginning to end." Earlier in Peking, when Pham Van Dong had met Pol Pot, he had "only friendly words and stretched arms" for the latter. Compared with the previous meeting in Hanoi, that was "a 180-degree turn." Yet the difficulties of the CPV were not over. Far from it. Although the CPK was now an ally of the CPV in the fight against common enemies (Lon Nol, Nguyen Van Thieu, and the Americans), it continued to oppose furiously all CPV attempts to establish Vietnamese domination over Cambodia, and in particular over the Cambodian Communist party.

The CPK leaders first struck at the "tap ket." These were the Khmer-Vietminh, as Sihanouk called them, that is, the Cambodian Communists who had fought alongside the Viet-Minh, accepted CPV leadership, and gone to North Vietnam with the Vietnamese Communists in 1954 after the conclusion of the Geneva agreement. They were accused of being "cau an," a Vietnamese term for seeking peace and tranquility, whereas their comrades had remained behind to carry on the struggle, endured hardships, and suffered harsh repressions by Sihanouk after 1963. Worse still, they were dubbed "Hanoi Khmers" and considered as agents of Vietnam and instruments of the CPV's schemes aiming at annexing Cambodia and establishing a "Federation of Indochina."

To avoid the risks of infiltration, the CPK leaders systematically excluded the Hanoi returnees from positions of power and influence in the CPK apparatus, dispersed them, and between 1971 and 1973 subjected them to bloody purges. One of the victims of these purges was Son Ngoc Minh, who had led the Khmer Issarak movement in Cambodia in 1945–1954, and who was the equivalent of the Laotian Kaysone Phomvihane. The CPV thus lost the key man for its designs in Cambodia.

The CPK leadership also adopted strong measures to prevent the establishment on Cambodian territory of a "parallel state." These measures affected not only the "locally manufactured Vietnamese" (local Vietnamese armed by Hanoi), but eventually were extended to the troops from North Vietnam. As a Vietnamese commentator remarked, following the Indochinese summit of 1970, one would expect full cooperation between the Vietnamese and Cambodian parties, yet

> soon, unusual signs became visible: Vietnamese fighters were forbidden to have any contact with the Khmer population in spite of moving expressions of hospitality. What is more serious is that entire Vietnamese columns were ambushed in areas where all Lonnolian forces had been swept clear, and the attackers could be no one else than the Red Khmers. These Khmers did not hesitate to seize food, weapons, and other equipment from their Vietnamese comrades.[33]

The CPK explained their attitude as reaction to the behavior of the Vietnamese troops and cadres. They said that although these troops and cadres were given hospitality by the Cambodians on their arrival on Cambodian territory, they behaved "like a great power, like colonialists, lords and masters of Kampuchea. . . . worse than the French colonialists." They said that, worse still, in November 1970 the CPV attempted to assassinate Pol Pot and Nuon Chea (deputy secretary of the party) during a meeting between these two men and Nguyen Van Linh (future secretary general of the CPV) and Tran Nam Trung (a general and well-known leader of the NLFSVN) at Stung Chinit, near the Vietnamese headquarters.

By 1973 it was clear that the CPV had no control, or even influence, on the CPK. Its pleadings with CPK leaders to participate in the peace negotiations fell on deaf ears, and these leaders also steadfastly refused to let the CPV negotiate on their behalf. Thus between 1970 and 1973, instead of scaling down their fighting, they intensified it. The CPV leaders were extremely angry, but there was little they could do. In February and March 1973 it became clear that, in spite of assurances by Le Duc Tho to Kissinger, "Hanoi could not deliver the Khmer Rouge," and Nixon's belief that the Khmer Rouge was "controlled by Hanoi and amenable by Moscow" was ill-founded.[34]

According to the confession of a North Vietnamese prisoner captured by the Khmer Rouge, Vietnamese cadres had been told that Cambodians must be forced to accept the Paris agreement and that "after finishing the war in Indochina, we will become the big brother of Indochina. . . . As a big brother we shall have to govern the younger brothers and not allow them to do anything at will."[35] This is precisely what the CPK did not want, and as it turned out, what Hanoi found very difficult to achieve.

Thus after the Paris and Vientiane peace agreements had been signed, the CPK forces went on fighting and fought even harder. In July the congress of the United Front resolved that it would never negotiate and would fight on until total victory was achieved. This they did on April 17, two weeks before North Vietnamese troops took Saigon, and one month before the Pathet Lao backed by Vietnamese "volunteers" took Vientiane.

By contrast, in Laos the CPV encountered no difficulty in carrying out its role of "big brother of Indochina." In February 1976, less than two months after the founding of the Lao People's Democratic Republic, a delegation of the Lao new government headed by Kaysone Phomvihane was invited to Hanoi. The joint communique issued on this occasion proclaimed the determination of the two parties to promote the "militant and fraternal solidarity" between "the three countries of Indochina," and to "closely coordinate" their actions against imperialism and "the reactionaries at their service."[36] This in fact was a revival of the CPI in a new form. In July 1977 a Vietnamese delegation led by Pham Van Dong arrived in Vientiane to formalize the full control of Laos by Vietnam through the signing of a Treaty of Friendship and Cooperation (July 17, 1977) between the two countries, together with a treaty on the delimitation of their frontiers and a number of other agreements.

The Treaty of Friendship and Cooperation formalized the "special relationship" between the two countries. Under article 1 the two countries would do "all in their power" to preserve and develop the "special relationship" between them. Under article 2 the two countries pledged to "cooperate closely to strengthen their defense." Under article 5, Laos pledged to "cooperate" with Vietnam to "give support to the struggle of the peoples of Southeast Asia for independence, democracy, peace, and true neutrality."[37] This means that Laos had to support Vietnam's forward policy in Southeast Asia and, for the first time in its history, participated in an imperialist scheme.

The text of the treaty on the delimitation of frontiers has not been made public, which is an indication of its highly sensitive nature, especially in regard to the national sentiment of the Laotian people. According to Amphay Doré, the Vietnam-Lao frontiers were moved westward into Lao territory fifteen to thirty kilometers; hundreds of Laotian villages that did not want to live under Vietnamese administration had to move, and tens of thousands of Vietnamese families settled on the evacuated territory.[38] Since the Ho Chi Minh trail ran through this territory, and, according to the disclosures of Colonel Vo Bam mentioned earlier, the corridor through which this trail ran was fifty to 80 kilometers wide, it can be surmised that the width of the stretch of territory ceded by Laos, which must include this historic trail, was more than thirty kilometers.

Thus Vietnamese control over the external and internal affairs of Laos was formalized by the establishment of a "special relationship." Amphay Doré said:

> this relationship translated into new terms adapted to the new situation the networks which the Communist party of Indochina had established in the "three brother countries." They were "special" because they were "organic," just as "three heads of the snake" belong to the same body. To characterize the relations between Laos and Vietnam, a text published thereafter said that the two countries were "bound to each other like skin and flesh." "Privileged" could not adequately describe the nature of the link.[39]

In concrete terms, Laotian officials were told to be "cooperative toward the Vietnamese," and those who were uncooperative or lukewarm were sent to "reeducation" in special camps, or even to North Vietnam. Even the king of Laos did not escape this treatment.[40] Those who showed anti-Vietnamese feelings were discarded and could "say goodbye to their careers." "Parallel ministries" were installed in the offices formerly occupied by USAID, and the Vietnamese nationals in Laos considered themselves to be in "conquered territory."[41]

The "special relationship" between Laos and Vietnam enabled the latter to use Laotian territory to dispatch troops quickly and conveniently toward the south, down the Mekong valley, and also to deploy troops along the Mekong River facing Thailand, as well as on the portion of Lao territory adjoining Thailand on the other side of the river. This had ominous implications for Cambodia and Thailand, as well as for Laos. Soon, indeed, Laos would have to join Vietnam in its conflict with Cambodia and Thailand, and Laotians troops would have to take part and die in the war resulting from this conflict.[42]

The CPV's total control of Laos, both de facto and de jure, was achieved smoothly, without generating waves, by the use of special tactics: the fashioning of a pliable instrument, the Pathet Lao, and the application of the technique of "special relationship." But when it tried the same in Cambodia, the CPV ran into strong resistance. To overcome this resistance, it first tried diplomacy, then political subversion, and when these methods failed, it resorted to war.

During their negotiations with Hanoi, the Cambodians demanded not only the recognition of Cambodia's frontiers existing before 1975 (the so-called Brevie Line, laid down by Governor General Jules Brevie in 1939), but also the evacuation of all Vietnamese troops from Cambodian territory. The negotiations failed.[43] The basic cause of conflict between Hanoi and Phnom Penh was, however, the CPK leaders' adamant refusal to concede "big brother" status to the CPV by accepting the same kind of "special relationship" existing between Vietnam and Laos, which in their eyes meant a reconstitution in fact of the CPI and of the Indochinese Federation, the latter under Vietnamese instead of French direction. Pol Pot had already made clear to the CPV leaders in 1965 and 1969 that the CPV would not accept the status of "younger brother" or "son" of the CPV.

The CPV leaders later accused the Chinese of encouraging the Cambodians in order to divide the Indochinese. But there was no need of Chinese encouragement for this. Cambodians, whatever their political colors, harbored a deep mistrust of the Vietnamese. The history of Vietnam's expansion at the expense of Cambodia from the seventeenth century onward was enough to convince them, whether it was Sihanouk or

Pol Pot, that the Vietnamese were "swallowers of Khmer land," a term used by both of them. The CPK stubbornly refused to take the Laotian road of "special relationship" and rectification of borders according to the wishes of the CPV leaders, and insisted on "normal" relations, that is, relations of equality between states and parties, instead of full and docile alignment on Hanoi.

At the same time Pol Pot carried out a massive purge of the "Hanoi Khmers." By early 1978 all the Khmers who had been sent down the Ho Chi Minh trail had been murdered. The bodies of the convicted bore the inscription: "Convicted for sympathy with Vietnam." A Vietnamese army paper said that Pol Pot "ordered the arrest of all leading cadres of all the divisions and units that had been trained in Vietnam. . . . All Khmer cadres who returned to Vietnam to participate in the fight against the U.S. aggressors and their puppets to save the country had been mur- dered. . . . Anyone who happens to speak a single word of Vietnamese is considered as commiting a crime."[44]

Pol Pot, not unreasonably, suspected that the Hanoi Khmers were pro- Hanoi, and feared that from their ranks the CPV could draw the men who could exert influence on the policies of the CPK, or recruit the men for fighting the CPK in the name of purity of Leninism and proletarian in- tenationalism. In liquidating them, he eliminated the danger of infiltration by the CPV, a coup, or physical liquidation. Three attempts at assassi- nation instigated by the CPV (July 1975, September 1976, and April 1976) and several coup attempts (1973, 1975, and 1978) had convinced the CPK leaders that the CPV wanted to eliminate them at all costs.[45]

To the CPV, the CPK leaders practiced "narrow nationalism"—a great Leninist sin—and in undermining "the traditional solidarity" between the three peoples they were "committing a crime which is encouraged by the imperialists and world reactionaries , and for which they must be held fully responsible to their own people and to history."[46] As the document suggests, now the CPV would see to it that the "crime" of the CPK lead- ers be punished by "their own people," and to put in place a Cambodian government willing to sign with Vietnam the same kind of treaties that Laos had accepted.

In the view of the CPV leaders, the Lao-Vietnamese treaties were in keeping with the declarations of Moscow of 1957 and 1960 according to which the Communist parties were "duty bound to support and assist one another." These treaties responded to "the earnest aspirations and vital interests of each people." In particular, the treaty on the delineation of the Lao-Vietnamese borders—which, significantly, the Lao government had not dared to render public—was "a splendid illustration of how to settle problems of national interests in a spirit of harmoniously combining genuine patriotism with pure proletarian internationalism" and also "a brilliant example" of the policy of friendship and good neighborhood.[47] Since the CPK leaders refused to endorse such a view, they had to be removed.

By June 1977 the CPV leaders had concluded that there was in the CPK "an evil faction bent on harming the traditions of fraternal solidarity and amity" between Cambodia and Vietnam.[48] From then onward, Hanoi radio called on the Cambodians to rise against their government. In September Hanoi launched a large-scale military operation. The Vietnamese troops penetrated twenty kilometers inside Cambodian territory, then withdrew. The purpose of the operation was not military but political. In withdrawing, the Vietnamese troops brought out some 150,000 Cambodians, the future "people" who were to "punish" the Pol Pot gang and provide "popular support" and "Cambodian" armed forces for the Cambodian team riding in with Vietnamese tanks.

Meanwhile, on December 31, from Peking the government of Democratic Kampuchea (Pol Pot) publicly denounced the Vietnamese as carrying out "a systematic and large-scale invasion" of Cambodia, of seeking to "occupy, annex, and swallow up Kampuchean land," both now and in the future, and, to that purpose, of having "continuously exerted pressure of coercion on Kampuchea over the past decades." It said that Vietnam had "long ago the strategic design of turning Democratic Kampuchea into a member of Indochinese Federation and a slave of Vietnam,"[49] It accused the Vietnamese of being "as ungrateful as crocodiles,"[50] and of "behaving like a superpower in Southeast Asia, walking in the footsteps of Hitler."[51] It also announced that it had decided to suspend diplomatic relations with Vietnam.

The bridges had thus been burned. From now on, events would move quickly. In January the Vietnamese staged a second and bigger offensive, penetrating thirty kilometres inside Cambodia on a front twenty kilometres wide. This attack was repulsed by the Cambodians, who were heavily armed by the Chinese. It prompted Pol Pot to intensify his purges of the ranks of the CPK, forcing many members, among them Heng Samrin, the future president of the Vietnam-backed government, to take refuge in Vietnam. On February 5, Pol Pot refused Vietnam's proposals of peace negotiations. In March at an important meeting, the CPV central committee adopted a plan to get rid of the Pol Pot government.[52]

According to Nayan Chanda, citing sources close to Vietnam, the plan, in typical CPV fashion, called for a three-pronged—diplomatic, political, military—offensive against the Pol Pot government. On the diplomatic front, it was decided that an offensive would be launched to convince the Southeast Asian countries of Vietnam's pacific intentions. Pham Van Dong toured Southeast Asia in the autumn in 1978 for this purpose. Dong knew then that a massive invasion was about to be started against Cambodia.

To cover its rear against a possible strong reaction by China, Hanoi needed assurances of Soviet support. This led to Vietnam joining the Council of Mutual Economic Assistance (Comecon) on June 28, then signing a Vietnamese-Soviet Treaty of Friendship and Cooperation on November 3.[53] Peking was prompt to point out that this treaty irrefutably "smelled of gun powder."[54]

With regard to the political part of the plan, the CPV needed levers— a man and a political organization. The man was Heng Samrin. The next step was to create an appropriate organization supposedly representing the will of the Cambodian people. This was accomplished on December 3 with the founding of the National United Front for the Salvation of Kampuchea (NUFSK). The CPV had its man. It had its political organization. The final step would be a popular uprising and a "request" from Cambodians for help to start the military phase of the plan. To prepare for this, since April Hanoi radio hd been calling on the Cambodian troops to rise up against their government.

Less than three weeks after the creation of NUFSK, on December 25 the CPV struck. In a massive military offensive involving 180,000 troops, Vietnam invaded Cambodia, and on January 7 it "liberated" Phnom Penh and installed a Cambodian government headed by Heng Samrin. On February 17 Pham Van Dong landed at Phnom Penh with a delegation. The next day Heng Samrin and Dong signed a Treaty of Peace, Amity and Cooperation on the pattern of the Viet-Lao Treaty of July 17, 1977.[55]

The rapidity of the signing suggests that the text had already been prepared by the Vietnamese, and all the Cambodians had to do was to append their signatures to it. In this they had little choice, as they owed their lives, their positions, and their protection to the Vietnamese.

The treaty legalized the presence of some 180,000 Vietnamese "volunteers" and Vietnam's preeminent position in Cambodia. Under article 2 of the treaty, the two parties pledged "to lend mutual support and aid in every field and in all necessary forms to strengthen their defense capacities." Like Laos, de facto as well as de jure, Cambodia was now squarely aligned on Vietnam. In another form, the Federation of Indochina and the CPI had now been fully reconstituted. The name for this new form is "special relationship"—of a very special kind (see map 1).

The CPV had not expected more than strong verbal protests from China and ASEAN for its action against the Pol Pot government. However, the invasion of Cambodia led to military action by China against Vietnam on February 19, and, since then to steadfast Chinese and ASEAN support for the anti-Vietnamese Cambodian forces, which was to make of Cambodia a "Vietnam's Vietnam."

By its action in Cambodia, Vietnam was going to get mired in a people's guerrilla war against Cambodian nationalist forces supported by a powerful and determined neighbor—China—and enjoying in a neighboring country—Thailand—the same kind of sanctuary and bases that North Vietnam once enjoyed in Cambodia in its war against South Vietnam, and that made it unbeatable. At the same time, as a result of its blatant invasion and occupation of Cambodia, it was to be isolated internationally by skilled diplomatic maneuvering by China and the ASEAN countries. All the international goodwill it had earned during its fight against France and then the United States were quickly dissipated.

As Sihanouk had said, Cambodia was but a kitten compared to the Vietnamese lion, but the Cambodian kitten had its eyes fixed on the Chinese dragon. It is strange that the CPV leaders had forgotten this basic fact, for when the DRV fought against the French or the Americans, it was also a kitten that had its eyes on the Chinese dragon. If this dragon could not crush its small challenging Vietnamese neighbor in one single blow, it could make life difficult for him in the short run, and nightmarish in the long run.

With an angry Chinese dragon next door, Vietnam would know no peace. That is a lesson from history that all Vietnamese, rulers or common people, know well. The CPV leaders, however, seemed to think they could ignore it, and that, under the protection of the red Russian bear, they could proceed safely with the digestion of their Laotian and Cambodian victims.

8

The CPV and Southeast Asia: Politics of Irreversibility

Until 1975 the CPV leaders were too busy with the liberation of Vietnam to concern themselves actively with Southeast Asia. The records show, however, that already in 1949, as the prospects of victory in Indochina became brighter, they began to turn their thoughts toward the region, and to set their strategic aims there.

Naturally, enough, it was Ho Chi Minh who, again, set the aims. This was quite in keeping with the role he himself had played in the region as a key agent of the Comintern in 1928–1931. In a speech to the cadres of the party in January 1949, he said: "We are an Indochinese party, but we have also the task of contributing to the liberation of Southeast Asia. This is because we are the largest party in Southeast Asia, and the first party to have conquered power in Southeast Asia."[1] At the Third National Congress of the party in September 1960, he said to view Vietnam as "the outpost of socialism in Southeast Asia,"[2] thus making clear that the CPV had a special interest in the region.

In conversations with foreign officials, the CPV leaders took no trouble to conceal their view. Thus Le Duc Tho, the chief CPV negotiator at the Paris peace negotiations in 1968–1973, told Kissinger that it was "Vietnam's destiny to dominate not only Indochina but all of Southeast Asia,"[3] And Pham Van Dong, speaking of Vietnam in the future, told William Sullivan, who accompanied Kissinger during a visit to Hanoi in 1973, that "We are the Prussians of Southeast Asia. We are a people of greater zeal, greater energy, greater intelligence than our neighbors." And referring specifically to the Thais, the Malays, and the Philippinos, he said: "We don't have to take military action to expand our sphere of influence," people will join us "merely because of our attraction."[4]

With Vietnamese and Southeast Asians, the CPV leaders spoke more

156

in ideological and revolutionary terms. Thus Truong Nhu Tang, a former minister in the South Vietnam revolutionary government, has reported that during his visits to Hanoi before 1975, he frequently heard high cadres of the Nguyen Ai Quoc School (which trained Southeast Asian revolutionary cadres) talk openly about the establishment of a "Federation of Southeast Asian Soviet Republics" by the year 2000.[5]

The CPV leaders' views regarding Southeast Asia were thus clearly expansionist and revolutionary. With such views, sooner or later a confrontation with ASEAN was inevitable. The occasion would be Vietnam's attempts to subjugate Cambodia. The study of this confrontation shows that, as in the case of China, the CPV would face politically sophisticated adversaries, and the politics it had used so effectively with the French and the Americans would not work so well when applied to fellow Southeast Asians.

Pham Van Dong was seriously mistaken in assuming that the countries of Southeast Asia would be naturally attracted to Vietnam, and that no military action was needed to expand Vietnam's influence. Indeed, before as after 1975, none of these countries showed any inclination for communism.

In April 1975, whatever their feelings toward communism, following the unexpected and total victory of the Vietnamese Communists, the ASEAN governments had to face the problem of how to deal with a Vietnam unified under a Communist Government. This question was discussed at a meeting in May 1975, two weeks after the entry of Hanoi's troops into Saigon. Although, as Roger Irvine has noted, "suspicion about Vietnam's future toward the region pervaded ASEAN's collective thinking" the ASEAN governments decided to give Vietnam the benefit of doubt, and declared their readiness to establish friendly relations with the states of Indochina.[6] Abdul Razak bin Hussein, prime minister of Malaysia, speaking on behalf of his colleagues, said that ASEAN "offered the hand of friendship and cooperation" to the Indochinese states.[7]

"A BREATHING SPELL"

In the ASEAN capitals, many believed that Hanoi would be forced to devote five to seven years to internal reconstruction and pacification of the South before it could turn its attention outward. This would give the region a "breathing spell."[8] However, this hope was quickly dispelled. After their entry into Saigon the CPV leaders clearly indicated that they intended to pursue a policy of "rushing headlong forward" (*politique de la fuite en avant*), as Richer has so aptly described it.[9]

The CPV leaders did not wait very long before bringing pressure to bear on their neighbors. Thus, on June 6 Le Duan said that the defeat of the United States had ushered in "a new period with promising perspectives for Southeast Asia."[10] A few days later, a commentary in *Saigon Giai Phong* (Liberated Saigon) told Thailand that the basic condition for normalization of relations was the termination of all American military presence on Thai soil, for "it is obvious that the Thai population will know how to force the government to adopt a resolutely anti-imperialist policy and to throw out the spies paid by the Americans."[11] The Philippines were told to "free themselves from the tutelage of Washington" and to "stop serving American interests," and the Marcos government was warned that it must take the aspirations of the Filipino people [for independence] into account "if it does not want to be eliminated."[12]

On February 11, 1976, Laos' prime minister Kaysone Phomvihane visited Hanoi. In the joint communique issued on this occasion, the two parties pledged to "coordinate closely" their actions against imperialism and "the reactionaries in its service."[13] Several months earlier, in June, these "reactionaries" had been named by *Nouvelles de la République démocratique du Vietnam* as Praman Adiraksan and Lee Kwang Yew, prime ministers of Malaysia and Singapore, respectively.[14] This time the army's newspaper *Quan Doi Nhan Dan* (People's Army) extended this appellation to all leaders of Southeast Asia.[15]

The violent attacks against the Southeast Asian leaders were made on the occasion of the ASEAN summit meeting at Bali on February 23, 1976, and constituted the CPV leaders' response to the overtures of that organization. Concerning the meeting itself, *Quan Doi Nhan Dan* said that it was called "at the instigation of the United States" and that ASEAN had "always served the neo-colonialist policy of the United States and acted on orders from Washington." It said Indonesia was the "pivot" of that organization and had acted as "the regional policeman" of the United States in its aggression against the Republic of Timor, and recalled that Indonesia had pleaded for aggression against the people of South Vietnam and had supported the Haiphong blockade."[16]

From another quarter through the voice of Kaysone Phomvihane of Laos, the CPV explained that Vietnam had refused to join ASEAN because it was "not nonaligned," that it was "an organization set up by the U.S. imperialists following the dissolution of SEATO," and that "the real nature of ASEAN is to defend the interests of U.S. neo-colonialism in Southeast Asia."[17]

In December the Fourth National Party Congress resolved that the party would "give unreserved support to the peoples of Southeast Asia in their struggle for national independence, democracy, peace and true neutrality."[18]

It was during this period that the CPV leaders had plans for a "Laosization" of Thailand. A French delegation visiting Laos in February 1976 was told by Premier Pham Van Dong that "Thailand will go the same way as Laos."[19] A member of the SRV's national assembly who defected in 1978 revealed that Tran Quynh, personal secretary of Le Duan, had told him that "the liberation of Thailand will be next" and that "it is a historical necessity and a responsibility of ours."[20] The existence of the plan was confirmed in August 1977 by a Pathet Lao officer who defected to Thailand.[21]

The plan, called Project Issane (North East), was to stage "popular uprisings" in the northeastern provinces of Thailand, supported by military moves from Laotian territory adjoining Thailand on the west side of the Mekong in the north and the south, that is, the regions of Sayaburi and Champassak, respectively. Preparations were started in May 1976 for the uprising of the population of Lao origin. In parallel, by May 1976 seven PAVN divisions had been deployed from the north to the south along the Mekong River in the areas of Huei Say, Oudomsay, Luang Prabang, Thakhet, Savannakhet and Champassak (see map 4).[22]

For the success of the plan, the thrust from Laos had to be combined with a thrust from the northwest of Cambodia. This meant cooperation from the Cambodians, but this cooperation was not forthcoming. On the other hand, a move against Thailand could be made only if Vietnam had a secure rear, that is, a friendly and cooperative China, and there was no certainty about this. In fact, as early as 1976 the CPV had already warned the deputies to the national assembly to expect trouble with China and Cambodia.[23] The CPV leaders thus had to shelve their plan of a thrust against Thailand. At the same time they were forced to modify their attitude toward ASEAN "from one of truculent criticism to one of coexistence and cooperation."[24]

In 1977 Vietnamese criticism of ASEAN declined in intensity and frequency. In 1978 as part of their three-pronged plan against Cambodia, the CPV leaders mounted a major diplomatic offensive in the direction of ASEAN. In July 1978 Deputy Foreign Minister Phan Hien visited the

ASEAN capitals. During his visit, he declared that Vietnam considered ASEAN a regional organization concerned primarily with economic development and was prepared to discuss "Zopfan" (Zone of Peace, Freedom, and Neutrality) on the basis "genuine neutrality."[25] Phan Hien was followed in September-October by Pham Van Dong, who offered to sign treaties of peace and nonaggression with Vietnam's neighbors. Dong gave the ASEAN governments the formal assurance that "we will not support subversive actions in neighboring countries, directly or indirectly."[26] That was only a few weeks away from Vietnam's massive invasion of Cambodia, and several months after the central committee (of which Dong was a leading member) had decided to settle the Cambodian problem by force.

Pham Van Dong's assurances are reminiscent of the lulling tactics used by the CPV in 1962, when it included in the platform of the Liberation Front of South Vietnam an item relating to "the application of a neutralist policy." Explaining this particular point fifteen years later, Le Duan said that

> with this limited objective, we divided the ranks of the puppets and tried to win to our side every force we could win, especially in Southeast Asia. Regarding our Southeast Asian neighbors, we made them understand that. . . . we do not advocate the "export of revolution" and the "export of socialism." This enabled us to win the neutral forces to our side. We thus knew how to divide and isolate our enemies.[27]

INVASION OF CAMBODIA AND AFTERMATH

Pham Van Dong had scored points over the Chinese who had failed to give firm assurances that China would stop supporting the Communist parties in the Southeast Asian countries. In the process, however, the CPV lost its credibility in the eyes of the ASEAN governments. An ASEAN leader remarked retrospectively that Pham Van Dong's visit could be interpreted as "a diplomatic wrapping designed to conceal a time bomb."[28] And when Vietnam blatantly and massively invaded Cambodia two months later, the ASEAN governments were "traumatized."[29] Commenting on the creation of the National United Front for the Salvation of Kampuchea (NUFSK), under whose cover Vietnam had staged its invasion of Cambodia, Singapore's minister of foreign affairs, S. Rajaratnam, said: "We are concerned because. . . . What happens today in Kampuchea may happen tomorrow in our countries,"[30] and the Malaysian minister of foreign affairs, Mohammed Mahatir, said that "it smacks of foreign intervention." [31]

The "shock waves" of Vietnam's brutal invasion led to a stiffening of ASEAN's attitude. On January 9, two days after the occupation of Phnom Penh by Hanoi troops, the Indonesian foreign minister, in his capacity as chairman of the ASEAN standing committee, declared that he "deeply deplored" the escalation and enlargement of the conflict between Vietnam and Cambodia, and expressed "grave concern" over the implications of this development. [32]

On January 12–13, the ministers of foreign affairs of ASEAN held a special meeting in Bangkok. In their joint communique they "strongly deplored the armed intervention" against Kampuchea, called for the immediate and total withdrawal of "all foreign forces," and "strongly" urged the Security Council of the United Nations to take "the necessary and appropriate measures" to restore peace, security, and stability in the area. [33] In March the ASEAN countries submitted a resolution to the Security Council calling for the withdrawal of all foreign forces, and allowing the Khmer people to decide their future free from foreign interference.

In June at their meeting in Bali, the ASEAN foreign ministers issued a stronger communique. However, they still refrained from naming Vietnam, thus leaving the door open for a possible accommodation with Hanoi. At this time, however, two new factors entered the picture. The Chinese had intervened militarily in favor of the Cambodians and launched a "punitive" action against Vietnam, and Vietnamese troops in pursuit of the remnants of the Cambodian forces had moved past Phnom Penh toward the frontiers of Thailand.

The ASEAN therefore deemed it necessary to issue a warning to Hanoi. In their joint communique, they stressed that "any incursion of any foreign forces into Thailand would directly affect the security of the ASEAN member states, and would endanger peace and security of the whole region." At the same time they "reiterated their firm support and solidarity with the government and people of Thailand, or any other ASEAN country" in the preservation of its independence, national sovereignty, and territorial integrity. [34]

At this point the ASEAN governments still refrained from naming Vietnam, speaking about Vietnamese aggression, or openly taking side in the Vietnam-Cambodian conflict. They were still hoping that Vietnam would exercise some restraint that would make a Vietnam-ASEAN confrontation avoidable. Developments in the next few months were, however, to cause a change in their attitude.

DEALING WITH THAILAND

In Cambodia the CPV leaders faced insoluble politico-military problems. To subjugate Cambodia they needed a political lever: a Communist party, or some other political organization, under its control. It had failed to set up in this country a lever similar to the one it had in Laos. The next option was a military solution. But a military solution was possible only with the cooperation or neutrality of Thailand. For ideological as well as historical reasons, however, Thai cooperation was out of the question.

There remained only one option: securing Thai neutrality through intimidation. Thus, on June 23, 1980 Vietnamese troops staged a major incursion into Thai territory: more than one regiment penetrated deep into Thailand and encircled the village of Ban Mak Moon, in the Arany-aprathet area, while some 10,000 Vietnamese troops from two divisions were deployed in the area on the other side of the border. At several points, the Vietnamese dug in and the Thais were unable to dislodge them. Thai intelligence sources said that the incursion had been "carefully thought out." Vietnamese prisoners confessed that they had been given specific order to penetrate into Thai territory, then withdraw "after having made their point." [35]

The Vietnamese incursion occurred at the precise moment when, in Jakarta, Vietnam's foreign minister, Nguyen Co Thach, stated categorically: "I wish to affirm here, again, that we shall not cross the border." [36] This is reminiscent of Pham Van Dong's assurances to the ASEAN governments during his tour of the region in the autumn of 1978.

The Vietnamese deliberate incursion into Thailand produced three major effects, all very unfavorable to Vietnam. It hardened the position of the ASEAN countries; it strengthened their unity; and it led to closer Thai-Chinese relations.

At their meeting in Bali on June 25, the ASEAN foreign ministers issued a communique that condemned the "act of aggression" by Vietnam, naming Vietnam for the first time, and using the term "aggression" also for the first time. It said that this "irresponsible and dangerous act" would have "far-reaching consequences," and constituted "a grave and direct threat" to the security of Thailand and the security of the region. It also made it clear that these acts "have further undermined Vietnam's own credibility and have undercut the trust and confidence that ASEAN has patiently attempted to forge with Vietnam." [37]

Vietnam's attack against Thailand also gave ASEAN something it had much difficulty in achieving until then: unity. The communique stated that any incursion of foreign forces into Thailand "directly affects the security of the ASEAN member-states," and expressed "ASEAN's firm support and solidarity" with the people and government of Thailand.[38]

From then on, it would be hard for the CPV leaders to divide the other ASEAN countries from Thailand. This was made perfectly clear in August when the Philippine foreign minister, in his capacity as chairman of ASEAN's standing committee, declared that "the unity and solidarity of ASEAN cannot and will not be broken," and they would "oppose any attempt to isolate Thailand from the rest of ASEAN."[39] It was at this meeting that the ASEAN countries decided to "freeze" their relations with Hanoi, and to consider that their number-one enemy was Vietnam and no longer China.[40]

Thailand could now have closer relations with China without risk of damaging its relations with the other ASEAN countries. It had established formal diplomatic ties with China on June 30, 1975, when Prime Minister Kukrit Pramoj led a delegation to Peking, just one month after Communist troops had moved into Saigon. Deng Xiao-ping said on this occasion that Kukrit Pramoj's visit had "turned a new page in the history of Thai-Chinese relations."[41] But the development of relations had been slowed down by the Chinese leaders' failure to give a firm pledge that they would stop supporting the Communist parties in the Southeast Asian countries.

On June 26, however, the Chinese foreign ministry issued a statement denouncing the Vietnamese attack against Thailand as "an act of aggression" and said that China would "resolutely support the people and government of Thailand.[42] Moreover, in private conversations with the Thai leaders during Deng Xiao-ping's visit in November 1978, the Chinese had already hinted to the Thai leaders that the Thai Communists might be on the same side as the Thai and the Chinese governments, and might consider Hanoi as the principal enemy if Cambodia came under the control of Vietnam and the Indochinese Federation was realized de facto.[43]

Clearly, Peking had advised the Thai Communists to cooperate with their government against the Vietnamese. As a result, many members of the Communist party of Thailand, including senior members, decided to abandon the armed struggle; by 1981 more than half the members who had joined the party since 1965 had returned to Bangkok.[44] The Chinese leaders would cap this success of the Thai government by giving the ASEAN governments the assurances they had been seeking. During a visit to Bangkok in February 1981, Zhao Zi-yang promised to "take further action to prevent our relations with the Communist parties of the ASEAN countries from affecting friendly relations between China and the countries of ASEAN." He also stressed that China "sincerely desire that these countries maintain internal unity and enjoy stability."[45]

The CPV's policy of "rushing headlong forward" had thus led to a de facto alliance between Thailand and China. One major consequence of this alliance was the possibility for anti-Vietnamese Cambodian forces backed by China to use Thailand as a base and a sanctuary in its resistance to Vietnam. Another consequence, which was naturally linked to it, was the possibility for Chinese aid to the Cambodian resistants to pass through Thai territory. This was admitted by Sihanouk as well as Deng Xiao-ping when both were in the United States in February 1979.[46] This, combined with China's determination to give firm backing to the anti-Vietnamese resistance, made the consolidation of Vietnam's position in Cambodia extremely difficult.

The situation was made worse for Vietnam by the decision of the ASEAN countries to switch from a position of neutrality to one of support for Democratic Kampuchea in spite of their aversion for Pol Pot. At their meeting in Kuala-Lumpur on June 25–26, the ASEAN ministers of foreign affairs declared in their joint-committee that they "strongly reaffirmed" their "continued total commitment" to "the exercise of the right to self-government of the Kampuchean people." They refused to recognize the Heng Samrin government, which they considered "a regime set up by an occupying force," and declared their support for Democratic Kampuchea "on the principle that foreign intervention must be opposed" and that "any change in the recognition of Democratic Kampuchea's credentials would be tantamount to condoning Vietnamese military occupation."[47] These were strong words.

The strong words would be followed by strong deeds, as from then on the ASEAN countries would engage in a determined—and successful—fight for the maintenance of the credentials of Democratic Kampuchea. But more than that, they would also take appropriate action to ensure the survival of this government by giving it strong political and even military support.

The CPV leaders thus had on their hands a "Vietnam's Vietnam." Nevertheless, they were determined to pursue their militant course and "rush headlong forward." While continuing their military actions in Cambodia, they engaged in political and diplomatic maneuvers with the aim of producing an "irreversible situation" there. The tactics they used were the same as those they had used so successfully against their earlier enemies—the French, the Americans, the Chinese Kuomintang—and they expected their enemies to get tired and give up in the end.

On the diplomatic front, the CPV declared the Heng Samrin government to be "the only legal and representative government of the Kampuchean people" and sought recognition of this "fact" by various international instances. To discourage its opponents, the CPV proclaimed that the situation in Cambodia was "irreversible." This was first asserted by Pham Van Dong at the Non-Aligned Countries' Conference at Havanna,[48] and was repeated over and over again by Hanoi afterward.

In addition to the "irreversibility" of the Cambodian situation, the CPV insisted on the recognition of the existence of the "Indochinese bloc" as "an undeniable reality of Southeast Asia" (see map 5),[49] and on negotiations between this group and ASEAN as two distinct and separate entities for the establishment of a zone of peace and cooperation between them. Furthermore, it declared that the "Indochinese group" belonged to the Socialist community, of which the Soviet Union was "the pillar." All this was formalized in the communique issued at the end of the Indochinese summit in February 1983, and repeatedly recalled since then in the half-yearly meetings of the ministers of foreign affairs of the three countries.[50]

With regard to the continued presence of Vietnamese "volunteers" in Cambodia, a special declaration on this question issued by the same summit said that these "volunteers from the Vietnamese army" were in the country "at the request of the government of the People's Republic of Kampuchea" (PRK) under the Vietnam-Kampuchea Friendship Treaty of February 1979, "to fulfil their internationalist obligations," to help Kampuchea to defend itself against "the interventions of the reactionaries among the Peking ruling circles and other reactionaries." They had stayed "at the request of the PRK," and would withdraw "at the request of the latter."[51]

Great efforts were also made by the CPV leaders to divide China from the ASEAN countries, and to split ASEAN. The ASEAN governments were told that the Indochinese bloc had no quarrel with ASEAN. Through a white paper issued by the government of the PRK they told the ASEAN governments that

> The Kampuchean problem. . .is not, as Peking proclaims, a problem between the countries of ASEAN and those of Indochina, but a problem between China and Kampuchea in particular, and between China and the three Indochinese states in general. The realities of the past five years have shown that no threat to ASEAN comes from Kampuchea, just as no threat comes from Vietnam and the USSR. The only threat to ASEAN is the hegemonist and expansionist policy of Peking which is opposed to the independence and the security of the three Indochinese countries, and to peace and stability in Southeast Asia.[52]

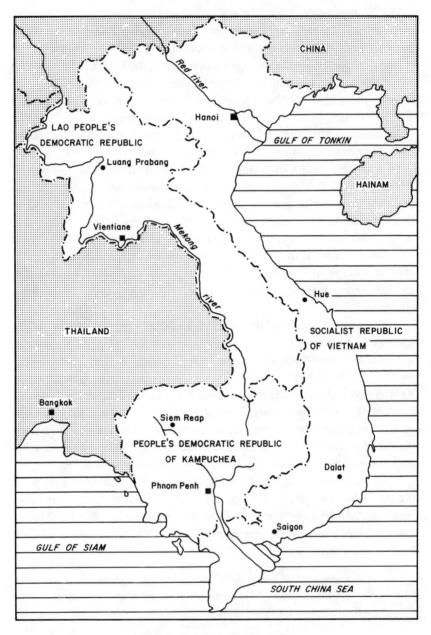

Map 5. Indochina bloc in 1980.

With regard to ASEAN itself, the efforts of the CPV leaders aimed at (1) isolating Thailand from the rest of the organization, and (2) exploiting the divergences between the member countries in order to prevent any common action by them. Thailand was singled out for fierce attacks, through the voice of Cambodia. The Cambodian white paper noted above said that "Thailand is the only country of Southeast Asia having expansionist and hegemonist ambitions," and Thailand had always been "the main and the most effective support of the imperialist and expansionist forces" against its neighbors. In particular since 1975, Thailand had become "the main base and the most effective tool of Chinese expansionism and hegemonism in the region."[53]

INDONESIA

The CPV leaders also tried to split Indonesia from the rest of the organization, especially after 1983. Attacks against Indonesia lessened after Hanoi's peace offensive of 1978. If the occupation of Timor was still referred to by Foreign Minister Nguyen Co Thach in his speech at the Delhi conference of nonaligned countries in March 1983, the phrase "by foreign forces" was used, and Indonesia was not named.[54] From 1984 onward, Hanoi's attitude toward Indonesia became more friendly.

In several ways Indonesia's position was different from that of other ASEAN countries. Since 1965 it had maintained a hostile attitude and had no diplomatic relations with China, and considered the latter a threat to the security of the region.[55] In its view, a strong and anti-Chinese Vietnam would be a convenient obstacle to Chinese expansion southward, and it was prepared to accept the maintenance of Vietnam's "influence over Laos and Cambodia."[56] In any case, geographically it was protected by the sea and was not on the front line. As Foreign Minister Mochtar Kutsumaadmadja summed up the situation very neatly: "Indonesia is more relaxed because we have the sea between us and Vietnam."[57]

Hanoi tried to exploit to the full special position of Indonesia in a number of ways. It treated this country visibly with more friendliness and consideration than the rest of ASEAN, trying to generate an impression of intimacy between the leaders of the "Indochinese bloc" and ASEAN, especially from 1984 onward, after the other ASEAN countries had agreed to consider Indonesia as their "interlocutor" in their "dialogue" with Vietnam. Hanoi therefore sought to give the impression that this "dialogue" was really ongoing and fruitful.

Since the Indonesians pursued what Weatherbee has called "a dual track diplomacy," Hanoi did everything to encourage them to continue on their second track, that is, their bilateral relations with Vietnam.[58] Its efforts were directed particularly at the Indonesian military leaders, among whom General Benny Murdani, who made two "private" visits to Hanoi between September 1981 and February 1984. He was then chief of the Indonesian intelligence service. During February 13–18 he made a four-day official visit to the Vietnamese capital as commander of the Indonesian armed forces.

Murdani's visit has been described as a "dramatic event." And indeed it was, as the general caused consternation in ASEAN circles by stating that "some countries say that Vietnam is a threat to Southeast Asia, but the Indonesian Army and people do not believe it."[59] The visit of General Murdani was followed by the holding of a joint seminar of the Vietnamese Institute of International Relations and the Indonesian Center for Strategic and International Studies in Hanoi later in the month.

The following year the exchange movement was intensified. In October an economic and commercial delegation was invited to Hanoi, followed by a delegation of the Indonesian Defense Institute, then in November by a group of editors representing the Indonesian Journalists' Association. Commenting on these visits, the *Jakarta Post* said that, to be blunt, commercially "Vietnam is not an attractive trading partner and we do not expect any significant results to come out of this mission," but journalistically it "provided a welcome alternative coverage of news and views" to Eastern and Western media. Militarily, it said that it was in Indonesia's own strategic interest "to include Vietnam, however difficult it might be, in a working regional order" and the long-term benefit of the missions was to "make them [the Vietnamese] aware of where their long-range interests lie."[60] This, of course, was sheer wishful thinking, as the CPV leaders were not likely to be swayed by the arguments of some good-willed journalists, Indonesian or other.

At the official level, General Murdani's visit was followed by that of Foreign Minister Mochtar Kusumaadmadja, who visited Hanoi on March 14–17. He received a warm welcome. Obviously the CPV leaders sought to win his heart as they had done previously with certain key French and American officials. In January in an interview with the Vietnam News Agency, Vietnam's foreign minister, Nguyen Co Thach, had already exonerated Indonesia from the crime of having taken part in the Vietnam war "as Thailand did," and said that Indonesia was the only country that had supported Vietnam during the war.[61]

On his return on March 17, Kusumaadmadja declared at the Jakarta airport that he had served as "go-between" for the United States and Vietnam concerning the problem of those Americans missing in action (MIAs) during the Vietnam war.[62] In addition to this question, he had surely discussed with the Hanoi government the question of normalization of Vietnam-U.S. relations, for he had told U.S. Assistant Secretary of State for Far Eastern Affairs Paul Wolfowitz in February that it was time for the United States to "seriously consider" normalizing diplomatic relations with Vietnam, as this would help in a solution to the Cambodian problem. Such normalization, he argued, "will make Vietnam renounce its present principles and pay more attention to national development." (By talking with authority about the position of Vietnam at a press conference on February 7, 1985, Kusumaadmadja showed he knew Vietnam well. He must have discussed this earlier and at length with Nguyen Co Thach.) Obviously, by making Indonesia the "go-between" for Vietnam and the United States, Hanoi enormously flattered the Indonesians' ego.

Although Hanoi was not able to cause Indonesia to break away or to publicly dissociate itself completely or partially from the position of ASEAN, it continued to maintain its special dialogue with that country. It could thus give the impression in its domestic and foreign propaganda that not all members of ASEAN were opposed to its position, and lessen the feeling of its isolation. This translated into the use of the statement that "a number of people in the ruling circles of ASEAN," or "certain countries of ASEAN" shared Vietnam's views.[63]

MALAYSIA

If, for the CPV leaders, Indonesia was the weakest link in the enemy chain, Malaysia was the next weakest. In some ways, Malaysia's position was similar to that of Indonesia. It had to cope for nine years with an extremely virulent Communist insurgency during 1948–1957. The insurgents were predominantly of Chinese origin. It considered that the domino theory was "utter rubbish" and believed that Vietnam would not attack Thailand, Malaysia, Indonesia, and the Philippines.[64]

In March 1980, together with Indonesia, Malaysia put forward the "Kuantan doctrine," according to which Vietnam should pursue a policy of neutrality between the Soviet Union and China, and should maintain peace on the Thai-Kampuchean border. In return, ASEAN would accept Vietnamese hegemony in Cambodia and take steps to ensure Vietnam's security regarding China. The idea was dropped as a result of strong opposition from Thailand and China.[65]

However, Hanoi's behavior led Malaysia to harden its position progressively. It was particularly irked by "Hanoi's utter disregard of the established rules of international relations and opinion."[66] Malaysia made it clear that it regarded the threat posed by the presence of Vietnamese troops in Kampuchea "as a threat to this country," and that the threat to Thailand was "real as far as Malaysia is concerned." The Vietnamese, it said, were "trying to prove that there is a military solution in the belief that they are militarily stronger."[67]

Hanoi also sought to neutralize Malaysia by playing on its fear of China and by giving it the impression that an accommodation with Vietnam was possible. Thus during the visit of Malaysia's foreign minister, Tengku Ahmed Rehauddeen, to Hanoi in February 1980, the CPV leaders assured him that Vietnam would respect the independence and territorial integrity of the ASEAN countries and that Vietnam supported the ASEAN's declaration on Zopfan. Rehauddeen came away with the impression that he had made a "historic visit" and that his conversations with Pham Van Dong and Nguyen Co Thach had been "fruitful and beneficial." The CPV leaders and he had agreed "to keep on talking."[68]

Hanoi blamed the impasse between ASEAN and Vietnam on China, which, it said, had sought to impede the dialogue between ASEAN and the Indochinese countries. This argument was stressed after the Delhi conference of the nonaligned countries in March 1983 had failed to take up a proposal for dialogue between ASEAN and the Indochinese countries put forward by Malaysia, because of China's violent opposition. It said that by this opposition China had "interfered in the internal affairs of the countries of Southeast Asia" and incited the ASEAN countries to oppose the Indochinese countries.[69]

SINGAPORE AND THE PHILIPPINES

In sharp contrast to Malaysia's hesitation, Singapore, like Thailand, advocated a policy of firmness and of keeping up strong pressure on Vietnam, diplomatically as well as militarily. Its position toward Vietnam has been characterized as "hard-nosed and tough-minded."[70] Singapore's leaders had no illusion about the intents of the new Vietnamese leaders. Prime Minister Lee Kwang Yew of Singapore declared that he believed in the "domino theory" and did not doubt that after catching its breath the new

Vietnam would "actively step up insurgency."[71] In December 1978 he welcomed the Communist break of unity as it would give the ASEAN countries five to ten years in which to strengthen their defenses.[72] He was acutely aware that "for at least ten years there is no combination of military forces that can stop or check the Vietnamese in any conflict."[73]

In 1975 Singapore did not favor making excessive concessions to Vietnam to induce it to join ASEAN. It was opposed to "to touting for new members."[74] And at the June 1979 ASEAN meeting at Bali, Singapore's S. Rajaratnam proposed that ASEAN side with the anti-Vietnamese Cambodian forces and provide material aid and arms to support the anti-Vietnamese resistance in Cambodia. From September 1981 to June 1982, Singapore played a major role in the establishment of the Coalition Government of Democratic Kampuchea (CGDK), which brought together the three bickering Cambodian anti-Vietnamese factions.

The formation of this government was achieved after much coming and going of the ASEAN leaders between their capitals and between them and Peking. By this act, willy nilly, not only Thailand but the other ASEAN countries were now associated with Peking. Thus any advantage Vietnam had obtained by its divisive and lulling tactics was cancelled by its intransigence and disregard for the views of the ASEAN countries. It now faced a de facto ASEAN-Chinese united front, which Peking had been trying to set up against it. For the first time in its history, the CPV found the Leninist tactics of united front used against it.

Among the ASEAN countries, the Philippines were the least worried about either the Vietnamese or the Chinese as an external threat to its security. Although internally it had a serious Communist insurgency problem, it was protected by the sea. It could thus afford to take a detached attitude, although, out of solidarity with the other ASEAN countries, it subscribed to all the measures taken by ASEAN against Vietnam. For their part, the CPV did not make great diplomatic efforts in the direction of Manila.

CPV TACTICS AGAINST ASEAN

Let us consider two other tactics used by the CPV leaders. One of them was aimed at preventing the ASEAN countries from gathering support for their actions against Vietnam in international forums, and the other at confusing and paralyzing the members of ASEAN.

With regard to the first, at the approach of an important international meeting at which the ASEAN countries were expected to present a motion condemning Vietnam, Hanoi would put forward a proposal that seemed to be reasonable and to demonstrate its willingness to negotiate a peaceful solution to the Cambodian problem. This was aimed at blocking the anti-Vietnamese move.

Thus, for example, in July 1982, in anticipation of the coming session of the United Nations General Assembly in the autumn, the Indochinese foreign ministers' conference put forward the idea of an international conference with the participation of "the two groups of countries"—Indochina and ASEAN—plus the countries that had participated in the conferences on Indochina in 1954, 1961–62, and 1973. It also proposed the establishment of a zone of security along the Thai-Cambodian border, as well as supervision by the United Nations.[75]

In September 1983, again in anticipation of the United Nations General Assembly session, the Indochinese foreign affairs ministers floated the idea of dialogue between the "two groups" of states at a regional conference, and announced their intent to make the necessary contacts to that end at the forthcoming session of the General Assembly. In February 1983, before the meeting of the conference of foreign ministers of non-aligned countries in Delhi, the Indochinese conference declared that Vietnamese "volunteers" would be withdrawn at the request of the Cambodian government.[76] Finally, at the Indochinese conference of August 1985, it was announced that Vietnamese volunteer forces would pursue their yearly partial withdrawals from Cambodia and "would conclude their total withdrawal by 1990."[77]

The other tactic used by the CPV was to confuse and divide a country by telling different people different things. It would send a high official to a country; he would ask to see different people and hold private talks with them. At these talks he would advance "ideas" that seemed conciliatory. Then he would see government officials and say something else, and no one was certain about Vietnam's real position. But the Vietnamese would generate the impression that there was a chance of peaceful settlement, which should be explored before any hard measure against Vietnam was contemplated.

Foreign Minister Nguyen Co Thach's maneuver in the autumn of 1984 is a typical illustration. Thach arrived in Bangkok at the end of September and asked to see the former prime minister, General Kriangsak Chamaman. They had a long conversation. Chamaman then told the press that the atmosphere for negotiations was better than in the past, that Hanoi had "softened" its stance.[78] Then Thach had talks with Deputy Prime

Minister Phichai Rattakun during which he apparently made a number of concrete and positive proposals. However, when Thach met with the press afterward he said he had no new peace plan to offer, that he had "nothing in his pocket," and that his talks with the Thai deputy prime minister were just "an exchange of ideas."[79] As *The Nation Review* commented, Thach had "floated ideas" to give the impression that "the chance of a breakthrough may not be very remote," but the overall outcome of his talks with the two Thai leaders was "to prevent anybody to shoot down his new "peace bid" prematurely and to sustain the "diplomatic offensive at least until the end of the UN General Assembly."[80]

Indeed, at the same time as Thach maneuvered in Bangkok, the Vietnamese delegation in New York asked the UN secretary general to circulate a document from Thach to all UN members. In this document it was claimed that there was progress in the process of negotiations between ASEAN and the Indochinese group as a result of his visit to Indonesia. Thach's assertion was, however, vigorously denied by ASEAN.[81]

As in the case of China, the CPV could not make much headway with the ASEAN countries. Unlike France or the United States, these countries could not be easily manipulated because their governments were not subject to the same kind of pressures as were the French or American government; their officials were more sophisticated in dealing with Vietnam and quickly saw through Hanoi's schemes; these countries were not wide open to Communist infiltration and propaganda and could thus not be divided; their public opinions were either opposed to Hanoi's schemes or could not be mobilized—no "teach in," no "sit in," no street demonstration—against their governments; and the governments of ASEAN were united and prompt in countering Hanoi's moves effectively.

ASEAN was particularly successful in the battle of the Cambodian government's credentials at the United Nations. There, in 1979 the ASEAN countries succeeded in having Pol Pot's government, and after 1982 the CGDK, recognized by the General Assembly as the legitimate government of Cambodia, with a large majority. This majority increased year after year. The votes in favor of the anti-Vietnamese Cambodian government were in 1979: 71 for; 35 against; 11 abstained; 11 nonvoting; in 1980: 74/35/32/12; in 1981: 79/36/30/10; and in 1982: 90/29/26/12.[82] From 1983 onward, Vietnam ceased to challenge the CGDK's credentials, possibly as Weatherbee has pointed out, because it wanted to avoid an embarrassing public setback.[83]

ASEAN also succeeded in mobilizing world opinion against Vietnam at the conference on Kampuchea and at the UN General Assembly. On

July 17, 1981 in spite of strong objections from Vietnam, the United Nations convened an International Conference on Kampuchea (ICK). Without naming Vietnam, it stated clearly that it was continued "foreign armed intervention" and the nonwithdrawal of "foreign armed forces" that had made it impossible for the Cambodian people to express their will in free elections. It called for a cease fire and the withdrawal of all "foreign forces" from Cambodia "in the shortest possible time." [84]

In addition to the ICK, from 1979 onward the UN General Assembly regularly passed a resolution expressing deep regret for "armed intervention by outside forces" in the internal affairs of Cambodia and calling for the immediate withdrawal of all "foreign forces" from Cambodia. [85] As is clear from Table 2 below, the increase in the number of countries that voted in favor of these resolutions was an eloquent demonstration of Vietnam's isolation in the world arena.

Although the resolutions of the UN General Assembly by themselves could not force Vietnam to evacuate Cambodia, they placed on it the onus of having to declare those resolutions "illegal," [86] and to accuse the United Nations of "taking sides with the expansionist forces." [87] More particularly, they highlighted the great diplomatic and moral isolation of Vietnam.

The ASEAN countries also succeeded in having economic aid to Vietnam cut off. The United States made it clear that no aid to Vietnam would be forthcoming so long as Vietnam's occupation of Cambodia continued, and China had stopped all aid to Vietnam even before Vietnam's invasion. The European community, as well as Australia, New Zealand, and Japan, after a joint meeting with ASEAN in Jakarta on April 4, 1980 declared their support for the position of ASEAN, and suspended their aid to Vietnam. Of the non-Communist countries, only Sweden continued its aid. The loss of external aid naturally aggravated Vietnam's already seriously deteriorating economic situation and rendered the CPV more and more unpopular among the Vietnamese people.

Table 2
Resolution Of The United Nations On The Situation In Kampuchea

Year	1979	1980	1981	1982	1983	1984	1985
For	91	97	100	105	105	110	114
Against	21	23	25	23	22	22	21
Abstain	29	22	19	20	11	18	16
Absent	9	11	12	9	19	8	7

Source: Thai Documents on Kampuchea, p. 141.

Last, the ASEAN government officials, especially Thai officials, became very familiar with Hanoi's tactics and were able to react promptly and to neutralize them very effectively.[88] What the Thais knew they naturally passed on to their ASEAN partners, and thus the ASEAN countries were able individually and collectively to neutralize Vietnam's maneuvers.

It is clear, however, that diplomatic actions aimed at isolating Vietnam internationally could not force Vietnam to withdraw its troops from Cambodia. Only defeating Vietnam militarily could achieve that. And neither the Cambodian resistance forces nor the ASEAN countries, singly or even collectively, had any hope of defeating the PAVN, the fourth largest army in the world, and the most battle experienced in Southeast Asia. Only one country—China—could pose a real military challenge to Vietnam. But China was more interested in accomplishing its modernization program, and, besides, it was official Chinese policy not to commit its troops to a war outside its borders, more particularly, far from its home bases.

On the other hand, so long as ASEAN, China, and other countries did not acquiesce in Vietnam's military occupation of Cambodia, and so long as an anti-Vietnamese Cambodian resistance continued to exist, Vietnam would not be able to consolidate its hold on Cambodia either. And, obviously, the longer the war lasted, the heavier would be the burden for Vietnam. It would thus be natural for ASEAN, in cooperation with China, to keep up the diplomatic, political, and military pressure on Vietnam.

Thus, while maintaining its diplomatic efforts aimed at isolating Vietnam internationally, the ASEAN gave the CGDK not only stronger political support, but also military assistance. The political elimination of Pol Pot in June 1982 and his withdrawal as leader of the Khmer Rouge and commander of their military forces in early September 1985 cleared the way for ASEAN to step up such assistance.

In an editorial on July 11, 1985, *The Straits Times* said that "all steps, military and diplomatic, have to be taken to keep pressure on Hanoi," and "aid, including military aid, to the Cambodian resistance forces has to be kept up."[89] This was obviously the message that Singapore's prime minister, Lee Kwang Yew, carried to Peking two months later, for he said on his return that ASEAN and other peace-loving countries in the region must help the resistance forces in Cambodia "to make Vietnam's occupation costlier," that "China should continue to pressurize the Vietnamese on their northern border," and Vietnam must "continue to be isolated in the UN and elsewhere."[90]

The key word here is "costlier," for obviously Vietnam's occupation of Cambodia was a costly affair, and especially it promised to be a long drawn-out one. This was realized clearly by its leadership. As General Tran Cong Man, editor of *Quand Doi Nhan Dan,* the army's paper, admitted to François Nivolon of the *Figaro,* after the Vietnamese big offensive of March 1985 against the Cambodian resistance bases in the Phnom Malai area: the big bases had been all destroyed, "but there are still small ones which we will have to clear up. And it will take time."[91] This sounded like a statement by the French high command in Indochina in 1947.

When the Vietnamese invasion of Cambodia was debated by the UN General Assembly in November 1979, Vietnam's permanent representative to the United Nations, Ha Van Lau, speaking of the Cambodian problem, told Singapore's representative, Tommy Koh, that "the world will have forgotten it in a week."[92] As of the end of 1985, not only had the Cambodian problem not been forgotten, but, instead, it had become a major international problem. Vietnam's war in Cambodia had already lasted five years, and it was not clear how the CPV leaders could make the world forget Cambodia, or disengage Vietnam from the Cambodian quagmire.

9

The CPV and the Soviet Union: Upholding the Purity of Marxism-Leninism

In its approach to the Soviet Union, the CPV's attitude was different from its attitude toward all other countries, whether colonialist or imperialist enemies (France, the United States), traditional enemies or rivals (China, Thailand), traditional victims (Laos and Cambodia), or potential victims (ASEAN countries). Towards the Soviet Union, the CPV was never antagonistic, inimical, or critical. Its fundamental attitude was one of admiration, gratitude, trust, full acceptance of the USSR as head of the international Communist camp, firm support for its policies, and great reliance on its aid.

Much of the CPV's attitude stemmed from its strong determination to be a pure Marxist-Leninist party and an exemplary member of the international Communist movement, during the lifetime of the Comintern as well as after the dissolution of that organization in 1943. Indeed, the CPV behaved as if the Comintern never ceased to exist. This is a fundamental fact that had many far-reaching consequences, and not only for the Vietnamese people. This aspect has been ignored, or at least neglected, in most writings on Vietnam in general, and on Vietnamese communism in particular.

To state that Ho Chi Minh and his companions were nationalists who were Communists, or Communists who were nationalists, and just stop there, without explaining what those statements really imply, would be inadequate, not to say misleading, in any interpretation of the events occurring in Vietnam, or resulting from events occurring in Vietnam, in the years following the birth of the Communist party of Vietnam (1930).

A full interpretation of the CPV's politics—foreign as well as domestic—requires an exposition of the implications of the fundamental fact that the CPV was a Communist party that always held fast to an absolute belief in the value of Marxism-Leninism and in the overriding necessity of maintaining its purity and that made Marxism-Leninism the guiding light of all its actions. To understand Vietnamese communism, we must therefore understand what unreserved acceptance of Leninism implied for the CPV. And for this, it is necessary to begin with a study of the Comintern, which was organically linked to Leninism.

THE COMINTERN

The Comintern was formally founded on March 4, 1919, but Lenin had begun to talk about the necessity of a new international as early as 1914.[1] In April 1917, after the collapse of the Left at the Zimmerwald congress, Lenin urged the foundation "right now, without delay" of "a new proletarian International," or rather to acknowledge publicly, without fear, that "this new International is already established and operating."[2]

Between 1914 and 1919, a number of ideas had matured in Lenin's mind. On the one hand, he had become very dissatisfied with the Second International ideologically and organizationally. On the other hand, he had worked out a new theory of capitalist development, that of imperialism. Lenin's ideas were formally expressed in a series of writings, in particular, in *Imperialism the Highest Stage of Capitalism* (1916), *The Tasks of the Proletariat in Our Revolution* (1917), and *The Proletarian Revolution and the Renegade Kautsky* (1918).

When World War I broke out in 1914, Lenin wanted the Socialists to consider it an "imperialist war" and to refuse to fight in "defense of the fatherland." His call was not heeded. Nationalism was still a stronger sentiment than proletarian internationalism. Socialists were to fight Socialists on the European battlefields. As a result, the Second International ceased to be an expression of international Socialist unity, and it was clear to Lenin that it could not be the effective instrument needed, especially by him, in the coming struggle for the proletarian world revolution.

Lenin's reflexions on the development of capitalism had led to the conclusion that capitalism had reached a new—its highest—stage, which was imperialism. This imperialism was spreading its nets over the whole world. It was decaying, "moribund," but while it existed, it was parasitic and oppressive on a world scale. The fight against capitalism had therefore to be waged also on a world scale. For this fight to be successful, the world proletariat needed an effective organization, which must be patterned on the Russian Bolshevik party.

In 1902 in *What's To Be Done?*, and in 1905 in *Two Tactics of Social Democracy*, Lenin had set forth his ideas on what kind of instrument (lever) was needed, and how to forge such an instrument for the seizure of power in Russia. That instrument was the Bolshevik party, with resolute, disciplined, dedicated professional revolutionaries thoroughly trained in all forms of struggle, operating on the principles of military discipline, secrecy, and "democratic centralism," very tight centralization and complete submission to a strong-willed and stable leadership endowed with dictatorial powers. With this party as lever and by using Bolshevik tactics, Lenin was able to seize power in Russia in November 1917. He thus became firmly convinced that bolshevism had created the ideological and tactical foundations for the Third International, that these tactics were "the only internationalist tactics," and could "serve as a model of tactics for all."[3]

Lenin's experience with the Second International convinced him that this "yellow" international was a weak and ineffective organization because of reformism, pacifism, petty bourgeois, narrow-minded nationalism, and opportunism, the refusal to accept the idea of violence and dictatorship, and the insistence on legality and parliamentary democracy. He was thus determined to keep out of his International "traitors" and "cowards" (like Plekhanov, Berstein, and Kautsky) who had committed the great sin of substituting petty bourgeois nationalism for internationalism, "deserting to the reformists' camp and renouncing revolution."[4] A still greater sin perhaps was that they, in particular Kautsky, held a majority in the Second International and prevented Lenin from imposing his own ideas about world revolution and bolshevism on this organization.

The second major factor that had a decisive influence on the founding of the Comintern and on its theory and practice was the situation prevailing in Europe, and more generally in the world, between 1917 and 1919. When Lenin surveyed the European scene at the end of September 1917, he believed that, for the Russian revolution as well as the world revolution, "the crisis has matured." The troop mutinies in Germany convinced him that there were "undisputable symptoms that a great turning point is at hand, that we are on the eve of a world wide revolution."[5]

In November, with the prospects of the Russian revolution brightening, Lenin became still more convinced that "the Socialist revolution will triumph all over the world for it is maturing in all countries."[6] Yet, by

1919 only in Russia alone did the revolution triumph. And it was the year when the situation was the most critical for the Russian revolution. The German revolution, whose victory Lenin considered vital for the consolidation of the revolution in Russia, did not succeed and Germany did not fall into Communist hands.

At the extraordinary Seventh Congress of the Russian Communist party in March 1918, before the signing of the peace treaty with Germany, Lenin painted a rather gloomy picture. He said that "when the Bolshevik party tackled the job alone, it did so in the firm conviction that the world revolution was maturing in all countries," and that "in the end, not at the beginning," the revolution would come. In the meantime, the Russian revolution was beset by difficulties, and "our salvation from these difficulties is in an all-European revolution." The German revolution had "the misfortune of not moving so fast" and "under all circumstances, if the German revolution does not come, we are doomed."[7] The Russian revolution would now retreat and wait for other Communist countries to come to its aid. The creation of the Communist International thus fitted into this picture.

As Lenin reflected on the failure of the Communists to capture power outside Russia, he saw that the reasons for this failure were of two kinds: tactical and organizational. Tactically, the major shortcomings were lack of flexibility and refusal of compromises. Organizationally, there was no strong and effective party on the model of the Russian Bolshevik party to direct the revolution. In particular, at the international level, Lenin had no control over the course of events in Germany because he did not have the instrument—the lever—for it. These shortcomings were to be corrected in two ways: on the one hand, by the creation of an appropriate instrument, the Communist International, which was to be modeled on the Russian Bolshevik party and controlled by Lenin; on the other hand by the provision of theoretical guidance to Communists on tactics by Lenin in *Left-Wing Communism: An Infantile Disorder*.

The failure of the Communists to seize power in Germany and the critical situation of the Russian revolution added to the imperative necessity and the utter urgency for Lenin to create an international Communist organization under his full control to ensure the security of the revolution. Although Lenin had seized power in Russia with relative ease, international developments made the position of the Russian Communist regime precarious. Communist Russia was isolated and insecure. In January 1918 Lenin said that the victory of socialism was "possible only on a world scale," that "the final victory of socialism in a single country is of course impossible."[8] And in July he compared Russia to a "besieged fortress" waiting for other detachments of the world Socialist revolution to come to its aid.[9]

It is against this historical and political background that we must consider the Comintern, and what its membership implied for the CPV, and hence for Vietnam and the Vietnamese people—institutionally, ideologically, politically.

Institutionally, under the twenty-one very stringent conditions for admission imposed by Lenin at the Second Congress in 1920, the CPV had to accept the principle of "democratic centralism," both internally and in relation to the organization. Condition 12 stipulated: "All parties belonging to the Communist International should be formed on the basis of the principle of "democratic centralism," and condition 16: "All the resolutions of the congresses of the Communist International, as well as the resolutions of the executive committee, are binding for all parties joining the Communist International." Under condition 21, "those members of the party who reject the conditions and theses of the Third International are liable to be excluded from the party."[10]

Lazitch and Drachkovitch have pointed out that in 1906, at the Stockholm Congress of Reconciliation and Reunification of Mensheviks and Bolsheviks, Lenin had defined the principle of "democratic centralism" as "election of the top party leaders from below, the essential and unconditional obligation to obey orders and regulations from above, and the existence of a strongly centralized party administration whose authority shall be generally recognized and respected during the period between congresses."

At the Second Congress of the Comintern in 1920, Lenin, however, omitted one of three essential parts, the one relating to election of top party leaders. Thus the new definition of "democratic centralism" read as follows: "The Communist party will be able to do its duty only if its organization is as centralized as possible, if it maintains iron discipline internally, and if its central organization, fortified by the confidence of the members, is equipped with all necessary powers and authority."[11]

According to the statutes of the organization adopted in 1920, the ten to twelve largest of the member parties had one representative each, whereas the country of the organization's headquarters had five representatives, and the smaller member parties were treated very undemocratically; their delegates had only consultative voices. Thus in 1920 the CPSU occupied five of ten or twelve seats, as well as the presidency of the ECCI. At the Third Congress, the CPSU had five representatives, and the other larger member parties two representatives each. At the Fourth Congress, the parties lost even the right to choose their own representatives to the ECCI. The latter would now be chosen by the congress as a whole.[12]

As McKenzie noted, the powers of the ECCI were considerable. According to article 29 of the statutes of 1928, "the leading organ of the Communist International in the period between two congresses is the executive committee which gives directives to all sections of the Communist International and controls their activities." Article 13 pointed out that the decisions of the ECCI were obligatory for all sections of the Comintern and were to be executed promptly."[13] Moreover, just as the ECCI was the supreme authority of the Comintern, in like fashion, the presidium, elected by the ECCI, was the supreme Comintern organ when the ECCI was not in session. In actual fact, the change in the statutes in 1928 enhanced the position of the presidium and weakened that of the ECCI. Moreover, instead of meeting monthly, the ECCI was to meet only twice a year.

Considering that the ECCI was dominated by the presidium and that the presidium was headed by a Russian (successively; Zinoviev, Bukharin, Molotov, Manuilsky, Dimitrov) who himself took orders from Lenin or Stalin, a Vietnamese who joined the CPV would in fact have to execute policies and directives emanating from Moscow and geared to Russian rather than to Vietnamese needs. This follows logically from conditions of admission 12 and 16 and the principle of "democratic centralism," as well as condition 17, according to which a member party was but a section of the Comintern, which Lenin had wanted to be "not simply a gathering of separate national sections, but a united world organization."[14]

The Comintern was viewed by its (Soviet) leaders as a single party and as an international army. "We must be a single party, with subdivisions in different countries" and "a united international party with branches in different countries," said Zinoviev at the Second Congress.[15] At the same congress Lenin said that a proletarian army existed everywhere, and it remained only to "organize a united army" whose task was "the world proletarian revolution, the creation of a world Soviet Republic."[16] A "general staff of the world revolution" was therefore needed to lead this international revolutionary army. "The Third International is the general staff of this army," said Kamenev.[17]

The subordination of the Communist parties to the Comintern was made total by conditions 1 and 15. Under condition 1 the general propaganda and agitation should bear really a Communist—and not a nationalist—character, and "correspond to the program and decisions of the Third

International," and under condition 15 all parties must "draw up a new program in conformity with the special conditions of the country and in accordance with the resolution of the Communist International." This means that the program of each party was subject to the approval of a Comintern congress or of the ECCI. Furthermore, as has been pointed out by McKenzie, article 29 of the statutes of 1928 required the central committee of each Communist party and of each sympathizing party to submit to the ECCI minutes of its meetings and reports of its work, whereas article 30 stated that the ECCI must give its consent before any congress of the party might be held.[18] But there was more.

Under article 30, the elected officials in the leading bodies of a Communist party might resign only with the consent of the ECCI; the consent of the central committee of the party concerned was insufficient. Finally, the "Organizational Structures of the Communist parties, the Method and Content of their Work" elaborated by the Third Comintern Congress in 1921 emphasized that a Communist party "is under the leadership of the Communist International," that "the directives and decisions of the International are binding on the party and also, it is evident, on each member of the party," and that the central committee of a Communist party is "responsible to the congress of the party and to the executive committee of the Communist International." Moreover, to ensure tighter control the Comintern frequently sent "emissaries" to the meetings of the national parties. None of the above was made in, by, or for Vietnam.

Thus, says McKenzie, the relations between the Comintern center (presidium, ECCI, political secretariat) and the several Communist parties were based on the oft-cited principle of proletarian unity and discipline. "According to this basic principle, the relations between the ECCI on the one hand, and any member party on the other hand, was not one between equals, but emphatically one between superior and inferior. Indeed, the presidium of the Comintern had made it perfectly clear that the relations between the Comintern and its sections "are not relations between two partners who are negotiating with each other but are based on the principle of international proletarian discipline."[19] In addition, as Lazitch and Drachkovitch have pointed out, under article 9 of the ECCI bylaws, the ECCI "has the right to demand of the parties belonging to the Comintern the expulsion of groups and/or individuals who violate international discipline, and to expel from the Communist International parties that contravene the decisions of the World Congress."[20]

It is thus clear that in adhering to the Comintern in 1930, not only did the CPV as a body automatically lose all strategic freedom and retain only tactical freedom—it could choose the means of its actions, but the ends (Vietnam's ends) were decided in Moscow, and by non-Vietnamese using criteria not dictated by Vietnam's interests—but also, each Vietnamese as an individual on joining the CPV would lose both strategic and tactical freedom in his life. This, formally, was the situation that prevailed until the dissolution of the Comintern in 1943. But, in fact, the CPV continued to follow the Moscow line thereafter. As Brimmell has pointed out, the line laid down by the Seventh Congress of the Comintern—United Front—was maintained until it was replaced by the new line—confrontation—signaled by Zhdanov in 1947 and conveyed to the Southeast Asian Communist parties at the International Youth Congress at Calcutta in February 1948.[21]

Thus the CPV had acted as if the dissolution of the Comintern in 1943 never occurred. The party's resolutions and the statements of the party leaders in 1943 and thereafter constantly stressed that the CPV always considered the international Communist movement a monolithic one, and made upholding the purity of Marxism-Leninism and respect of the principle of proletarian internationalism their overriding concerns. Thus, institutionally, by deliberate choice the CPV had put on a Leninist strait jacket. This is also true ideologically and politically.

On joining the Comintern, a Communist party had to renounce certain paths and commit itself to follow certain others. On the negative side, it must reject any idea of reform, peaceful change, and nationalism. The condition of admission 2 stated that every organization desiring to join the Communist International must remove from all responsible posts in the labor movements. . . . "all reformists and followers of the "center," and to have them replaced by Communists." Lenin's obsessive determination to bar reformism from the organization was so strong that he had it repeated in condition 7 (resolute break with reformism).

Next, condition 17 stated that the Communist International "has declared a decisive war against the entire bourgeois world, and all the Yellow Social Democratic parties. . . ." And under condition 6 a Communist party seeking affiliation with the Cointern must "renounce not only avowed social patriotism, but also the falsehood and hypocrisy of social pacifism." Communists must therefore reject what Lenin considered "petty bourgeois democracy," and nonrevolutionary (nonviolent) methods. It is a very important aspect, in view of the necessity to determine whether such terms as "nationalism," "independence," "moderation," "democracy," and "peaceful coexistence" can be used when speaking of Ho Chi Minh and of the Vietnamese Communists.

In adopting Leninism without reservations, the CPV committed itself to reject any thought of reformism, pacifism, nationalism, and to accept violence and dictatorship of the proletariat. The need to resort to violence was a constant major theme of Lenin's speeches and writings until his death in 1924. It was particularly expounded with force and clarity in *The State and Revolution* (1917), in which he contended that the state is "an organ of class rule, an organ for the suppression of one class by another,"[22] that the suppression of the bourgeois state by the proletarian state is "impossible without violent revolution,"[23] that the proletariat needs state power, defined as "a centralized organization of force, an organization of violence both to crush the resistance of the exploiters and to lead the mass of the population. . . ."[24]

In the same work, Lenin described democracy as "a state which recognizes the subordination of the minority to the majority, an organization for the systematic use of force by one class against another, by one section of the population against another."[25] Lenin contemptuously rejected "bourgeois" democracy because it is "democracy for the rich." Communist democracy is "democracy for the vast majority of people, and suppression by force, that is, exclusion from democracy, of the exploiters and oppressors of the people."[26]

In place of bourgeois democracy, Lenin would establish the "dictatorship of the proletariat." To him, "dictatorship presupposes and implies. . . . revolutionary violence of one class against another,"[27] and

> Dictatorship is rule based directly on force and unrestrained by any law.
>   The revolutionary dictatorship of the proletariat is rule won and maintained by the use of violence by the proletariat against the bourgeoisie, rule that is unrestricted by any laws.[28]

Another basic principle of Leninism is "internationalism," more specifically "proletarian internationalism." To Lenin, nationalism, more specifically "petty bourgeois nationalism," was one of the greatest obstacles to the development of the proletarian movement, at both the national and the international levels. He spent a great deal of time fighting it, inside and outside the Second International, especially from 1914 onward. In "The right of nations to self-determination" (1914), he said that the bourgeoisie always placed its national demands in the forefront and did so in categorical fashion. "With the proletariat, however, these demands are subordinated to the interests of class struggle," "the proletarians are opposed to nationalism of any kind," and "successful struggle against exploitation requires that the proletariat be free from nationalism . . ."[29] To him, the proletarian must be a true internationalist.

In "The tasks of the proletariat in our revolution" (April 1917), and especially in "The proletarian revolution and the renegade Kautsky" (November 1918), Lenin made clear what he meant by internationalism. He said in "The tasks of the proletariat . . ." that there is "one, and only one, kind of internationalism," and that is "working wholeheartedly for the development of the revolutionary movement in one's own country, and supporting (by propaganda, sympathy, and material aid) this struggle, this, and only this, line in every country without exception."[30] He denounced acceptance of the principle of "defense of the fatherland" in an imperialist war as "a betrayal of socialism."[31]

In "The proletarian revolution and the renegade Kautsky," Lenin again said that "recognizing defense of the fatherland means, in fact, supporting the imperialists, predatory bourgeoisie, and completely betraying socialism."[32] To argue that "it is my right and duty as a Socialist to defend my country if it is invaded by an enemy" is not arguing like a Socialist, an internationalist, and a proletarian revolutionary, but "like a petty bourgeois nationalist," he said. In his view, such an argument ignores internationalism. "My country is being wronged, that is all I care about. . . . that is where petty bourgeois nationalism lies."[33] The Socialist would argue differently, Lenin said. He would say that "my duty as a representative of the revolutionary proletariat is to prepare for the world proletarian revolution as the only escape from the horrors of world slaughter." To argue from the point of view of "my" country is to use "the argument of a wretched, stupid, petty bourgeois nationalist"; a Socialist must argue "from the point of view of my share in the preparation, in the propaganda, and in the acceleration of the world proletarian revolution." That is what internationalism means, Lenin said.[34]

In the "Preliminary draft theses on the national and colonial questions" for the Second Congress of the Comintern, Lenin took up the question of nationalism, and internationalism again, and more concretely. He said:

> Petty bourgeois nationalism proclaims as internationalism the mere recognition of the equality of nations, and nothing more. Quite apart from the fact that this recognition is purely verbal, petty bourgeois nationalism preserves national interests intact, whereas proletarian internationalism demands first, that the interests of the proletarian struggle in any country should be subordinated to the interests of that class struggle on a world wide scale, and second, that a nation which is achieving victory over the

bourgeoisie should be able and willing to make the greatest national sacrifices for the overthrow of international capital.[35]

On this point, Lenin was very categorical. Further on in the same theses, he said that neither propaganda nor the most solemn declarations were of any value whatsoever "unless it is proved in practice, indeed, that the Communists and workers' leaders are able to place above everything else in the world the development and the victory of the proletarian revolution, and to make the greatest sacrifices for it. . . ."[36]

Unreserved acceptance of the Leninist principle of internationalism would carry with it the acceptance of its Leninist corollaries: the promotion of world revolution, the establishment of a world Soviet republic, and the defense of the Soviet Union.

"The Leninist theory of proletarian revolution is the theory of Socialist victory on an international scale, it is the theory of the international proletarian revolution," said Zinoviev.[37] Lenin was "the model itself of the international revolutionary," and his doctrine is applicable not only to Russia, but to the whole world. And the disciples of Lenin must "firmly reject the thought that it is possible to remain Leninist if one takes away even the slightest part of the internationalism which Leninism represents."[38] Lenin himself frequently stressed the international nature of the revolution and of the revolutionary methods he advocated. He said that Bolsheviks were "partisans of world revolution and revolutionary methods,"[39] and the Socialist revolution that had begun in Russia was "only the beginning of the world revolution."[40]

The corollary of the necessity of world revolution is naturally the establishment of a world Soviet republic. Indeed, Lenin clearly thought in terms of such a Soviet republic, a Communist state embracing the whole world. In a letter to the workers and peasants of the Ukraine in 1919, he said: "We are opposed to national enmity and exclusiveness. We are internationalists. We stand for the close union and the complete amalgamation of the workers and peasants of all nations in a single Soviet republic."[41]

In 1914 when the question of the right of peoples to self-determination was a hot topic, Lenin made it clear that he favored the right of peoples to secession. But what he had in mind was "recognition of the right of all nations to self-determination. . . . then, a close unbreakable alliance in the class struggle of the proletarians of all nations in a given state."[42]

Lenin made clear that what he prescribed was valid for all Communists, in particular those of the colonial countries. In 1920 in the "preliminary draft theses on the national and colonial questions," he said that the salvation of all the liberation movements lay in the Soviet system's victory over world imperialism. Consequently,

> one cannot at present confine oneself to the base conception or proclamation of the need for closer union between the working peoples of the various nations; a policy must be pursued that will achieve the closest alliance with Soviet Russia, of all the national and colonial liberation movements. . . . Federation is a transitional form to the complete unity of the working peoples of all nations.[43]

Lenin concluded that "under present-day international conditions there is no salvation for dependent and weak nations except in a Union of Soviet Republics."[44] He called on Communists in all lands to "help us now to organize a united army for the accomplishment of our tasks," and those tasks were the world proletarian revolution and the creation of a world Soviet republic.[45]

In *Left-Wing Communism: An Infantile Disorder* (1920), Lenin said that "repudiation of the party principle and of party discipline is tantamount to disarming the proletariat," and "whoever brings about the slightest of the iron discipline of the party of the proletariat . . . is actually aiding the bourgeoisie against the proletariat."[46]

In other words, any violation of party discipline, however slight, is treason. Considering what has been said above concerning the Comintern, to respect proletarian discipline means to follow the instructions of the Comintern, including instructions to defend the Soviet Union, "the fatherland of Socialists." And such instructions were not lacking in the following years.

Thus in 1922 the Fourth Congress of the Comintern passed a resolution making it mandatory for the workers of other countries "to fight for the Soviet Union."[47] In 1927 the eighth plenum passed a special resolution calling for the defense of the Soviet Union from the attacks supposedly planned by the capitalist countries, and the Comintern regularly instructed its followers "to display their revolutionary zeal by fighting for the defense of the USSR."[48] In 1928 the Comintern program enjoined the proletariat of the world to defend the Soviet Union as "the bulwark of the world revolution."[49] Finally, in 1935 the Fifth Congress adopted the United Front line. Dimitrov, who introduced it, explained that it was "the principal device for carrying out the main objective of defending the Soviet Union against Fascist aggression." The United Front line was to remain in effect until 1947.[50]

After the dissolution of the Comintern in 1943, although theoretically the Communist parties were free to choose their strategy and tactics, in fact, as Desanti has pointed out, Moscow continued to exercise control. This was done, this time bilaterally, through the "relations with brother parties section" of the CPSU, in the name of the necessity to "coordinate" the activities of the international Communist movement.[51]

Other new forms of "coordination" were devised, the Cominform being one of them. Although its membership was limited to East European countries, it was believed to be "the reincarnation of the Communist International."[52] Indeed, between 1947 and 1957, in particular in 1947–1948, it undoubtedly played such a role in the eyes of the Southeast Asian parties, since the Zhdanovian confrontational line was strictly followed by these parties after the meeting of the Calcutta conference. After the dissolution of the Cominform in 1957, the new form was the world conferences of the Communist parties. Through these conferences, in 1957 and 1960, the new line—peaceful coexistence—was officialized, and the policies of the world Communist parties were "coordinated" with that of Moscow.

MORAL AND TACTICAL ASPECTS OF LENINISM

So far, we have examined the ideological and strategic implications of the CPV's membership of the Comintern and its unreserved acceptance of Leninism. But, as Zinoviev has pointed out, Leninism is both "the theory and the practice of Marxism."[53] We must therefore also examine the constraints to which the CPV was subjected from the point of view of tactics. Since the question of means is inseparable from that of morals, we must examine the moral and tactical aspects together.

Lenin expressly discussed the problem of Communist morality in a speech to the youth leagues in Moscow in 1920. To him, class struggle was the criterion in questions of morality. The class struggle was continuing, and "it is our task to subordinate all interests to that struggle. Our Communist morality is also subordinated to that task. We say: Our morality is what serves to destroy the old exploiting society and to unite all the working people around the proletariat, which is building up a new Communist society." To a Communist, "all morality lies in this united discipline and conscious mass struggle against the exploiters. We do not believe in any eternal morality, and we expose the falsehood of all fables about morality," Lenin said. "Communist morality is based on the struggle for the consolidation and completion of communism." That is also the basis of

Communist training, education, and teaching.[54] This means considering what helps advance class interests and the victory of communism as moral, and inversely.

As regards truth, Lenin said that "there is no such thing as abstract truth. Truth is always concrete." To him, "all things are relative, all things flow, all things change."[55] It follows that what is true at one moment ceases to be true at another. Thus a Communist can assert, and/or believe, that he always speaks the truth, even when he says something that absolutely contradicts what he has said earlier, or that he will deny vigorously later. This, combined with the morality rule noted above, allows, and even incites, Communists to lie, deceive, and cheat, all not only with a clear conscience, but also with a feeling of satisfaction and pride for having advanced the cause of communism. This is perhaps one of the least known and least understood aspects of Vietnamese communism.

On the other hand, for Lenin, it is impossible to be politically neutral. The very term "apolitical" or "nonpolitical" [education] is "a piece of bourgeois hypocrisy," he said. In particular, on the issue of the dictatorship of the proletariat, "each man must choose our side or the other side. Any attempt to avoid taking sides must end in fiasco."[56] Proletarian dictatorship—that is, rule based directly on force and unrestrained by any laws—is not only "an absolute legitimate means" of overthrowing the exploiters and suppressing their resistance, but also the unique means. "There can be no alternative" and "dreams of some third way are reactionary, petty bourgeois lamentations."[57] Thus one must be either for or against communism; approve and support communism or be crushed and destroyed. Again, this is one of the least known and least understood aspects of Vietnamese communism.

It is in the light of the Leninist/Bolshevik attitude toward morality and of the rule that if one is not for, then one is against communism, that we should consider the tactics Lenin advocated in his various writings. It is not possible to deal with all those tactics here. We focus only on those that obviously had been the most eagerly and thoroughly studied by the CPV leaders, as can be judged from the frequent references by these leaders to them, or the most systematically used by these leaders, as can be observed from their acts.

One important Leninist tactic, and for a party in a colonial country, perhaps the most important one, is the "minimum program," two-stage tactic, which consists of achieving the proletarian dictatorship in two stages: (1) a bourgeois democratic revolution, and (2) a Socialist revolution. The first stage was considered by Lenin to be "absolutely necessary in the interests of the proletariat."[58] During this stage, the Communists would fight only for a minimum program and demand immediate political and economic reforms. These, however, are transient Socialist aims. Their purposes are to "extend the boundaries of bourgeois democracy" and pave the way for the next stage, which is the Socialist stage, the one in which the Communists would seize power and establish the dictatorship of the proletariat.

Those who have no knowledge of the Communists' ultimate aim would find their demands moderate and reasonable, and would cooperate with them in a United Front, all the more so as, in addition to democratic reforms, the Communists stand also for national independence. Thus the bourgeois democratic revolution would become a national democratic revolution; its immediate aim would become the recovery of national independence and the establishment of a democratic republic. To Communists, however, the democratic republic is only a transient form, which must lead to the Socialist republic. Furthermore, this Socialist republic will join the other Socialist republics in a world Soviet republic, under this or some other name.

The communists, however, would say nothing about their plan for the next stage. They would not wave the two flags—national independence and proletarian dictatorship—at the same time. Indeed, the second flag would be carefully hidden first, to be unfurled only after stage one has been completed. Thus those inside and outside the country who have no inkling of the Communists' plans would cooperate with them and carry them to power. Once in power, the Communists would immediately implement Lenin's ideas on the dictatorship of the proletariat. It would then be too late for those who realize that they have been deceived to do anything about it.

The Bolshevik tactics by which the CPV achieved power were spelled out by Lenin in the following main writings:

1. "Two Tactics of Social Democracy" (1906).
2. "Lessons of the Moscow Uprising" (1906).
3. "On Compromises" (1917).
4. "The Russian Revolution and Civil War" (1907).
5. "Marxism and Insurrection" (1917).
6. "Can the Bolsheviks Retain Power?" (1917).
7. "Left-Wing Communism: An Infantile Disorder" (1920).

A careful examination of these texts is indispensable for a full understanding of the CPV's tactics—domestic or foreign—for it is clear from these writings, as well as from the acts of Ho Chi Minh and his disciples, that, in its march to power, the CPV had very thoroughly studied and "creatively" applied the rules laid down by Lenin.

Lenin insisted particularly on the necessity for Communists, while holding firm to principles, that is, to their ultimate aims, to adopt utmost tactical flexibility. "Only one thing is lacking," to enable Communists to march forward more confidently and more firmly to victory, he said, and that is "the universal and thorough awareness of all Communists in all countries of the necessity to display the utmost flexibility in tactics." The Communist has the duty, as a Communist, "to master all forms, to learn how, with maximum rapidity, to substitute one form for another, and to adapt our tactics to any such change that does not come from our class or our effort."[59]

To him, revolutionaries who are incapable of combining illegal forms of struggle with every form of legal struggle are "poor revolutionaries indeed."[60] It is a necessity, an "absolute necessity," for the Communist party to resort to "change of tack, to conciliation and compromises." In a very important passage, which was frequently quoted or paraphrased by the CPV leaders, Lenin said:

> To carry on a war for the overthrow of the international bourgeoisie, a war which is a hundred times more difficult, protracted and complex than the most stubborn of ordinary wars between states, and to renounce in advance any change of tack, or any utilization of a conflict of interests (even if temporary) among one's enemies, or any conciliation or compromise with possible allies (even if they are temporary, unstable, vacillating or conditional allies), is that not ridiculous in the extreme? Is it not like making a difficult ascent of an unexplored and hitherto unaccessible mountain and refusing in advance to move in zigzags, ever to retrace one's steps, or even to abandon a course once selected, and to try others?[61]

Another important tactic advocated by Lenin and applied systematically by the CPV leaders is the exploitation of the contradictions and divisions among the enemies. The following passage was also frequently quoted or paraphrased:

> The more powerful enemy can be vanquished only by exerting the utmost effort, and by the most thorough, careful, attentive, skillful and obligatory use of any, even the smallest, rift between the enemies, any conflict of interests among the bourgeoisie of the various countries and among the various groups or types of bourgeoisie within the various countries, and also by taking advantage of any, even the smallest, opportunity of winning

a mass ally, even unreliable and conditional. Those who do not understand this reveal a failure to understand even the smallest grain of modern Marxism, of modern scientific socialism in general.[62]

Another Leninist tactical rule is that a revolutionary must always maintain the offensive; "win the first success and then proceed from success to success, never ceasing the offensive against the enemy, taking advantage of his confusion."[63] He must surprise the enemy while his forces are scattered, prepare the way for new successes, however small, but prepare daily, keep up the moral superiority resulting from the first success in order to rally the vacillating elements.[64] In time of war, said Lenin, it is not only of the utmost importance to imbue one's own army with confidence, but it is important also to convince the enemy and all neutral elements of this strength, for "friendly neutrality may sometime decide the issue."[65] Another rule connected with winning daily successes is that of winning "branch after branch, sphere after sphere."[66]

The revolutionary must also learn to retreat, for "victory is impossible unless one has learned how to attack and retreat properly."[67] And he must accept battle only when he is sure of winning. "To accept battle at a time when it is obviously advantageous to the enemy, but not to us, is criminal," said Lenin. Political leaders of the revolutionary class are "absolutely useless if they are incapable of changing tack, or offering conciliation and compromise in order to take evasive action in a patently disadvantageous battle."[68]

If we compare the Leninist ideas described earlier with the basic thinking of the CPV leaders discussed in chapters 2 and 3, we cannot fail to see a striking parallelism. The claim of the CPV leaders that in the fifty-five years of the party's existence they always took care not to deviate from pure Marxism-Leninism is thus well founded. It may be pertinent to ask here that if this claim is true for the period 1930–1943, when the CPV was a member of the Comintern and bound by its twenty-one very strict admission conditions, can it be true also for the post-1943 period, when the Comintern had ceased to exist and the Communist parties had regained their freedom?

A clear and very cogent answer to the above question has been provided by Desanti.[69] For a quarter of a century, the Comintern had trained a whole generation of leaders of the brother parties in the spirit of proletarian internationalism. This "internationalism" meant above all "unconditional fidelity to Soviet policy." This "unconditional fidelity" was the "ombilical cord" that attached each Communist party bilaterally to the CPSU through its relations with brother parties section. The "Cominternians" of the 1920s were revolutionaries by training, character, and drive. They spoke not in terms of "the party," but of "the movement." Essentially, they were "internationalists whose fatherland was the revolution." They were Stalinists issued from the same mold. And, in turn, they trained a second generation, the "grandsons of the Comintern."

Orthodoxy was ensured in particular by training in the special schools established in Moscow for foreign Communists, especially for those from the Orient: the University for the Toilers of the East (KUTV), the Sun Yat-sen University, the Lenin School for higher cadres.[70] The KUTV trained many of the future Asian leaders. Speaking to the students of this university in May 1925, Stalin stressed that its aims were to turn its students into "cadres competent to attend to the [revolutionary] needs of the toiling masses of the colonies and dependent countries," to "forge them into true revolutionaries."[71]

The programs of those schools were orientated toward the training of professional revolutionaries, but, as Desanti has stressed, they sought especially to inculcate faith to strip the students of bourgeois ideology and forge them "anew." Above all, they taught them discipline of thought and work, and stubborn courage in the pursuit of their aims.[72] This training, which created in the future cadres habits of thought, explains the persistence of the "ombilical cord" and uniformity, for these cadres were fashioned in the same "Comintern mold."[73]

With regard to Vietnam, the man who served as "ombilical cord" and ensured discipline and the "unconditional fidelity" of the CPV to Moscow, the Stalinist Cominternian who made the present generation of Communist leaders "the grandsons of the Comintern," was undoubtedly Ho Chi Minh.

Ho had declared absolute faith in Lenin and in Leninism. He was trained at both the KUTV and the Lenin School. He had spent more time in Moscow than any other Vietnamese Communist. He had worked for the ECCI. And he was Stalinist enough to be allowed by Stalin to be a representative of the Comintern with the CPV and a Comintern agent in China and Southeast Asia. His credentials as "man from Moscow" were impeccable. And he was the man who ensured strict Leninist/Stalinist orthodoxy during the lifetime of the Comintern and after its dissolution.

One need only leaf through the pages of the "history of the party" (*Lich Su Dang Cong San Viet Nam*), and glance at the party resolutions, or the speeches of Ho Chi Minh and other CPV leaders intended for internal guidance since the foundation of the party, to see the close alignment of the CPV's positions at various periods with those of Moscow. The party's resolutions echoed the resolutions of the CPSU.

In the light of what has been said about Leninism and the basic thinking of the CPV, it is now possible to give an answer to the question of whether the terms "nationalism," "independence," "moderation," "peaceful co-existence" can be used when speaking of Ho Chi Minh and the CPV leaders. The answer is both yes and no. It is yes if one proceeds from a static and tactical viewpoint, that is, from the view of a particular moment in time and excluding from consideration the broader picture. If such a viewpoint is adopted, then in 1945, or 1954, or 1968, or 1973, Ho Chi Minh and the CPV would inevitably appear as nationalists fighting for the independence of Vietnam, prepared to sit down and talk about the conditions for an honorable peace based on a reasonable compromise. That was what they said, and what they seemed to be doing.

However, if one looks at the situation from a dynamic and strategic point of view, that is, from the point of view of a whole period, and taking into consideration the ultimate aims of Ho Chi Minh and the CPV, what Ho and his disciples would call "the revolution," that is, the world revolution, the picture then changes completely. The answer to the question is then no, because what Ho and his disciples said to non-Communists was only a small part of what they told their fellow Communists to achieve by all means and at all costs in the name of pure Leninism.

One of the authors considered to be a great expert on Vietnam, Bernard Fall, said in 1969 about Ho Chi Minh's decision to fight before 1949:

> Yet, he fought on and against a French Communist-backed government, for nothing else but purely national objectives, and that fact is terribly important to this very day. He was not interested in proving that capitalism was on the way to the scrap heap of history; that "liberation war" (the word, of course, was used but, thank God, had not yet been discovered by the Pentagon) was the wave of the future; or that the French (and the U.S., which began backing them in 1950) were "paper tigers." He fought because he felt that Viet-Nam must be one single state because it was un-viable as a divided one and because the French were tramping upon Viet-namese national dignity.[74]

These words sound very odd today, to say the least, in the light of what Ho and the CPV leaders had said and done since 1925, and especially since 1975. They are blatantly contrary to the facts now known to all, and knowable to experts then.

Other authors have offered more subtle interpretations. Huynh Kim Khanh has put forward the thesis of "grafting" of Leninism onto Vietnamese nationalism by Ho Chi Minh, and called the period 1939–1940 "the final glory of the Moscow-oriented Communists."[75] William Duiker has written about the "symbiotic relationship between nationalism and communism," and from 1940 on, of a "deliberate shift of emphasis from ideology to nationalism."[76] Douglas Pike has said of Vietnamese communism that the system that communism has brought to Vietnam "in spite of its alien genesis has now become authentically Vietnamese and well rooted in the soil of earlier culture," and that the CPV retained power and popular support "with policies contradictive to international advice": their success was achieved "in spite of, and not because of, their ties with international communism."[77]

All the above interpretations have one thing in common: they are blatantly contrary to the interpretations given by Ho Chi Minh and by the CPV leaders concerning themselves, and they contradict what we know now about the relationship between Leninism and Vietnamese communism as explained by the Vietnamese Communists.

In a survey of Vietnam's external relations to 1984, a Communist author noted that "a number of Western observers have remarked that Vietnam forsook the Communist doctrine to adopt a nationalist policy." In fact, it only made "limited concessions" to the Chinese and "temporary concessions" to the French. These were "diplomatic maneuvers" to gain time and win the world's sympathy. And by 1950 "our position of principle [real basic aims] in external relations could now be fully expounded, *which could not be done formerly, for strategic reasons.*"[78]

One could cite a more authoritative voice, that of Le Duan, who was general secretary of the CPV from 1960 until his death in 1986. In his political report to the Fifth Party National Congress in 1982, he said:

> Looking back on more than half a century of activities of the Communist party of Vietnam, we are happy to note that since its foundation, parallelly to a judicious internal policy, our party has always applied a judicious foreign policy. The Leninist foreign policy advocated by comrade Ho Chi Minh is an integral part of the strategy and tactics of our party *at all periods* of development of the Vietnamese revolution."[79]

Thus those who continue to assert today that the Vietnamese Communists were "nationalist first, Communist second," or that they had forsaken communism for nationalism, claim thereby to be better Leninists than the Vietnamese Communists themselves.

There has been a great deal of attention given to the question of whether the CPV was "pro-Peking," "pro-Moscow," or "simply pro-Hanoi," as Lacouture has asserted of Ho Chi Minh.[80] Labels such as "pro-Soviet" or "pro-Chinese" or "neutral," often applied by Western analysts to various Communist parties, may not only be inaccurate but misleading, said Smyser in a study bearing the rather significant title *The Independent Vietnamese*. The DRV certainly did not take positions mainly for the sake of moving toward Peking or Moscow, although this was "a factor." It made decisions on the basis of "its own objectives" in South Vietnam, and on the basis of "its concept of how the Communist world should be organized."[81]

Although Smyser's interpretation is perhaps the closest to the truth, it still does not correspond to all the truth. But let the Vietnamese speak for themselves. In the report just mentioned, Le Duan, who spoke for the CPV since he was its chief after Ho's disappearance, tells us that "solidarity with the Soviet Union *has always been* the cornerstone of the foreign policy of our party and of our state."[82] This should not be surprising since the CPV was a party that took pride in being always completely faithful to pure Leninism.

The CPV certainly acted in perfect independence in adhering to the international Communist movement, but once they had done so and decided to be a "true" Marxist-Leninist party, that is, a party embracing bolshevism without reservations, it *ipso facto* lost its independence and became a prisoner in a prison of its own making.

The CPV's decisions must be judged, as it judged them, in the light of conformity or nonconformity to pure Marxism-Leninism, that is, to Leninist/Bolshevik ideological orthodoxy in theory, and to Leninist/Bolshevik strategy and tactics in practice. Seen in this light, the independence of the CPV was the independence of Faustus, or of the driver of a Soviet trolleybus who was quite happy with his Soviet transport company.

To judge the CPV in the light of its own words and deeds of the past fifty-five years, it was certainly the purest Marxist-Leninist party of the whole international Communist movement, as well as its most contented prisoner. Once it had jumped in with both feet, there was no way out. Being true believers in Marxism-Leninism, these Communists, however, did not give any indication that seeking a way out was necessary, desirable, or even thinkable.

10

Conclusion: History in Retrospect

We have seen how, by applying Leninist/Bolshevik strategy, and especially Leninist/Bolshevik tactics, Ho Chi Minh and the CPV leaders obtained uneven results depending on whether they were dealing with Western and democratic nations, or with Asian and/or Communist countries.

With the Western nations, the CPV could exploit the naiveté, wishful thinking, or ignorance of certain key officials and of ill-informed public opinion, by generating the belief that its members were Asian nationalists fighting for the emancipation of colonial people, while knowing perfectly well that independence was only a stage on the road to world revolution, which was the strategic, that is, the real, aim. They thus received widespread sympathy and support, and were able to divide the public opinion of those nations. This, no doubt, was one of the major reasons for their spectacular successes.

With Asian and/or Communist nations, the situation was different. Leninist/Bolshevik strategy and tactics were not very effective because the local conditions were not favorable. In the case of the Chinese, the CPV had to cope with people who were also Asian and/or Communist. They were just as subtle, if not more so, than the Vietnamese.

With regard to the nationalist Chinese, the Chungking government, as well as the Yunnan warlords, used Vietnam for their own purposes. The CPV cannot be said to have been successful in exploiting them for its own ends. When the Chinese troops left, Vietnam was handed over to France. Of course, the CPV emerged as the party wielding government power in North Vietnam, but this was thanks essentially to the Japanese and the Americans rather than to the Kuomintang Chinese.

With regard to the Chinese Communists, they were just as subtle as their nationalist compatriots. In addition, they had much more experience than the CPV in the use of Leninist/Bolshevik strategy and tactics in fighting external enemies, experience dating back to the early 1920s, whereas the CPV dated only to 1945. They were also the inventors of protracted war and masters of this technique. Finally, being a state under dictatorship, Communist China was not open to CPV infiltration, subversion, or divisive action. Its government was not subject to the pressure of domestic or international public opinion. Externally, instead of being isolated by the CPV, it was on the contrary successful in isolating the latter. For the first time in its history, the CPV was on the defensive. In Leninist theory, this is a deadly weakness.

One of the main reasons for the international isolation of the SRV was its obviously expansionist policy after 1975 at the expense of its immediate neighbors, Laos and Cambodia, and the threat represented for Southeast Asian countries by its Communist messianism. From 1975 and especially from 1978 onward, the Vietnamese Communists were considered by international public opinion no longer as nationalists fighting for the independence of Vietnam, but as expansionists. Whether this expansionism was motivated by nationalism or communism, or both, was irrelevant. It was fiercely denounced by current or potential victims alike, and universally condemned by international public opinion. One of the major ingredients of Leninism/Bolshevism—an outwardly just cause—was thus missing. The CPV could not apply Leninism/Bolshevism with full success because mass support in the opponent camp was lacking.

Another important condition for the successful application of Leninist/Bolshevik strategy and tactics was also missing. The Cambodian and the Southeast Asian countries were not Western-Style parliamentary democracies; public opinion in those lands could not be easily infiltrated and manipulated. The CPV could not freely use agit-prop techniques against their governments. This, combined with the fact that these governments were much more alert and more capable of reacting promptly than Western governments, made it impossible, or extremely difficult, for the CPV to apply Leninist/Bolshevik strategy and tactics with great success. Thus, instead of successfully isolating its adversaries internationally, the CPV became the victim of international isolation. Again, it was on the defensive.

With regard to the Soviet Union, the situation was rather different. The Soviets were not tactical but strategic allies of the CPV, that is, the CPSU-CPV alliance was not temporary and conditional but stable and unconditional. To them, proletarian internationalism applied, although perfect mutual confidence and candidness did not always prevail. Ho Chi Minh, for example, could not refrain from the urge to use everything and everyone—including Stalin—for his purposes, and Stalin responded with his usual mistrust of everyone. An example (noted in an earlier chapter) was given by Khrushchev in his memoirs.

During a secret visit to Moscow some time between 1950 and 1954, Ho tried the autographed photograph technique with Stalin. But unlike the innocent American General Chennault, Stalin was not so unsuspecting. As Khrushchev told it:

> I first met [Ho] when Stalin was still alive. . . . During our conversation, Ho Chi Minh kept watching Stalin with his unusual eyes. . . . I remember once he reached into his briefcase and took out a copy of a Soviet magazine—I think it was *The USSR Under Construction*—and asked Stalin to autograph it. . . . He liked the idea of being able to show people Stalin's autograph back in Vietnam. Stalin gave Ho the autograph but shortly afterward had the magazine stolen back from him because he was worried how [Ho] might use it.[1]

Obviously it takes a Communist to understand the hidden motives of another Communist, and Stalin was too experienced for Ho Chi Minh to outwit him!

In the same memoirs, speaking of the CPV fight against the French in 1954, Khrushchev said that "An important war is going on, and the Vietnamese are putting up a good fight. The French are taking heavy losses."[2] And of the CPV's war against the United States, he said: "There is more at stake in this war than just the future of the Vietnamese people. The Vietnamese are shedding their blood and laying down their lives for the sake of the world Communist movement."[3] If one modifies this sentence to read: "The CPV is making the Vietnamese people shed their blood and lay down their lives for the world Communist movement," then, in retrospect, this is the stark truth about Vietnam, not just between 1945 and 1975, but also since then. After making the Vietnamese people fight two bloody and devastating wars, against France, then against the United States, from 1975 onward the CPV made the Vietnamese people fight a third war, apparently against Cambodia, but in fact against China. This was the third permanent member of the United Nations' Security Council against which the CPV had led Vietnam to war.

In the light of what has been happening since 1975, and of what we know now about the policies, motivations, and basic thinking of the leaders of the CPV, as set against the background of their unreserved adoption of Leninism/Bolshevism and what that means, it is possible to look back at the history of Vietnam over the past fifty-five years and ask some pertinent questions concerning the CPV's foreign politics, in particular from the point of view of the interests of Vietnam and of the Vietnamese people, as opposed to those of the CPV and of the world communist movement.

WHAT WAS GAINED?

What has been gained by Vietnam and the Vietnamese people from their CPV-led wars? If one is to judge by the fate of the Vietnamese people since 1975, the answer is nothing, or even less. Vietnam in 1984 was among the poorest countries of the world; in terms of income per capita it occupied the 162nd rank among 170 countries;[4] according to *Le Monde*, this income was only 100 dollars per year.[5] According to *Newsweek*, in 1983 a civil servant in Vietnam earned only the equivalent of 3 dollars per month, or 36 dollars per year, and 10 cents per day.[6] It is highly significant, not to say tragic, that in 1976 at the IV National Congress of the CPV, Le Duan deplored the fact that "the war has practically destroyed everything the people have built at the cost of immense efforts, thereby delaying by a few five-year plans the progression towards large-scale production and upsetting established methods of economic management."[7] And when he made statistical comparisons, he used 1960 as a base year.[8] More significant and more tragic still, in August 1985 the Voice of Vietnam broadcast an article with the title "Forty Years of Victory of Vietnamese Revolution"; it used prewar 1939 as the base year for its statistical comparisons to show that great progress had been achieved.[9]

Comparison with Southeast Asian countries would show how different political choices by their leaders produced different economic results for their peoples. None of the Southeast Asian countries had chosen the road selected by Ho Chi Minh and his disciples: they all rejected Leninism/ Bolshevism with its accent on violence, and total and immediate break with the former colonial power. As a result, the economic lot of the peoples of these countries was immeasurably better than that of the Vietnamese, as reflected in the differences in incomes per head shown in Table 3.

All reports on Vietnam since 1975 concur on one point: the economic situation in Vietnam deteriorated dramatically after 1975, and there was no sign as of 1985 that the economy was on an upward course. If anything, the war in Cambodia and the interruption of economic aid from

Table 3

Per Capita Incomes of Southeast Asian Countries (in US $)

Countries	1977	1982
Singapore	2700	5302
Malaysia	860	1800
Philippines	410	731
Thailand	240	609
Vietnam	190	160

Source: Far Eastern Economic Review, Asia Year Book 1977 and 1984. In 1960, all Southeast Asian countries had roughly the same per capita income: US $100.

non-Communist countries following Vietnam's occupation of that country, made considerably worse a situation that was already almost hopeless.

Another major cause of the economic plight was the destructions wrought by practically uninterrupted warfare since 1945. Under Communist leadership, Vietnam was a country ravaged by war for a longer time than any other country in the twentieth century. And as of 1985 there seemed to be no end. War, whatever the reason, means loss of lives and property, and more particularly disinvestment in terms of human and physical capital.

There are no precise authoritative figures concerning the loss of human lives in Vietnam's wars against France and the United States. A few figures, taken from various estimates, however, give an idea of the extent of the losses. According to Azau, the first Vietnam war cost one million lives. The French side (France plus associated states) accounted for 300,000 deaths. The Vietnamese side (DRV) thus lost 700,000 lives. These figures do not include civilian losses.[10]

With regard to the second Vietnam war, according to Pike, the Vietnamese Communist side lost one million men. In proportion to the total population, if compared to the United States, that would be equivalent to a loss of 15 millions Americans if North Vietnam alone was taken into account.[11] In Table 4, South Vietnam Allan Goodman has given the following figures (from January 1, 1961 to March 29, 1973 alone).

Physical losses are more difficult to estimate. But it is obvious that there would be little left in any country that is at war almost continuously for half a century. According to Pike, material losses resulting from U.S. air strikes against North Vietnam were 400 million dollars, against a GNP of 1.7 billion dollars—by Vietnamese standards—a quarter of physical property. A rough idea of the loss of physical assets by Vietnam is given

Table 4
Human Costs of War to South Vietnam

ARVN killed in action	166,429
ARVN wounded in action	453,039
Civilians killed	415,000
Civilians wounded	935,000
Civilian refugees	8,819,700

Source: Allan G. Goodman, *The Lost Peace* (Stanford: Hoover Institution Press, 1978), Appendix A.

by the U.S. pledge of 5 billion dollars (in 1973) in aid for postwar reconstruction. By Vietnamese standards, that was an imposing sum, but it surely does not represent real losses, considering the country's almost total economic paralysis since 1975 due to extensive destruction of the already very inadequate infrastructures.

More important than the loss of physical capital was the loss of human capital resulting from forty years of practically uninterrupted warfare, and almost total concentration on war to the exclusion of training experts in fields other than military combat, a task that is essential to any nation that wishes to improve its living conditions. The results of these years of neglect were obvious, even to the war-obsessed and war-hardened leaders of the CPV, especially after the spectacular failure of the third five-year plan in 1980.[12]

By the time certain CPV leaders became really aware of the economic consequences of long wars, it was, however, too late. The destruction they had wrought on the country, physically, politically, socially, and economically, was too extensive to be easily repaired. In revolutionary terms, the Leninist/Bolshevik revolution had been really successful. But the momentum was too great for it to be stopped, let alone reversed—if one could imagine that the first generation of Ho Chi Minh's disciples, "the grandsons of the Comintern," would ever think of renouncing pure Marxism-Leninism.

WAS WAR NECESSARY?

The second question one could and should ask now is: Was it necessary for the Vietnamese people to resort to war to achieve national independence and improve their living conditions? To give a firm answer, again one would have to look at Vietnam's Southeast Asian neighbors. All these countries achieved national independence and improved their living conditions without war. Indeed, they were able to do so sooner and faster than Vietnam precisely because they had achieved independence *with* rather than *against* the colonial nations, and had not followed the Communist road.

As Brimmell has pointed out, the real, though unwitting, liberator of Southeast Asia was Japan. It had demonstrated the mythical nature of European superiority and removed Europe from the Asian scene in 1942, and in the process made any return of Europe impossible. After having performed its historical mission, Japan was itself removed from the scene. The final stage of the resurgence of Southeast Asia began in 1943 and was over in essence by 1948. "The battle had been won by then, and with no assistance from communism. In fact, communism was irrelevant, save as a complicating and delaying factor, in the achievement of independence."[13]

That view expressed by Brimmell applies in the case of Vietnam in the light of what we know now about General de Gaulle's plans in December 1945, that is, a full year before the outbreak of the war. From the revelations of General de Boissieu and others at a workshop on Indochina at the Institut Charles de Gaulle in February 1981, and from those made by Admiral D'Argenlieu in his memoirs,[14] it is clear that what Ho Chi Minh found necessary to fight a war to obtain, namely national independence and reunification, de Gaulle was already prepared to concede to Prince Vinh Sang, ex-Emperor Duy Tan, in the autumn of 1945. Indeed, there was an agreement between the prince and the general, and the agreement was firm enough for the ex-emperor to draw up a program,[15] which he expected to carry out after his return to Vietnam in the company of de Gaulle himself some time in early 1946.

But if de Gaulle was prepared to give ex-Emperor Duy Tan what he steadfastly refused to concede to Ho Chi Minh for many years, it was because the ex-emperor, like Sihanouk of Cambodia, wanted to achieve his nation's independence *with* France and *not against* France. We noted earlier how warmly de Gaulle had received Sihanouk in the summer of 1946 while firmly refusing to see Ho Chi Minh. De Gaulle's attitude was summed up in a sentence that he constantly repeated to Henri Laurentie, director of political affairs at the Ministry of Overseas France, in August 1946: "Laurentie, do not give Cochinchina to Ho Chi Minh."[16]

In addition to the sentimentalism of de Gaulle, which was shared by many of his compatriots, there was another and still greater obstacle to an agreement between France and Vietnam; in a French union led by a capitalist and bourgeois France for which the Soviet Union was a potential enemy, there was no room for a Communist member state, whatever Ho Chi Minh might say to Sainteny and whatever the latter might think, believe, or hope at the time. Alfred Georges put this very well in *Charles de Gaulle et la guerre d'Indochine:*

> Let us look squarely at the truth: a Communist system could not conciliate the total planning of its economy with the respect of the private property of the colonists. Between a Communist state which subordinates individual freedom to the reason of state and a western nation where individual had primacy over all the rest, the opposition is irreducible. The one could not prosper if it had not eliminated the other from its field of action.[17]

On the other hand, "a Communist government could not accept to leave its diplomacy in the hands of a non-Marxist nation, or accept to see its army and its diplomacy teleguided by a so-called capitalist state.[18] And conversely, of course.

Indeed, in addition to Cochinchina, the negotiations between Ho Chi Minh's government and the French government in 1946 at Dalat and at Fontainebleau broke down essentially on the question of Vietnam's diplomacy and defense. It was natural for Ho, in the light of the Leninist conception of self-determination—to secede from the colonial nation, then join the world Soviet republic—to insist on total independence in matters of defense and diplomacy, just as it was natural for Georges Bidault, then France's prime minister and foreign minister, to instruct the French delegation, verbally through Max Andre, chief delegate, to "secure all necessary guarantees so that in external matters Vietnam could not become a pawn in the Soviet hand, a satellite of Moscow."[19]

If in the first Vietnam war the CPV made the Vietnamese shed their blood and lay down their lives primarily not for national independence but in the interests of the world Communist movement, so in the second Vietnam war, they again made the Vietnamese shed their blood and lay down their lives to prove that imperialism headed by the United States could be attacked and defeated without the risks of a general war, that is, of involving the Soviet Union in a direct military confrontation with the United States. This was the CPV's interpretation of the reference to peaceful coexistence in the resolutions adopted by the world congresses of Communist parties in 1957 and 1960.

Khrushchev was not quite convinced that the CPV's interpretation was right, but his dispute with the Chinese prevented him from firmly blocking the CPV forward policy from the end of 1959 onward. On the other hand, President Kennedy's policy of acceptance of a coalition government for Laos, and his sounding out of Hanoi on agreeing to the same for South Vietnam encouraged the CPV leaders in their conviction that the United States was not really determined to go all the way to prevent a Communist takeover of South Vietnam. Moreover, at the Vienna Soviet-American summit in 1961, Kennedy's failure to make the status quo in Vietnam a major condition of detente between the Soviet Union and the United States strengthened Hanoi's position in resisting Khrushchev's pressure against the taking of South Vietnam by escalating military action.

The first two Vietnam wars were fought according to Leninist principles: tactically in the name of nationalism, but stratgically in the interests of the international Communist movement. The third war, outwardly against Cambodia but in fact against China, also followed the same principles. To the Vietnamese people it was presented as a war for the defense of their fatherland against a traditional national enemy. But, at the same time, for the CPV leaders it was a war against "the reactionary elements in the Chinese ruling circles" who acted in collusion with international imperialists and had betrayed the cause of socialism. Whatever the motives, it promised to be a protracted and, for the Vietnamese people, a very costly war. In contrast to the wars against France and the United States, the prospects of a decisive victory in this war against China were slim. Vietnamese lives and treasury were being thrown down a seemingly bottomless pit, and Vietnam's development was again delayed, this time one does not know by how many five-year plans.

In retrospect, in view of the militancy of the CPV leaders, and of their determination to accelerate the world revolution, one could look at the three wars in a different light, from the viewpoint of the peoples of Vietnam and of Southeast Asia. Considering that not only the CPV leaders were determined to impose Leninism/Bolshevism on all Vietnam and Indochina, but also planned to set up a Federation of Soviet Republics of Southeast Asia by the year 2000 (see chapter 7), it is pertinent to ask the question: What would have happened if France, the United States, and China had not intervened in Indochina?

Regardless of how one would judge French and American motives, the answer to the question is obvious. The CPV leaders would have achieved their aims thirty years sooner, and in much better condition. With regard to Vietnam, they would have imposed communism on Vietnam thirty years sooner, and more easily—without encountering any resistance.

Millions of Vietnamese would have lived under Communist rule, accepted communism, and served international Communist purposes instead of enjoying economic well-being and relative freedom for thirty years.

As regards Southeast Asia, the CPV leaders would have a unified Vietnam, with all its resources intact at their disposal, free access from Vietnam's southern coast to all Southeast Asian countries, in particular Malaysia, and free access by land to Thailand. They would have started their "revolutionary mission" for the establishment of the Federation of Soviet Republics of Southeast Asia sooner, at a time when none of the Southeast Asian governments could offer the national independence, the necessary political freedom, and especially the economic well-being and social reforms that would divert their people from revolutionary thoughts and save them from becoming easy preys of Communist propaganda and agitation. Popular discontent resulting from insecurity, poverty, social inequality, and stringent limitations of personal freedom necessitated by the need for governments to maintain public order would have produced political and social unrest, which would have made rapid political, economic, and social progress, and hence effective resistance to communism, impossible.

Whatever one may think about the three wars, then, one must admit that one of their major results was that the peoples of Vietnam, and especially those of Southeast Asia, had been given a very precious breathing space. The stark contrast between the growing economic prosperity of non-Communist Southeast Asia and the increasing economic decline of Communist Vietnam is the most eloquent demonstration of the truth that communism is not a cure but a cause of poverty.

WERE THE GOALS REACHED?

One last question, and in the light of the views held by many about Vietnam for nearly half a century, the most important one: Has Vietnam achieved what so many Vietnamese had given their lives for, and what so many generous people in the world had wished that they would obtain—national independence? The answer is a clear no. Whoever one may think is responsible for it, Vietnam is today in fact a dependency of the Soviet Union.

To say that Vietnam has become a Soviet dependency is simply to describe a reality. It does not imply that this dependency has been imposed on the CPV. In fact, the CPV leaders' unreserved adoption of Leninism/Bolshevism resulted from a perfectly independent and free choice, made out of very deep convictions, but deep convictions based disastrous illusions. However, once the choice had been made, certain constraints, strategic as well as tactical, became inevitable. The CPV, as a party, lost its strategic freedom, whereas the individual member of the CPV lost both strategic and tactical freedom in relation to the CPSU.

The situation prevailing since 1975 has been rather paradoxical. Now that the war was over and there was no more compelling need to rely on foreign powers, one would expect Vietnam to exercise the right for which it had fought so hard for many years. But, instead, Vietnam has become more dependent on a foreign power than ever. It is beyond the scope of this chapter to deal with Vietnam's foreign relations since 1975 in general, and with the Soviet Union in particular. We mention only a few major facts, especially in the military and economic fields, that highlight this dependency and that are drawn from two remarkable studies by Thai Quang Trung and Vo Nhan Tri in *Indochina Report,* published by the Information and Resource Center of Singapore.[20]

Militarily since 1975 and especially since 1978, the SRV has been integrated more and more tightly into the Soviet defense system. Many features of this integration recall the pattern of dependence of South Vietnam on the United States between 1954, and especially between 1965 and 1973. Reports about the Soviet military presence in Vietnam have centered on the use of Cam Ranh Bay as a major Soviet forward naval base. But, in fact, the whole of Vietnam, and indeed Indochina, has become a Soviet military base ominously flanking China, casting a huge shadow over Southeast Asia and the southwestern Pacific, and threatening the sea lanes of the whole area (see map 6).

Since November 3, 1978 the SRV was bound to the Soviet Union by a Treaty of Friendship and Cooperation, which was in fact a treaty of military alliance. The treaty, originally directed at China, has, however, become the instrument of greater Soviet strategic designs. As Thai Quang Trung puts it neatly:

> As Cam Ranh Bay has become the largest Soviet forward base outside the Soviet Union, Socialist Vietnam has been smoothly integrated as a bulwark State in the encirclement security policy against China, as well as a kind of relay-State in the Soviet global system, the major objective of which is to acquire supremacy upon the seas. Furthermore, as "a reliable impregnable outpost of socialism in Southeast Asia," Vietnam is assigned today to play the role of a guardian-State of the Soviet system in the region as well as a legionnaire-State, carrying out a policy of selective regional destabilization. In sum, because of its multiple functions, Socialist Vietnam is per-

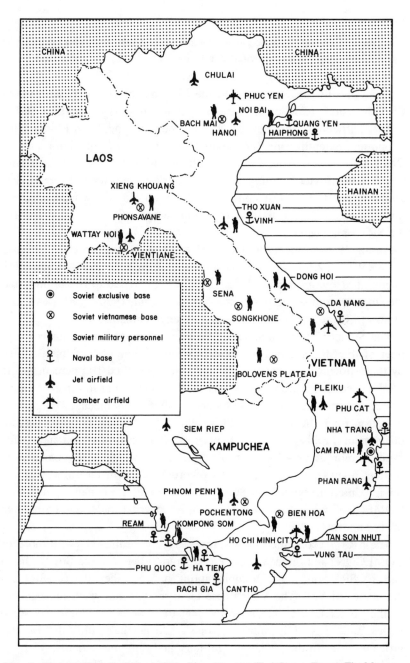

Map 6. Soviet military facilities in Indochina. (*Source:* Thai-Quang-Trung, The Moscow-Hanoi Axis and the Soviet Military Build-up in Southeast Asia, *Indochina Report,* No.8, October 1986, Singapore. Courtesy of Information and Resource Center)

haps of greater strategic value than any other Soviet footholds in the Third World, and even more vital than Cuba.[21]

Economically since June 1978, the SRV has been integrated into the CMEA system (Council of Mutual Economic Assistance, or COMECON), particularly through the USSR-Vietnam Long-Term Program for Economic, Scientific and Technological Cooperation, signed in Hanoi on October 31, 1983. After China cut off all aid to the SRV in the spring of 1978, the Soviet Union became the latter's main source of foreign aid; after the non-Communist countries suspended aid following Vietnam's invasion of Cambodia, the Soviet Union became still more important for the SRV as a source of aid.

During 1976–1980, for its second five-year plan, the Soviet Union gave the SRV US $2.6 billion in economic aid; during the 1981–1985 period of the third five-year plan, the amount was increased to 6.5 billion; and the amount promised for the fourth five-year plan, 1986–1990, was 13.05 billion.[22] These are substantial sums by any standards.

The Soviet Union has naturally become the major, or exclusive, supplier of the SRV for many important goods. Some idea of this is given by the following figures. In 1984 the USSR supplied 100 percent of the SRV's needs in oil products and cast iron, 80 percent of fertilizers, almost 80 percent of rolled steel, 80 percent of nonferrous metals, 100 percent of cotton fiber. In return, the SRV sent to the Soviet Union 60 percent of its natural rubber exports, about 60 percent each of its tea and coffee exports, more than 30 percent of its jute exports, and 100 percent of its parquet planks exports.[23] In terms of proportions, in the same year the Soviet Union accounted for 80 percent in value of Vietnam's trade with COMECON, 60 percent of the total of its external trade, and 65 percent of its imports.[24]

The SRV's economic plans were closely "coordinated" with those of COMECON, and there was close cooperation between the Soviet Union and the SRV, but it was a cooperation "between the rider (USSR) and the horse (SRV)." The Vietnamese claimed that they were independent of the Soviet Union, and it is true that they were recalcitrant on some issues, said V.N. Tri; "however, one could not help think that on significant issues in the economic, military and diplomatic fields, Vietnam could not adopt an independent position of the Soviet Union," especially since its membership of COMECON and the signing of the Treaty of Friendship and Cooperation, and the resulting setting up of a whole institutional mechanism of cooperation between Vietnam and other

COMECON member countries, "above all between Vietnam and the Soviet Union."[25]

The close "coordination" of the SRV's military and economic policies with those of the Soviet Union had to be preceded by close "coordination" of foreign policies. This was very well summarized in the following statement: "The Vietnamese side expressed total support for the Soviet Union's foreign policy . . ." (Joint USSR-Vietnam Communique following the visit of a Soviet state delegation).[26]

Foreign Minister Nguyen Co Thach has said that "Vietnam would be nothing without the Soviet Union."[27] But more than for Vietnam, the alliance with the Soviet Union was, as *Quand Doi Nhan Dan,* the army's paper, expressed it, "a life-and-death matter for the revolution," that is, for the CPV itself.[28]

In 1945–1947 the negotiations between Ho Chi Minh and France broke down on the question of Vietnam's right to independence. Ho Chi Minh then appealed to the Vietnamese to endure sacrifices, shed their blood, lay down their lives, and fight hard for this sacred right. Now, after two wars and thirty years of fighting, suffering, and dying, the Vietnamese people found themselves tied to another power by bonds not much different from those they had wanted to shake off from their French colonial master. But there is one very big difference: the lot of the Vietnamese people, as different from that of the CPV leadership, had become worse than under French rule.

Vietnam in 1985 was no more independent than it was in 1945. The Vietnamese people had fought hard, but gained nothing, except new and worse masters, domestic and foreign. The only winners were the CPV, who had retained, reinforced, and extended their power, and the Soviet Union, which had gained a first-class military base, replaced France as the dominant power in Indochina, and become the major factor in the strategic picture of Southeast Asia in place of the United States. This was surely not what the Vietnamese people had sought or wanted. But, in terms of pure Leninism, this was certainly a great success. And to the CPV leaders, that was what really mattered, for it proved that in their foreign politics they had thoroughly grasped Leninism and applied it fully and "creatively," in the interests of the international Communist movement and the world revolution.

Notes

Introduction

1. In the words of a French influential journalist, Jean Lacouture, in *Ho Chi Minh* (Paris: Seuil, 1969), p. 249.

2. Foreign Broadcast Information Service, *Daily Report, Asia and Pacific.*

Chapter 1

1. For text of this treaty, see: S. M. Bao Dai, *Le Dragon D'Annam* (Paris: Plon, 1980), Annex I.

2. For a detailed study of the Vietnamese nationalist movement, see: William Duiker, *The Rise of Nationalism in Vietnam, 1900–1941* (Ithaca: Cornell University Press, 1976).

3. V. I. Lenin, *Speeches at Congresses of the Communist International* (Moscow: Progress Publishers, 1972), 108–110.

4. In: Xenia Joukoff Eudin and Robert C. North, *Soviet Russia and the East, 1920–1927* (Stanford: Stanford University Press, 1957), 386.

5. On this and on the subsequent events involving the French and Japanese moves leading to Japan's occupation of Indochina, see: General Georges Catroux, *Deux actes du drame indochinois* (Paris: Plon, 1959); Admiral Jean Decoux, *A la barre de l'Indochine: histoire de mon gouvernement général 1940–1945* (Paris: Plon, 1952); J. M. Pedrazzini, *La France en Indochine, de Catroux à Sainteny* (Paris: Arthaud, 1972).

6. On Japanese designs concerning Southeast Asia, see: Willard H. Ellsbree, *Japan's Role in Southeast Asian National Movements 1940 to 1945* (New York: Russell and Russell, 1953).

7. On American policy toward Indochina in 1940–1945, see: Edward R. Drachman, *United States Policy Toward Vietnam 1940–1945* (Rutherford, NJ: Farleigh Dickinson University Press, 1970).

8. The day of entry of French troops into Hanoi, General Leclerc appeared on the balcony of the French mission's headquarters. To the acclaim of the French crowd he said only: "Hanoi, last stage of the liberation." In: Jean Sainteny, *Histoire d'une paix manquée, Indochine 1945–1947* (Paris: Faillard, 1967 (1948)), 209.

9. For texts of these agreements, see: Sainteny, *Histoire*, 199–201; see also: Gareth Porter, ed., *Vietnam, A History in Documents* (New York: NAL, 1981), 42.

10. See: Alfred Georges, *Charles de Gaulle et la guerre d'Indochine* (Paris: Nouvelles editions latines, 1974); Alfred Grosser, *La quatrième république et sa politique extérieure,* Paris: Armand Colins, 1967); Institut Charles de Gaulle, *Le général de Gaulle et l'Indochine 1940–1946* (Paris, Plon: 1982).

11. On the Dalat and Fontainebleau negotiations, see: Henri Azau, *Ho Chi Minh, dernière chance* (Paris: Flammarion, 1968).

12. On the military aspect of the war, see: Jacques Suant, *Vietnam 45–72* (Paris: Arthaud, 1972); General Yves Gras *Histoire de la guerre d'Indochine* (Paris: Plon, 1979).

13. General Paul Ely, chief of staff of the French forces from October 1953 to 1954, stresses in his memoirs that the French military problem in Indochina was always that of manpower. See: Général d'Armée Paul Ely, *L'Indochine dans la tourmente* (Paris: Plon, 1964). On France's internal politics, see: Georges and Grosser, *Charles de Gaulle.*

14. For text of this agreement, see Bao Dai, *Le Dragon,* Annex 3.

15. On the U.S. involvement, see the Senator Gravel edition, *The Pentagon Papers,* vol. 1 (Boston: Beacon Press, 1971); Russell Fifield, *Americans in Southeast Asia* (New York: Crowell, 1973).

16. On the Geneva Conference on Indochina, see: Jean Lacouture and Philippe Devillers, *La fin d'une guerre: Indochine 1954,* Paris: Seuil, 1960; Robert F. Rankle, *Geneva 1954: The Settlement of the Indochinese War* (Princeton, NJ: Princeton University Press, 1969); *Pentagon Papers.*

17. On the post-Geneva developments, see: Russell Fifield, *The Diplomacy of Southeast Asia: 1945–1958* (New York, Harper, 1958); Jean Lacouture, *Le Vietnam entre deux paix* (Paris: Seuil 1965); Donald F. Lach and Edmund S. Wehrle, *International Politics in East Asia since World War II* (New York: Praeger, 1975); R. B. Smith, *An International History of the Vietnam War,* Vol. I (New York: St. Martin's 1983); William J. Duiker, *The Communist Road to Power in Vietnam* (Boulder, CO: Westview Press, 1981).

18. On the Sino-Soviet conflict, see: Francois Feijto, *Chine/URSS, de l'alliance au conflit, 1950/1977* (Paris: Seuil, 1978); Jacques Levesque, *Le conflit sino-soviétique* (Paris: Presses Universitaires de France, 1979).

19. See: Allan Goodman, *The Lost Peace, America's Search for a Negotiated Settlement of the Vietnam War* (Stanford: Hoover Institution Press, 1979).

20. See the revelations of Kenneth O'Donnell, appointment secretary to Kennedy, in: John Galloway, *The Kennedys and Vietnam* (New York: Facts on File, 1971); of Chester Cooper, a White House insider, in: *The Lost Crusade* (London: McGibbon and Kee, 1970); of Roger Hillsman, ex-state department high official, in: Michael Charlton and Anthony Moncrieff, *Many Reasons Why, The American Involvement in Vietnam* (London: Solar Press, 1978).

21. Lyndon Baines Johnson, *The Vantage Point* (London: Weidenfeld and Nicholson, 1972).

22. Johnson sent special ambassadors all over the world to explain his desire to avoid a wider war. On this, see Cooper, *Lost Crusade.* On the use of Canadian

and other channels, see: George C. Herring, ed., *The Secret Diplomacy of the Vietnam War* (Austin: University of Texas Press, 1983).

23. See: Général Van Tien Dung, *Et nous prîmes Saigon* (Paris: Les éditions le Sycomore, 1979).

Chapter 2

1. Pham Van Dong, in *Notre Président Ho Chi Minh* (Hanoi: Editions en langues étrangères, 1970), 11.

2. Ibid., 220.

3. Detailed biographical data on Ho's life can be found in: Bernard B. Fall, *The Two Vietnams, A Political and Military Analysis* (New York: Praeger, 1963) and *Last Reflections on a War* (New York: Doubleday, 1964); Jean Lacouture, *Ho Chi Minh* (Paris: Seuil, 1967); Nguyen Khac Huyen, *Vision Accomplished, The Enigma of Ho Chi Minh* (New York, Macmillan, 1971); Huynh Kim Khanh, *Vietnamese Communism 1924–1945 (Ithaca: Cornell University Press, 1982);* Robert F. Turner, *Vietnamese Communism, Its Origin and Development* (Stanford: Hoover Institution Press, 1975); Pham Van Dong, *Notre Président;* Tran Dan Tien and others, *Avec l'Oncle Ho* (Hanoi, Editions en langues étrangères, 1972).

4. One is a little brochure by the Nghe-Tinh section of the CPV's Committee for the Study of the History of the Party (Uy Ban Ngien Cuu Lich Su Dang, Tinh Uy Nghe Tinh), *Nhung mau chuyen ve thoi nien thieu cua Bac Ho* (Stories about the young days of Uncle Ho) (Hanoi: Nha Xuat Ban Su Thuc, 1970). Another is the complete works of Ho Chi Minh. The first three (of five volumes) contain detailed chronologies of Ho's life from his birth to 1945; *Ho Chi Minh Toan Tap* (Complete works of Ho Chi Minh), published between 1980 and 1984; these are referred to as *HCM-Toan Tap.* Also see: Hong Ha, *Bac Ho tren dat nuoc Le-nin* (Uncle Ho in Lenin's land) (Hanoi: Nha Xuat Ban Thanh Nien, 1980).

5. Turner, *Vietnamese Communism,* 3.

6. This school trained future colonial high officials, including Vietnamese-born ones, whom the CPV was to label "traitors" in 1945. See: Vu Ngoc Chieu and Nguyen The Anh, *Another School for Young Nguyen Tat Thanh* (Paris: Tu Sach Van Hoa, 1983).

7. Various authors have given different figures: 19 in Turner, *Vietnamese Communism* 93; 23 in K. C. Chen, *Vietnam and China, 1938–1954* (Princeton, NJ: Princeton University Press, 1969), 38; 32 in Huynh Kim Khanh, *Vietnamese Communism,* who adds that the CPV has claimed to have found as many as 76 (p. 58).

8. Lacouture, *Ho Chi Minh,* 20.

9. Bernard Fall, commenting on Ho's association with the French cook Escoffier of the Carlton Hotel in London, later speculated that at this school Ho took a "quickie course" in pastry—an absurdity, as this was a marine trade school. See: Fall, *Two Vietnams,* 86, and *Last Reflections on a War,* 64.

10. Fall said that Ho chose that name because he did not want to embarrass his family for accepting such a lowly job (*Last Reflections on a War*, 65). This shows a total ignorance of Vietnamese customs, according to which Hai (Two) is reserved for the eldest son, and Ba is quite respectable.

11. The exact date is given by the Nghe Tinh Study Committee (67). This is the first time that Ho's precise departure date from Vietnam has been given. Various authors, including CPV high cadres, have given fanciful dates: Fall spoke of "early 1912" (*Last Reflections on a War*, 65); Lacouture, of "the very last days of 1911" (*Ho Chi Minh*, 15); Pham Van Dong, of "the end of 1911" (*Notre Président* 67).

12. *Tap Chi Cong San* (5–1980) said Ho went to the United States "in late 1913," was in New York (where he attended a meeting in Harlem, and was a laborer in Brooklyn), visited Boston and San Francisco. *Toan Tap* (Vol. 1, 546) said Ho went to the United States "at the end of 1913," and stayed in New York "for a time."

13. Letters to Phan Chu Trinh, *HCM-Toan Tap*, Vol. 1, 476–479.

14. See: Michele Zecchini's testimony in *Planète Action* (Paris), special issue on Ho Chi Minh, March 1970.

15. At that time there was no way for Ho's Vietnamese companions to know this. See Lacouture, Ho Chi Minh, 18–19.

16. *HCM-Tuyen Tap*, Vol. II, 519.

17. See *President Ho Chi Minh's Testament* (Hanoi: Foreign Languages Publishing House, 1969).

18. Zecchini, *Planète Action*, 27.

19. Lacouture, *Ho Chi Minh*, p. 34.

20. Ibid., 35.

21. *HCM-Tuyen Tap*, Vol. II, 518 ff.

22. Ibid.

23. Tran Dan Tien, *Avec l'Oncle Ho*, 55; Fall, in *Two Vietnams*, said Ho reached Leningrad on January 23, 1924, "and immediately proceeded to Moscow" (p. 92).

24. Hong Ha, *Bac Ho*.

25. Ibid., 23.

26. Interview with Charles Fourniau of *L'Humanité*, in *HCM-Tuyen Tap*, Vol. II, 524.

27. *HCM-Toan Tap*, Vol. I, 191, 132.

28. *HCM-Tuyen Tap*, Vol. II, 524.

29. *HCM-Toan Tap*, Vol. I, 550.

30. Ibid.

31. A. Reznikov, *The Comintern and the East, Strategy and Tactics*, (Moscow: Progress Publishers, 1978), 162–163.

32. Zecchini, *Planète Action*, 28.

33. Text in *HCM-Toan Tap*, Vol. II, 174 ff.

34. According to Turner, *Vietnamese Communism*, 100,000 piastres; according to Nguyen Khac Huyen, *Vision*, 150,000 piastres. Whatever the sum, it was very large for that time, as a buffalo cost only 5 piastres.

35. Nguyen Khac Huyen, *Vision*, 27–28.

36. Thomas Hodgkin, *Vietnam: The Revolutionary Path* (London: Macmillan, 1981), 223.

37. David Halberstam, *Ho Chi Minh* (Paris: Editions Buchet-Chastel, 1972), 58.

38. Fall, *Le Viet Minh* (Paris: Armand Colin, 1960), 35.

39. *HCM-Toan tap*, Vol. II, 365.

40. Ibid.

41. Fall said that Ho fled back to the Soviet Union "across the Gobi desert," in *Two Vietnams*, 94.

42. Ibid. 367–368.

43. Two members of the CPV who had known Ho in Thailand during this period have left very vivid accounts of his activities there. See: Le Manh Trinh and Tran Lam's stories in Tran Dan Tien *L'Oncle Ho*, 191 ff.

44. *HCM-Toan Tap*, Vol. II, 302.

45. Reznikov, *Comintern*, 169.

46. Lacouture, *Ho Chi Minh*, 43.

47. J. H. Brimmell, *Communism in Southeast Asia* (London: Oxford University Press, 1959), 58.

48. *HCM-Toan Tap*, Vol. III, 466.

49. Ho's escape from Hongkong is a long story impossible to tell fully here. For details, see: Lacouture, *Ho Chi Minh*, 51 ff, and Tran Dan Tien, *Avec l'Oncle Ho*, 172–173.

50. Mrs. Loseby confirmed the story in 1969. Officially, Ho died on June 26, 1932. See: Huynh Kim Khanh, *op. cit., Vietnamese Communism*, 179.

51. Lacouture, *Ho Chi Minh*, 57.

52. Fall, *Two Vietnams*, 57.

53. Huynh Kim Khanh, *Vietnamese Communism*, 179–186.

54. Charles B. McLane, *Soviet Strategies in Southeast Asia* (Princeton, NJ: Princeton University Press, 1966), 149.

55. Tran Dan Tien, *Avec l'Oncle Ho*, 143 ff.

56. *HCM-Toan Tap*, Vol. III, 460.

57. Huynh Kim Khanh, *Vietnamese Communism*, 188.

58. Dominique Desanti, *L'Internationale communiste* (Paris: Payot, 1970), 234.

59. Ibid., 198; *Le Courrier du Vietnam*, 2–1984, 11.

60. Lacouture, *Ho Chi Minh*, 57.

61. Fall, *Last Reflections*, 79.

62. Reznikov, *Comintern*, 164–167.

63. *HCM-Toan Tap,* Vol. III, 116 ff.

64. "The Chinese Revolution and the Vietnamese Revolution," written in 1961, for the fortieth anniversary of the CCP, in *Vi doc lap tu do, vi chu nghia xa hoi* (For independence and freedom, for socialism) (Hanoi: Nha Xuat Ban Su That, 1970) 239 ff. This article was not reprinted in *Tuyen Tap* after 1975.

65. *HCM-Toan Tap,* Vol. III, 470.

66. Ibid.

67. *HCM-Toan Tap,* Vol. III, 471.

68. *50 d'activités,* 61–62.

69. Ibid., 61–62.

70. According to Vu Anh, in Lacouture, *Avec l'Oncle Ho,* 261.

71. *50 d'activités du Parti communiste du Vietnam* (Hanoi: Editions en langues étrangères, 1980), 69.

72. *HCM-Toan Tap,* Vol. II, 457.

73. "The road that led me to Lenin," *HCM-Tuyen Tap,* Vol. II, p. 176.

74. *HCM-Toan Tap,* Vol. I, 191. The article first appeared in *Pravda* on January 27, 1924.

75. Ibid., 232.

76. William Duiker, *The Communist Road to Power in Vietnam* (Boulder, Colorado: Westview Press, 1981), 20.

77. Phan Van Dong, *Notre Président,* 93.

78. Ibid.

79. Ibid.

80. *HCM-Toan Tap,* Vol. II, 181.

81. *HCM-Tuyen Tap,* Vol. I, 306.

82. Phan Von Dong, *Notre Président,* 93.

83. *HCM-Toan Tap,* Vol. II, 216.

84. Ibid., 385.

85. *President Ho Chi Minh's Testament.*

86. Phan Van Dong, *Notre Président,* 184.

87. *HCM-Tuyen Tap,* Vol. II, 419.

88. *HCM-Tuyen Tap,* Vol. I, 230.

89. *HCM-Tuyen Tap,* Vol. II, 70–71.

90. Tran Dan Tien, *Avec l'Oncle Ho,* 316.

91. Ibid., 225, 272.

92. Ibid., 158, 174.

93. Ibid., 271.

94. Ibid., 213.

95. Ibid., 296.

96. Quoted by Halberstam, *Ho Chi Minh,* 90.

97. Tran Dan Tien, *Avec l'Oncle Ho,* 205.

98. Ibid., 300.

99. Ibid., 327.

100. Lacouture, *Ho Chi Minh*, 103.

101. Ibid., 120, 150, 190.

102. Jean Sainteny, *Au Vietnam face à Ho Chi Minh* (Paris: Seghers, 1970), 11.

103. Nguyen Khac Huyen, *Vision*, 319.

104. R. Harris Smith, *OSS, The Secret History of America's First Central Intelligence Agency* (Berkeley: University of California Press, 1972), 349–350.

105. Philippe Devillers, *Histoire du Vietnam de 1940 à 1952* (Paris: Seuil, 1952, 106.

106. Yves Gras, *Histoire de la guerre d'Indochine* (Paris: Plon, 1979), 20–21.

107. Nguyen Khac Huyen, *Vision*, 65, 102.

108. Huynh Kim Khanh, *Vietnamese Communism*, 1.

109. In Daniel Guérin, *Au service des colonisés*, quoted by Lacouture, *Ho Chi Minh*, 22.

Chapter 3

1. The first was Ho's address in February 1951 to the congress of the party at which the party resurfaced as Vietnam Workers' Party. The second was in his preface to the Russian edition of his *Selected Works* (1957).

2. Huynh Kim Khanh, *Vietnamese Communism 1924–1945* (Ithaca: Cornell University Press, 1982), 125.

3. Jean, Lacouture, *Ho Chi Minh*, 47.

4. Bernard B. Fall, *The Two Vietnams, A Political and Military Analysis* (New York: Praeger, 1963), 95.

5. *Tap Chi Cong San*, 5, 1980, 68–87.

6. *Ho Chi Minh Toan Tap* (Collected works of Ho Chi Minh), Vol. II, 8.

7. See details in Huynh Kim Khanh, *Vietnamese Communism*, chapter 11, and *50 ans d'activités du Parti Communiste du Viet Nam* (Hanoi: Editions en langues étrangères, 1980), 23ff.

8. Alain Ruscio, *La C.G.T. et la guerre d'Indochine 1945–1954* (Paris: Institut C.G.T. d'histoire sociale, 1984), 27.

9. J. H. Brimmell, *Communism in Southeast Asia* (London: Oxford University Press, 1959), 94.

10. Text in *Lich Su Dang Cong San Viet Nam* (History of the Communist party of Vietnam), Vol. I (1927–1945), 17–24. From here on: LSDCSVN (emphasis added).

11. Milton Sachs, "Marxism in Vietnam," in Frank Traeger, *Marxism in Southeast Asia, A Study of Four Countries, 1965* (Stanford: Stanford University Press, 1957), 116.

12. "L'Internationale communiste et la révolution indochinoise," *Le courrier du Vietnam*, 2–1984.

13. A. Reznikov, *The Comintern and the East, Strategy and Tactics* (Moscow: Progress Publishers, 1978), 165–166.

14. Ibid., 166.

15. Ibid., 167.

16. Figures compiled from *50 ans d'activités*, and Le Duan's Political Report to the Fifth National Congress of the party, 1982.

17. On the CPV leadership, see Douglas Pike, *History of Vietnamese Communism, 1925–1976* (Stanford: Hoover Institution Press, 1978), J. P. Honey, *Communism in North Vietnam* (Westport, CT: Greenwood Publishers, 1963), chapter 2.

18. See various resolutions of the party in LSDCSVN: October 1930 (p. 61), March 1935 (p. 132), September 1937 (p. 176), July 1939 (p. 200), November 1939 (p. 271), and Ho Chi Minh, "Leninism and the Struggle for Liberation of Oppressed Peoples," written for *Pravda* on April 1955 (*HCM-Tuyen Tap*, Vol. II, 15 ff).

19. Ibid., 183.

20. Ibid., 156.

21. Parti Communiste du Vietnam, IVè Congrès National, *Documents* (Hanoi: Editions en langues étrangères, 1977) 164.

22. Dang Cong San Viet Nam, *Luan Cuong Chinh Tri Nam 1930 (Political Platform, 1930)* (Hanoi: Nha Xuat Ban Su That, 1982), 7.

23. Le Duan, *Ecrits* (Hanoi: Editions en langues étrangères, 1976), 61.

24. Truong Chinh, *Ecrits* (Hanoi: Editions en langues étrangères, 1977), 739.

25. Le Duan, *Ecrits*, 85.

26. Truong Chinh, *Ecrits*, 316–317.

27. Le Duan, *Ecrits*, 8.

28. Ibid., 38.

29. Truong Chinh, *Ecrits*, 38.

30. Ibid., 56.

31. Ibid., 243.

32. Ibid., 340.

33. *HCM-Tuyen Tap*, Vol. I., 466.

34. IVè Congrès National, *Documents*, 38.

35. Pham Van Dong, quoted by Robert F. Turner, *Vietnamese Communism, Its Origin and Development* (Stanford: Stanford University Press, 1975), 112.

36. LSDCSVN, 136.

37. Ibid., 38.

38. Ibid., 44.

39. Ibid., 83.

40. Truong Chinh, *Ecrits*, 461.

41. LSDCSVN, Vol. I, 163.

42. Truong Chinh, *Ecrits*, 753.

43. *HCM-Tuyen Tap*, Vol. II, 380.

44. Le Duan, *Ecrits*, 50.

45. LSDCSVN, Vol. I, 61.

46. Ibid., 108.

47. Ibid., 132–133.

48. Ibid., 143.

49. *HCM-Tuyen Tap*, Vol. I, 261–162.

50. Le Duan, *Ecrits*, 100.

51. Truong Chinh, *Ecrits*, 418.

52. Pham Van Dong, *Mot so van de nha nuoc* (A number of problems concerning the government) (Hanoi: Nha Xuat Ban Su Thuc, 1980), 23.

53. Truong Chinh, *Ecrits*, 644.

54. Ibid., 644.

55. Ibid., 678.

56. Ibid., 667.

57. Ibid., 678.

58. Le Duan, *Ecrits*, 27.

59. Ibid., 217.

60. Ibid., 27.

61. Truong Chinh, *Ecrits*, 668.

62. Ibid., 673.

63. Ibid., 673.

64. Pham Van Dong, *Mot so van de nha nuoc*, 375.

65. Vo Nguyen Giap, *Ca nuoc dong long bao ve vung chac to quoc Viet Nam Xa Hoi Chu Nghia* (The whole country united in defending the Vietnam Socialist fatherland) (Hanoi: Nha Xuat Ban Su That, 1979), 15.

66. Truong Chinh, *Ecrits*, 75.

67. Ibid., 90.

68. Ibid., 675.

69. Ibid., 230.

70. Vo Nguyen Giap, *La guerre de libération nationale au Viet Nam*, in *Ecrits*, (Hanoi: Editions en langues étrangères, 1977), 338–339.

71. Ibid.

72. General Vo Nguyen Giap, *Guerre du peuple, armée du peuple* (Hanoi: Editions en langues étrangères, 1961), 105.

73. Henry Kissinger, *White House Years* (Boston: Little, Brown, 1979), 259.

74. Vo Nguyen Giap, interview with Oriana Fallaci, in *Interview with History* (Boston: Houghton Mifflin, 1976), 86.

75. Jean Sainteny, *Histoire d'une paix manquée, Indochine 1945–1947* (Paris: Faillard, 1967), 167.

76. Fallaci, *Interview*, 86.

77. Quoted by Turner, *Vietnamese Communism*, p. 112.

78. Ibid., 266.

79. Le Duan, *Ecrits*, 34.

80. Ibid.

81. Ibid., 150.

82. Ibid., 11.

83. Truong Chinh's famous *La résistance vaincra* (The resistance will win) has been reprinted in full in *Ecrits*, and Vo Nguyen Giap's writings, *La guerre de libération nationale* and *Guerre du peuple armée du peuple*, have already been referred to.

84. Archimedes L. Patti, *Why Vietnam? America's Albatros.* (Berkeley: University of California Press, 1980), 4.

85. Henri Azau, *Ho Chi Minh, dernière chance,* (Paris: Flammarion, 1968), 159.

86. Truong Chinh, *Ecrits*, 159.

87. Cited in Yves Gras, *Histoire*, 152.

88. Cited in Bernard B. Fall, *Le Viet Minh* (Paris: Armand Colin, 1960), 184.

89. Fallaci, *Interview*, 87.

90. Vo Nguyen Giap, *Ecrits*, 357.

91. Pham Van Dong, *Ecrits*, 252.

92. Hoang Quoc Viet, "Rapport politique du Comité Central du Front de la Patrie du Viet Nam," in IIIè Congres du Front de la Patrie, *Documents*, 93.

93. Le Duan, *Ecrits*, 177.

94. Ibid., 358.

95. Ibid., 177.

96. Sainteny, *Histoire*, 239.

97. Patti, *Why?*, 334.

98. J. P. Honey, *Communism in North Vietnam* (Westport, CT: Greenwood Press, 1963), 18.

99. Ibid., 37.

100. Pike, *History*, 64.

101. See his articles in *Renmin Ribao* of November 29, 1979 (reproduced in *Beijing Information*, December 10, 1979).

Chapter 4

1. Enrica Colotti-Pischel, quoted in Jean Lacouture, *Ho Chi Minh* (Paris: Seuil, 1967), 219.

2. Lacouture, *Ho Chi Minh*, 216–218.

3. *HCM-Tuyen Tap*, Vol. I, pp. 242, 247.

4. Ibid., 55 ff.

5. In particular, the resolution of the First Congress at Macao in 1935. *Lich Su Dang Cong San Viet Nam* (History of the Communist party of Vietnam) Vol. I, 107 ff. Hereafter: LSDCSVN.

6. Huynh Kim Khanh, *Vietnamese Communism, 1924–1945* (Ithaca: Cornell University Press, 1982), 284–285.

7. Ibid., 315.

8. K. C. Chen, *Vietnam and China, 1938–1954* (Princeton, NJ: Princeton University Press, 1969); Archimedes L. A. Patti, *Why Vietnam? America's Albatros* (Berkeley: University of California Press, 1980).

9. This and other subsequent details related to this period are from Patti's memoirs, unless otherwise indicated.

10. Patti, *Why?*, 53.

11. Huynh Kim Khanh, *Vietnamese Communism*, 317. Khanh translated "liên quân" as "brigade," but the correct translation should be "joint forces" or "combined forces," which is, of course, far more impressive, as it conveys the impression of an alliance.

12. Patti, *Why?*, 67.

13. R. Harris Smith, *OSS, The Secret History of America's First Central Intelligence Agency* (Berkeley: University of California Press, 1972), 326.

14. David Halberstam, *Ho Chi Minh* (Paris: Editions Buchet-Chastel, 1972), 95.

15. Patti, *Why?*, p. 129.

16. R. Harris Smith, *OSS The Secret History of America's First Intelligence Agency* (Berkeley: University of California Press, 1972), 333.

17. Patti, *Why?*, 135.

18. Charles Fenn, *Ho Chi Minh* (New York: Charles Scribner, 1973), 81.

19. Ibid.

20. Ibid., 77.

21. Patti, *Why?*, 134.

22. Smith, *OSS*, 352. Conein was to be mentioned later in stories about the coup against President Ngo Dinh Diem in 1963 as the CIA agent in charge of liaison between the Vietnamese generals and Ambassador Henry Cabot Lodge.

23. Fenn, *Ho Chi Minh*, 82.

24. Smith, *OSS*, 351, 357.

25. Patti, *Why?*, 86.

26. Ibid., 85.

27. Ibid., 88.

28. Patti, *Why?*, 129.

29. Patti, *Why?*, 369.

30. Ibid., 203.

31. Ibid., 245–246.

32. Ibid., 372–373.

33. Ibid., 373–74.

34. Ibid., 246.

35. Ibid., 374.

36. Ibid., 223–224. The text of Vietnam's declaration of independence can be found in Gareth Porter, *Vietnam, A History in Documents*, (New York: NAL, 1981), p. 28.

37. Ibid., p. 145.

38. Smith, *OSS*, 334.

39. Letter from Moffat in Hanoi to the State Department, December 1946. In Porter, *Vietnam*, 355.

40. Smith, *OSS*, 355; Philippe Devillers, *Histoire du Vietnam de 1940 á 1952* (Paris: Seuil, 1952), 202.

41. Fenn, *Ho Chi Minh*.

42. Ibid., 73.

43. Fenn, *Ho Chi Minh*, 78–79.

44. Patti, *Why?*, 58.

45. Fenn, *Ho Chi Minh*, 82. GBT stands for Gordon-Bernard-Tan, a group named after its three men who worked for OSS.

46. Patti, *Why?*, 135.

47. Ibid., 136.

48. Mrs. Le Thi Anh, "Revolution," in Al Santoli, *To Bear Any Burden* (New York: Dutton, 1985), 34.

49. Devillers, *Histoire*, 141–142.

50. S. M. Bao Dai, *Le Dragon d' Annam* (Paris: Plon, 1980), 119.

51. Patti, *Why?*, 188.

52. Ibid., 392.

53. Smith, *OSS*, 356–357.

54. Ibid., 354.

55. Vo Nguyen Giap, *Des journées inoubliables* (Hanoi: Editions en langues ét rangères, 1975), 4.

56. *50 ans d'activités*, 94.

57. Bao Dai, *Le Dragon*, 139–140.

58. See in particular: Ho Chi Minh's address to the Second National Party Congress in February 1951; *HCM-Tuyen Tap*, Vol. I, 468 ff.

59. Robert F. Turner, *Vietnamese Communism, Its Origin and Development* (Stanford: Hoover Institution Press, 1975), 35.

60. Devillers, *Histoire*, 133.

61. *Lich Su Dang Cong San Viet Nam* (History of the Communist Party of Vietnam), Vol. 1, 386.

62. *50 ans d'activités*, 81.

63. *HCM-Tuyen Tap*, Vol. I, 486.

Chapter 5

1. Pham Van Dong, *Mot so van de nha nuoc* (Hanoi: Nha Xuat Ban Su Thuc, 1980), 382.

2. *Lich Su Dang Cong San Viet Nam* (History of the Communist Party of Vietnam), Vol. I, 25. Hereafter: LSDCSVN.

3. On Comintern policy, see: J. H. Brimmell, *Communism in Southeast Asia,* (London: Oxford University Press, 1959); Charles B. McLane, *Soviet Strategies in Southeast Asia,* (Princeton, NJ: Princeton University Press, 1966); A. Reznikov, *The Comintern and the East, Strategy and Tactics* (Moscow: Progress Publishers, 1978); Kermit E. McKenzie, *Comintern and World Revolution 1928–1943* (New York: University of Columbia Press, 1964); Dominique Desanti, *L'Internationale communiste* (Paris: Payot, 1970); on the CPI and Comintern, see Huynh Kim Khanh, *Vietnamese Communism 1924–1945,* (Ithaca: Cornell University Press, 1982); Robert F. Turner, *Vietnamese Communism, Its Origins and Development* (Stanford: Hoover Institution Press, 1975).

4. Le Parti communiste du Vietnam, *Jalons historiques* (Hanoi: Editions en langues étrangères, 1982), 7.

5. LSDCSVN, Vol. I, 191.

6. Ibid., 194.

7. Ibid., 197; Ho's report to the ECCI on the situation in 1936–1939.

8. Ibid., Vol. I, 251, 257.

9. Ibid., 296–297.

10. Ibid., 322.

11. Ibid., 380.

12. *50 ans d'activités du Parti Communiste du Viet Nam* (Hanoi: Editions en langues étrangères, 1980), 69.

13. LSDCSVN, Vol. I, 381–383.

14. Jean Sainteny, *Histoire d'une paix manquée* (Paris: Amiot Dumont, 1973), 68. (From here on referred to as Sainteny I.)

15. Archimedes L. Patti, *Why Vietnam? America's Albatros,* (Berkeley: University of California Press, 1980), 129.

16. Ibid., 65.

17. Text in *De Gaulle et l'Indochine* (Paris: Institut Charles de Gaulle, Plon, 1982), Annex 2.

18. Patti, *Why?,* 126.

19. In conversation with Patti in Hanoi; Patti, *Why?,* 179.

20. Sainteny I, p. 70.

21. LSDCSVN, Vol. I, 363.

22. S. M. Bao Dai, *Le Dragon d'Annam* (Paris: Plon, 1980), 140.

23. Patti, *Why?*, 201.

24. Sainteny I, 97–99.

25. Patti, *Why?*, 207–210.

26. Vo Nguyen Giap, *Des journées inoubliables* (Hanoi: Editions en langues étranqères, 1975), 21.

27. Ibid., 144–146.

28. Patti, *Why?*, 343.

29. Ibid., 343–344.

30. Ibid., 360–361.

31. LSDCSVN, Vol. II, 9.

32. Ibid.

33. *Patti, Why?*, 369–370.

34. Admiral d'Argenlieu, *Chronique d'Indochine 1945–1947* (Paris: Albin Michel, 1985), 259.

35. Sainteny I, 181–183.

36. D'Argenlieu, *Chronique*, 180, 183.

37. Ibid., 98–100.

38. Ibid., 104–105.

39. Ibid., 139.

40. Ibid., 220.

41. Sainteny I, p. 184.

42. *HCM-Tuyen Tap*, Vol. I, 472.

43. Ho Chi Minh, *Vi doc lap tu do, vi chu nghia xa hoi* (For Independence and Freedom, for Socialism) (Hanoi: Nha Xuat Ban Su That, 1970) 162.

44. LSDCSVN, Vol. II, 16, 26.

45. Vo Nguyen Giap, *Des journées inoubliables*, 185, 187–188.

46. LSDCSVN, Vol. II, 94–95.

47. Text in Sainteny I, 199–201.

48. D'Argenlieu, *Chronique*, 207, 215.

49. Ibid., 198.

50. Ibid., 212–213.

51. Ibid., 198.

52. Ibid., 221.

53. Sainteny I, 215.

54. Sainteny, *Au Vietnam Face à Ho Chi Minh* (Paris: Seghers, 1980), 84 (From here on cited as Sainteny II).

55. Ibid., 86.

56. *HCM-Toan Tap*, Vol. IV, 173.

57. See their testimonies in *Planète Action,* special issue on Ho Chi Minh, March 1970.

58. Sainteny I, 105.

59. Henri Azau, *Ho Chi Minh, dernière chance* (Paris: Flammarion, 1968), 150.

60. Ibid., 279.

61. Sainteny II, 100.

62. Sainteny I, 99.

63. See story in *Planète Action.*

64. Ibid., 100.

65. Sainteny II, 189.

66. Text of de Gaulle's speech in Norodom Sihanouk, *Souvenirs doux et amers* (Paris: Hachette, 1981), 317–319.

67. Mourad Bourboune in *Planète Action,* 76.

Chapter 6

1. *Lich Su Dang Cong San Viet Nam* (History of the Communist Party of Vietnam). Hereafter: LSDCSVN. Vol. I, 180.

2. Ibid., 299–302.

3. Vo Nguyen Giap, in Tran Dan Tien and others, *Avec l'Oncle Ho* (Hanoi: Editions en langues étrangères, 1972), 292.

4. These and other details concerning the relations between Chang Fa-kwei and the Vietnamese nationalists in China are drawn from K. C. Chen *Vietnam and China, 1938–1954* (Princeton, NJ: Princeton University Press, 1969), 65, unless otherwise stated.

5. Ibid., 67.

6. Ibid., 81.

7. *HCM-Tuyen Tap,* Vol. I, 343.

8. Archimedes L. Patti, *Why Vietnam? America's Albatros* (Berkeley: University of California Press, 1980), 115.

9. V. N. Giap, *Des journées inoubliables* (Hanoi: Editions en langues étrangères, 1977), 61.

10. Chen, *Vietnam and China,* 115.

11. Ibid., 118.

12. Chen, *Vietnam and China,* 126.

13. Giap, *Des jounéers inoubliables,* 61.

14. Ibid., 96.

15. LSDCSVN, Vol. II, 183.

16. Giap, *Des journées inoubliables,* 78.

17. Ibid., 91.

18. Chen, *Vietnam and China,* 145.

19. Ibid., 123.

20. Ibid., 82.

21. Ibid., 149.

22. Text in Nguyen Khac Huyen, *Vision Accomplished, The Enigma of Ho Chi Minh* (New York: Macmillan, 1971), 102.

23. LSDCSVN, Vol. II, 185.

24. Giap, *Des journées inoubliables*, 61.

25. Chen, *Vietnam and China*, 126.

26. Thierry D'Argenlieu, *Chronique d'Indochine 1945–1947* (Paris: Albin Michel, 1985), 143, 159.

27. Giap, *Des journées inoubliables*, 101.

28. Ibid., 102.

29. Ibid., 101.

30. Patti, *Why?*, 338.

31. S. M. Bao Dai, *Le Dragon d'Annam* (Paris: Plon, 1980), 140.

32. LSDCSVN, Vol. II, 175; Ho Chi Minh, *Vi doc lap tu do Vi chu nghia xa hoi* (Hanoi: Nha Yuat Ban Su That, 1970), 240–241.

33. Tan Dan Tien and others, *Avec l'Oncle Ho* (Hanoi: Editions en langues étrangères, 1972), 291–293.

34. Ibid., 113, 163.

35. Chen, *Vietnam and China*, 41–42.

36. Ho was seen at Chou's residence several times in 1939; testimony of Professor Franklin Lien Ho, who was then deputy minister for economy of the Chinese government. Chen, *Vietnam and China*, 34.

37. Giap, *Guerre du peuple, armée du peuple* (Hanoi: Editions en langues étrangères, 1961), 20–21.

38. *La vérité sur les relations vietnamo-chinoises durant les trente dernières années* (Hanoi: Ministère des affaires étrangères, 1979). (From here on cited as *La vérité.*)

39. *On the Vietnamese Foreign Ministry's White Bokk concerning Vietnam-China Relations* Beijing; Foreign Language Press, 1979), 12–13. (From here on cited as *On Vietnam's White Paper.*)

40. *La vérité*, 20.

41. Ibid., 12.

42. Ibid., 36.

43. Ibid., 33.

44. François Joyaux, *La Chine et le règlement du premier conflit d'Indochine* (Paris: Presses Universitaires de France, 1979), 179.

45. Ibid., 227.

46. On the Geneva Conference, see: Jean Lacouture and Philippe Devillers, *La fin d'une guerre: Indochine 1954* (Paris: Seuil, 1960); Robert F. Randle, *Geneva 1954, The Settlement of the Indochinese War* (Princeton, N.J.: Princeton University Press, 1969).

47. Ho Chi Minh, *Vi doc lap, vi tu do*, 164.

48. *La vérité*, 34.

49. Ibid., 45.

50. Ibid., 44.

51. Ibid., 46–47.

52. Ibid., 47–48.

53. Ibid., 51.

54. Ibid., 52.

55. The Egyptian was Mohammed H. Heikal, who cited Chou En-lai in a book entitled *Les documents du Caire* (Paris: Flammarion, 1972), cited in *La vérité*, 53.

56. La vérité, 53.

57. Ibid., 55.

58. Ibid., 58.

59. Ibid., 61.

60. For details, see: P. J. Honey, *Communism in North Vietnam* (Westport, CT: Greenwood Press, 1963); Donald S. Zagoria, *Vietnam Triangle, Moscow, Peking, Hanoi* (New York: Pegasus, 1967); Robert A. Rupen and Robert Farrel, *Vietnam and the Sino-Soviet Dispute* (New York: Praeger, 1967).

61. On the Sino-Soviet dispute, see also: François Feijto, *Chine-URSS, de l'alliance au conflit, 1950/1977* (Paris: Seuil, 1978); Jacques Levesque, *L'URSS et sa politique internationale de 1917 à nos jours* (Paris: Armand Colin, 1980); John Gittings, *Survey of Sino-Soviet Dispute* (London: Oxford University Press, 1968).

62. Le Duan, *Ecrits* (Hanoi: Editions en lanques étrangères, 1967), 57.

63. Ho "disappeared" between November 10 and December 23, 1957. He went secretly to Moscow and refused to come home until his terms were met. See Honey, *Communism,* 52 ff.

64. Lecture at the Nguyen Ai Quoc School on March 13, 1963, in Le Duan, *Ecrits,* 59 ff.

65. On American policy toward Vietnam and China in this period, see: Sundershan Chawla, Melvin Gurtov, and Alain Gerard Marsot, *Southeast Asia under the New Balance of Power* (New York: Praeger, 1970); Philippe Richer, *Jeu de quatre en Asie du Sud-Est,* (Paris: Presses Universitaire's de France, 1982); Henry Kissinger, *White House Years* (Boston: Little, Brown, 1979) and *Years of Upheaval* (Boston: Little, Brown, 1982).

66. See Chawla Sundershan and others, *Southeast Asia under the New Balance of Power* (New York: Praeger, 1974), 148–149.

67. Harish Kapur, *The Awakening Giant, China's Ascent in World Politics* (Alphen aan den Rijn, The Netherlands: Sijhoof and Noordhoof, 1981), 53.

68. *La vérité,* 62–70.

69. Ibid., 64.

70. Ibid., 68–70.

71. Ibid., 82–84.

Chapter 7

1. Amphay Doré, *Le partage du Mékong* (Paris, Editions de l'encre, 1980), 57.

2. *50 ans d'activités du Parti Communiste du Viet Nam* (Hanoi: Editions en langues étrangères, 1980), 31.

3. Ibid., 58.

4. Ibid., 62.

5. Ibid., 80.

6. Ibid., 112.

7. Ibid.

8. SRV Ministry of Foreign Affairs, "Facts about the Indochinese Federation question," April 17, 1978, in *Kampuchea Dossier I, Vietnam Courier,* Hanoi, 1980, 98.

9. Ibid., 98–99.

10. On these and other events related to Cambodia, see: Philippe Richer, *L'Asie du Sud Est* (Paris: Imprimerie Nationale, 1988), 252ff.

11. 2,000–4,000 according to Richer, *L'Asie,* 359; 5000 according to Doré, *Le partage,* 59.

12. Mangkra Phouma, *L'agonie du Laos* (Paris: Plon, 1976), 66.

13. On these and other events of Laos, see: Richer, *L'Asie.*

14. *Vietnam Courier,* 5-1984.

15. Général Van Tien Dung, *Et nous prîmes Saigon* (Paris: Sycomore, 1979), 17.

16. See Doré, *Le partage,* Phouma, *L'agonie.*

17. *50 ans d'activités,* 236.

18. Doré, *Le partage,* 63.

19. Norodom Sihanouk, *L'Indochine vue de Pékin* (Paris: Seuil, 1972), 51.

20. Ibid., 155.

21. Norodom Sihanouk, *Souvenirs doux et amers* (Paris: Hachette, 1981), 223, 226.

22. Sihanouk, *Souvenirs;* see chapter: "Pourquoi j'ai aidé les révolutionnaires vietnamiens."

23. Ibid., 345–348.

24. *Les peuples indochinois vaincront* (Hanoi: Editions en langues étrangères, 1970).

25. *Kampuchea Dossier I,* 150.

26. Sihanouk, *L'Indochine,* 369–372.

27. Ibid., 169.

28. Sihnaouk, *Souvenirs,* 369, 372.

29. Ministère des Affaires étrangères du Kampuchea démocratique, Departement de Presse et d'Information, *Livre noir: Faits et preuves des actes d'agres-*

sion et d'annexation du Vietnam contre le Kampuchea, Septembre 1978, reprinted by Editions du centenaire, Paris, 1979. From here on cited as *Black Paper.*

30. Ibid., 13.

31. Ibid. All facts related concerning CPV attitude toward the CPK are from the *Black Paper,* 28–60.

32. Ibid., 34–35.

33. Hoang Nguyen, "The Vietnam-Kampuchea conflict," in *Le conflit Vietnam-Kampuchea* (Hanoi: Editions en langues étrangères, 1979), 8.

34. William Shawcross, *Sideshow, Kissinger, Nixon, and the Destruction of Cambodia* (New York: Simon and Scguster, 1979), 283, 285.

35. Ibid., 281.

36. Vietnam News Agency, February 11, 1976.

37. Text of this treaty in *Bulletin du Vietnam* (Paris), numéro spécial, September 1977.

38. Doré, *Le partage,* 211.

39. Ibid., 178.

40. See: Phouma, *L'agonie,* chapter XI.

41. Doré, *Le partage,* 154, 213; Phouma, *L'agonie,* 184.

42. Ibid., 229.

43. On the CPK-CPV rift, see: "Indochine: première guerre entre états communistes," in *La documentation française,* No 373, October 12, 1979. David Elliott, ed. *The Third Indochina Conflict* (Boulder, CO: Westview Press, 1981).

44. Shawcross, *Sideshow,* 386.

45. *Black Paper,* 55, 60, 76.

46. *Kampuchea Dossier I,* 117.

47. Ibid., 113.

48. *Le Monde,* January 7, 1978.

49. Statement of the government of Democratic Kampuchea, December 31, 1977, in *Kampuchea Dossier I,* 146.

50. Ibid., 148.

51. Ibid., 150.

52. Nayan Chanda, "Timetable for a take-over," *Far Eastern Economic Review,* reproduced in *Documentation française.*

53. Text in *Bulletin du Vietnam* (Paris), nouvelle série, November 16–30, 1978.

54. *Pékin Information,* November 27, 1978.

55. Text in *Bulletin du Vietnam,* February 15–28, 1979.

Chapter 8

1. Speech to Sixth Congress of party cadres, January 18, 1949. *HCM-Tuyen Tap,* Vol. I, 446 (emphasis added).

2. *HCM-Tuyen TAP,* Vol. II, 186.

3. Henry Kissinger, *White House Years* (Boston: Little, Brown, 1979), 441.

4. U.S. G.P.O., *U.S. Policy toward Indochina since Vietnam's Occupation of Kampuchea,* hearings before the Subcommittee on Asian and Pacific Affairs of the Committee of Foreign Affairs, House of Representatives, Ninety-seventh Congress. October 15, 21, 22, 1981, 141.

5. Ibid.

6. Roger Irvine, "The formative years of ASEAN, 1967–1975," in Alison Broinowski, ed., *Understanding ASEAN* (London: MacMillan, 1982), 40.

7. *International Herald Tribune,* May 14, 1975.

8. Irvine, *Formative Years,* 41.

9. Richer, *Jeu de quatre en Asie du Sud Est* (Paris: Presses Universitaires de France, 1982), 133.

10. *Nouvelles de la République démocratique du Vietnam* (Paris), June 15, 1975.

11. *Le Monde,* June 11, 1975.

12. Ibid.

13. Vietnam News Agency, February 11, 1976.

14. *Nouvelles de la République démocratique du Vietnam,* June 25, 1975.

15. *Quand Doi Nhan Dan,* quoted by Vietnam News Agency, February 22, 1976.

16. Quoted by Vietnam News Agency, February 22, 1976. In 1970 Indonesia trained Cambodian troops for action in Cambodia and at the 11th conference of foreign ministers of ASEAN in Jakarta in May 1970, it called for the withdrawal of "foreign"—i.e., North Vietnamese—troops from Cambodia.

17. Vietnam News Agency, July 2, 1976.

18. Parti Communiste du Vietnam, IVè Congrès National, *Documents,* (Hanoi: Editions en langues Etrangères, 1977), 162.

19. Amphay Doré *Le partage du Mékong* (Paris: Editions de l'encre, 1980), 179.

20. Nguyen Cong Hoan, "Promises," in Al Santoli, ed., *To Bear Any Burden* (New York: Dutton, 1985), 288.

21. Doré, *Le partage,* 183.

22. Ibid., 180.

23. Nguyen Cong Hoan, "Promises."

24. Michael Richardson, "ASEAN and Indochinese Refugees," in Alison Broinowski, *Understanding Asean* (London: Macmillan, 1982), 93.

25. Allen Gyngell, "Looking Outwards: ASEAN's External Relations," in Broinowski, *Understanding ASEAN,* 131.

26. *International Herald Tribune,* December 18, 1978.

27. Le Duan, *Phan dau xay dung nuoc Vietnam Xa Hoi Chu Nghia giau manh* (Struggling for a rich and beautiful Socialist Vietnam) (Hanoi: Nha Xua Ban Su That, 1979), 16–17.

28. *Le Monde,* December 21–22, 1978.

29. Ibid., February 12, 1979.

30. Cited in *Beijing Information,* January 8, 1979.

31. *Malaysia,* February 1979.

32. Ministry of Foreign Affairs, *Documents on the Kampuchean Problem 1979–1985,* September, Bangkok, Thailand, 73. From here on cited as *Thai Documents.*

33. *Thai Documents,* 74. On this and subsequent actions, see also Irvine, *Formative Years.*

34. Ibid., 77.

35. *The Globe and Mail* (Toronto), June 15, 1980.

36. *Journal de Genève,* July 7, 1980.

37. *Thai Documents,* 81.

38. Ibid.

39. Ibid., 87.

40. *Journal de Genève,* July 5, 1980.

41. *Peking Information,* July 4, 1975.

42. *The Globe and Mail* (Toronto), June 26, 1980.

43. P. R. Paringaux, citing an ASEAN minister, in *Le Monde,* November 28, 1978.

44. *International Herald Tribune,* January 1, 1983; *Le Monde,* March 23, 1981, December 1982.

45. *International Herald Tribune,* February 2, 1981.

46. *Le Monde,* February 3, 1979; *Le Devoir* (Montreal), February 10, 1979.

47. *Thai Documents,* 82–83.

48. *Le Devoir,* September 8, 1979.

49. Editorial, *Courrier du Vietnam,* 1-1982.

50. See: *Pour la paix et la stabilité en Asie du Sud-Est,* (Hanoi: Editions en langues étrangères, 1984), 32–33. From here on cited as *Indochinese Documents.*

51. Ibid., 38–40.

52. Khmer White Paper, July 10, 1984, in *Courrier du Vietnam,* 9-1984, 9.

53. Ibid., 8.

54. *Indochinese Documents,* 49.

55. On Indonesia's position, see: Donal Weatherbee, "The diplomacy of stalemate," in *Southeast Asia Divided: The Asean-Indochina Crisis* (Boulder, CO: Westview Press, 1985); also Jay Taylor, *China and Southeast Asia: Peking's Relations with Revolutionary Movements* (Stanford: Hoover Institution Press, 1965), chapter 2.

56. *Journal de Genève,* June 16, 1980.

57. *Indonesia Weekly Bulletin* (Bern, Embassy of Indonesia), July 2, 1982.

58. Weatherbee, *Diplomacy,* 22.

59. Ibid., 20.

60. *Jakarta Post*, October 14, 1985, as reported in FBIS, October 22, 1985.

61. Vietnam News Agency, January 19, 1985, as reported by FBIS, January 22, 1985.

62. Ibid.

63. *Indochinese Documents*, 11, 19.

64. Statement of Malaysia's deputy prime minister, Datuk Mahatir Mahommed, in Stockholm in 1979. *Malaysia*, December 1979.

65. Gyngell, "Looking Outwards," 133; Weatherbee, *Diplomacy*, 12.

66. Statement by Malaysia's foreign minister Tengku Rihauddeen; Kuala Lumpur Radio, January 9, 1985, as reported in FBIS, January 9, 1985.

67. Kuala Lumpur Radio, March 11, 1985, as reported in FBIS, March 13, 1985.

68. *Malaysia*, February 1980.

69. Communique of the Conference of Indochinese Foreign Ministers, April 1983, in *Indochinese Documents*, 59.

70. Richardson, "ASEAN," 102.

71. *International Herald Tribune*, July 7, 1975.

72. Ibid., December 12, 1978.

73. *Far Eastern Economic Review*, January 24, 1980.

74. Broinowski, *Understanding Asean*, 32.

75. *Indochinese Documents*, pp. 7 ff.

76. Ibid., 36 ff.

77. Phnom Penh SKP, October 16, 1985, as reported in FBIS, August 16, 1985.

78. *Bangkok World*, September 29, 1984, as reported in FBIS, October 1, 1984.

79. *The Nation Review*, October 3, 1984, as reported in FBIS, October 3, 1984.

80. Ibid.

81. *The Nation* (Bangkok), October 8, 1984, as reported in FBIS, October 8, 1984.

82. *Thai Documents*, 140.

83. Weatherbee, *Diplomacy*, 140.

84. Texts in *Thai Documents*, 123–125.

85. Ibid., 126 ff.

86. *Indochinese Documents*, 15.

87. Nguyen Co Thach's speech in the UN General Assembly in October 1984; Vietnam News Agency, October 10, 1984, as reported in FBIS, October 12, 1984.

88. See: Pichai Rattakun, Thailand's deputy prime minister, "Negotiations with

Vietnam," in *The Nation Review* (Bangkok), February 16, 1985, as reported in FBIS, February 26, 1985.

89. *The Straits Times,* July 11, 1985, as reported in FBIS, July 12, 1985.

90. Singapore Radio, September 1985, as reported in FBIS, September 27, 1985.

91. *Le Figaro,* March 21, 1985, as reported in FBIS, March 28, 1985.

92. *Thai Documents,* 9.

Chapter 9

1. Lenin, "The war and Russian social democracy," *Selected Works,* 3 vols. (Moscow: Progress Publishers, 1977), Vol. I, 164. From here on cited as Lenin SW.

2. Lenin SW.III, 57.

3. Lenin, "The proletarian revolution and the renegade Kautsky," SW.III, 68–70.

4. Lenin, "Proletarian revolution,"SW.III, 63.

5. Lenin, "The crisis has matured," SW.II, 342.

6. Lenin, "Can the Bolsheviks retain power?" SW.II, 383.

7. Lenin, SW.II, 352–355.

8. Lenin, speech to All-Russia Congress of Soviets, Soldiers' and Peasants' Deputies, January 1918, SW.II, 506.

9. Speech in Moscow, July 1918, SW. II, 715.

10. Text of the rules of admission in Robert V. Daniels, *A Documentary History of Communism,* Vol 2 (New York: Vintage Russian Library, 1960), 44 ff.

11. Branko Lazitch and Milovan M. Drachovitch, *Lenin and Comintern,* Vol. I (Stanford: Hoover Institution Press, 1972), 324.

12. Kermit McKenzie, *Comintern and World Revolution, 1928–1943, The Shaping of Doctrine* (New York: Columbia University Press, 1964), 26 ff.

13. Ibid., 27.

14. Ibid.

15. Quoted in Lazitch and Drachovitch, *Lenin,* 325.

16. Lenin, *Speeches at Congresses of the Communist International* (Moscow: Progress Publishers, 1972), 48.

17. Quoted in Xenia Joukoff Eudin and Robert C. North, *Soviet Russia and the Far East 1920–1927, A Documentary History* (Stanford: Stanford University Press, 1975), 71.

18. For these and other references to the structures and procedures of the Comintern, see Mckenzie, *Comintern,* 31 ff.

19. Ibid., 33.

20. Lazitch and Drachovitch, *Lenin,* 326.

21. J. H. Brimmell, *Communism in Southeast Asia, A Political Analysis* (London: Oxford University Press, 1959), 130.

22. Lenin, "The state and revolution," SW.II, 241 ff, 242.

23. Ibid., 253.

24. Ibid., 255.

25. Ibid.

26. Ibid., 302.

27. Lenin, "Proletarian revolution," SW.III, 24.

28. Ibid., 23.

29. Lenin, "The right of nations to self-determination," SW.I, 579, 591–592.

30. Lenin, "The tasks of the proletariat in our revolution," SW.II, 52.

31. Ibid., 59.

32. Lenin, SW.III, 60.

33. Ibid., 64.

34. Ibid.

35. Ibid., 376.

36. Ibid., 387.

37. G. Zinoviev, *Le léninisme* (Paris: Bibliothèque communiste, 1926), 253.

38. Ibid., 269.

39. Lenin, "On compromises," *Letters on Tactics* (1916) (Moscow: Progress Publishers, 1976), 27.

40. Lenin, "For bread and peace" (1917), SW.II, p. 640.

41. Lenin, "Letter to the workers and peasants of the Ukraine," 1919, SW.III, 259, 263.

42. Lenin, "Right of nations to self-determination," SW.I, 600.

43. Lenin, "Theses for the Second Congress of the Communist International," SW.III, 374.

44. Ibid., 377.

45. Ibid., 404.

46. Lenin, "Left-wing communism: An infantile disorder," SW.III, 310–311.

47. McKenzie, *Comintern*, 54.

48. Ibid., 55.

49. Ibid., 94.

50. Charles B. McLane, *Soviet Strategies in Southeast Asia* (Princeton, NJ: Princeton University Press, 1966), 208.

51. Desanti, *op. cit.*, 357.

52. McLane, *Soviet Strategies*, 352.

53. G. Zinoviev, *Le léninisme* (Paris: Bibliothèque Communiste, 1926), 13.

54. Lenin, "The tasks of the Youth Leagues" (October 1920), SW.III, 418–419.

55. Lenin, "Two tactics of social democracy," SW.I, 483.

56. Lenin, speech at All-Russian conference of political workers (November 1920), SW.III, 428.

57. Lenin, speech at First Congress of the Communist International (March 1919), WS.III, 104.

58. Lenin, "Two tactics" (1906), SW.I, 452.

59. Lenin, "Left-wing communism. . . ." SW.III, 357–359.

60. Ibid., 352–353.

61. Ibid.

62. Ibid., 322.

63. Lenin, "Marxism and insurrection," SW.II, 331.

64. Lenin, "Can the Bolsheviks retain power?" SW.II, 387.

65. Lenin, "What is to be done?" SW.I, 192.

66. Ibid., 355 (emphasis added).

67. Lenin, "Left-wing communism . . .", SW.III, 297.

68. Ibid., 337.

69. Dominique Desanti, *L'Internationale communiste* (Paris: Payot, 1970), in particular chapter XIII.

70. On this, see: Desanti, *L'Internationale*, Chapter XIII; Eudin and North, *Soviet Russia*, 85 ff; Koudou Koudawou, Les écoles du Comintern, in *Annals of International Studies*, Vol. 15 (Geneva: Graduate Institute of International Studies, 1985), 99 ff.

71. Quoted in Eudin and North, *Soviet Russia*, 87.

72. Desanti, *L'Internationale*, 338–339.

73. Ibid., 326.

74. Bernard B. Fall, *Last Reflections on a War* (New York: Doubleday, 1964), 87.

75. Huynh Kim Khanh, *Vietnamese Communism, 1924–1945* (Ithaca: Cornell Univerisity Press, 1982), 249.

76. William J. Duiker, *The Communist Road to Power in Vietnam,* (Boulder, CO: Westview Press, 1981), 7, 68.

77. Douglas Pike, *History of Vietnamese Communism 1925–1976* (Stanford: Hoover Institution Press, 1978), xiii.

78. Nguyen Kien "A survey of Vietnam's external relations," in *Vietnamese Studies* (new series), No 6, 1985, (Hanoi: Xunhasaba), 16–21.

79. Parti Communiste du Vietnam, Vè Congrès National, *Rapport Politique* (Hanoi: Editions en langues étrangères, 1982) 148.

80. Jean Lacouture, *Ho Chi Minh* (Paris: Seuil, 1967), 215.

81. R. S. Smyser, *The Independent Vietnamese: Vietnamese Communism between Russia and China 1956–1969*. Southeast Asia, No. 55. Papers on International Studies, (Athens, OH: Ohio University, Center for International Studies, 1980).

82. Parti Communiste du Vietnam, IVè Congrès National, *Documents* (Hanoi: Editions en langues étrangères, 1977), 112.

Chapter 10

1. N. S. Khrushchev, *Khruschev Remembers* (Boston: Little, Brown, 1970), 481.

2. Ibid., 482.

3. Ibid., 487.

4. *Nouvel Observateur, Atlas économique,* 1982.

5. *Le Monde,* November 9, 1984.

6. *Newsweek,* May 23, 1983.

7. Parti Communiste du Vietnam, IVè Congrès National, *Documents* (Hanoi: Editions en lanques étrangéres, 1977), 36.

8. Ibid., 29.

9. Vietnam News Agency, August 28, 1985, as reported in FBIS, August 29, 1985.

10. Henri Azau, *Ho Chi Minh, dernière chance* (Paris: Flammarion, 1966), 308.

11. Douglas Pike, *History of Vietnamese Communism 1925–1976* (Stanford: Hoover Institution Press, 1978), 133.

12. On this and other economic aspects, see: Ton That Thien, "Vietnam's new economic policy," *Pacific Affairs,* Winter 1983–84.

13. J. H. Brimmell, *Communism in Southeast Asia* (London: Oxford University Press, 1959), 175.

14. See: General de Boissieu's testimony in: Institut Charles de Gaulle, *De Gaulle et L'Indochine* (Paris: Plon, 1982), 174 ff, Thierry d'Argenlieu, *Chronique d'Indochine 1945–1947* (Paris: Albin Michel, 1985), 113, 436 ff.

15. Text in Azau, *Ho Chi Minh,* Annex III.

16. *De Gaulle et l'Indochine,* 238.

17. Alfred Georges, *Charles de Gaulle et la guerre d'Indochine* (Paris: Nouvelles éditions latines, 1971), 116.

18. Ibid., 123.

19. Azau, *Ho Chi Minh,* 155.

20. Information and Resource Center, *Indochina Report,* No. 8, October 1986, Singapore.

21. Thai Quang Trung, "The Moscow-Hanoi axis and the Soviet military build up in Southeast Asia," *Indochina Report,* 30.

22. Vo Nhan Tri, "Milestones of Soviet-Vietnamese economic cooperation," *Indochina Report,* 40.

23. Ibid., 50.

24. Hanoi Radio, July 17, 1985, as reported in FBIS, July 22, 1985.

25. Vo Nhan Tri, "Milestones," 66.

26. Hanoi Radio, September 4, 1985, as reported in FBIS, September 5, 1985.

27. Quoted in Vo Nhan Tri, "Milestones," 66.

28. Quoted in Thai Quang Trung, "Moscow-Hanoi," 29.

Bibliography

Writings of Communist Party of Vietnam Leaders

Ho, Chi Minh. *President Ho Chi Minh's Testament*. Hanoi: Foreign Language Publishing House, 1969).

——. *Vi doc lap tu do Vi chu nghia xa hoi* (For independence and freedom, for socialism). Hanoi: Nha Xuat Ban Su That, 1970.

——. *Ve Le-nin va chu nghia le-nin* (On Lenin and Leninism). Hanoi: Nha Xuat Ban Su That, 1977.

——. *Ecrits 1920–1969*. Hanoi: Editions en langues étrangères, 1979.

——. *Tuyen Tap* (selected works), 2 vols., 1: 1920–1954, 2: 1955–1969. Hanoi: Nha Xuat Ban Su That, 1980.

——. *Toan Tap* (complete works), 5 vols., 1: 1920–1925, 2: 1925–1930, 3: 1930–1945, 4: 1945–1947, 5: 1948–1950. Hanoi: Nha Xuat Ban Su That, 1980, 1981, 1983, 1984, 1985.

Le Duan. *Ecrits*. Hanoi: Editions en langues étrangères, 1976.

——. *Phan dau xay dung mot nuoc Viet Nam Xa Hoi Chu Nghia giau dep* (Fighting for a rich and beautiful Socialist Vietnam). Hanoi: Nha Xuat Ban Su That, 1979.

Pham, Van Dong. *Ecrits*. Hanoi: Editions en langues étrangères, 1977.

——. *Mot so van de nha nuoc* (A number of government problems). Hanoi: Nha Xuat Ban Su That, 1980.

Truong, Chinh. *Ecrits*. Hanoi: Editions en langues étrangères, 1977.

(Général) Van, Tien Dung. *Et nous prîmes Saigon*. Paris: Les éditions Sycomore, 1977.

(Général) Vo, Nguyen Giap. *Guerre du peuple, armée du peuple*. Hanoi: Editions en langues étrangères, 1961.

——. *La guerre de libération au Viet Nam*. Hanoi: Editions en langues étrangères, 1970.

——. *Des journées inoubliables*. Hanoi: Editions en langues étrangères, 1975.

——. *Ecrits*. Hanoi: Editions en langues étrangères, 1977.

——. *Ca nuoc mot long bao ve vung chac to quoc Viet Nam Xa Hoi* (The

---

Due to the particular subject of this book, only limited use has been made of periodicals and newspapers. Therefore, they are not listed in the bibliography.

whole country united in solidly defending the Vietnam Socialist fatherland). Hanoi: Nha Xuat Ban Su That, 1979.

Documents of the Communist Party of Vietnam

Ban Tuyen Huan Trung Uong (Central Propaganda and Training Committee). *Lich Su Dang Cong San Viet Nam, Trich Van Kien Dang* (History of the Communist party of Viet Nam, extracts from Party documents), 3 vols., I: 1925–1945, II: 1945–1954, III: 1954–1976. Hanoi: Nha Xuat Ban Giao Khoa, 1979.

Editions en langues étrangères, *Notre Président Ho Chi Minh*. Hanoi, 1970.

Front de la Patrie du Viet Nam: IIIè Congrès, *Documents II*. Hanoi: Editions en langues étrangères, 1972.

Parti Communiste du Viet Nam: IVè Congrès National, *Documents* Hanoi: Editions en langues étrangères, 1977.

———. *50 ans d'activités du Parti Communiste du Viet Nam*. Hanoi: Editions en langues étrangères, 1980.

———. *Jalons historiques*. Hanoi: Editions en langues étrangères, 1982.

———. Vè Congrès National, *Rapport Politique*. Hanoi: Editions en langues étrangères, 1982.

Testimonies of People Having Direct Dealings with the Communist Party of Vietnam

(Admiral) d'Argenlieu, Thierry. *Chronique d'Indochine 1945–1947* (Paris, Albin Michel, 1985).

Bao Dai, S. M. *Le Dragon d'Annam* (Paris, Plon, 1980).

Fenn, Charles. *Ho Chi Minh, A Biographical Introduction*. New York: Charles Scribner, 1973.

Khrushchev, Nikita. *Khrushchev Remembers*. Boston: Little, Brown, 1970.

Kissinger, Henry. *White House Years*. Boston: Little, Brown, 1979.

———. *Years of Upheaval*. Boston: Little, Brown, 1982.

(Colonel) Patti, Archimedes L. *Why Vietnam? America's Albatros*. Berkeley: University of California Press, 1980.

Sainteny, Jean. *Histoire d'une paix manquée, Indochine 1945–1947*. Paris: Amiot Dumont, 1973.

———. *Au Vietnam face à Ho Chi Minh*. Paris: Seghers, 1980.

Sihanouk, Norodom. *L'Indochine vue de Pékin*. Paris: Seuil, 1972.

———. *Souvenirs doux et amers*. Paris: Hachette, 1972.

Testimonies of People Involved in Vietnam

(Général) Catroux, Georges. *Deux actes du drame indochinois*. Paris: Plon, 1959.

Cooper, Chester. *The Lost Crusade*. London: McGibbon and Keel, 1970.

(Admiral) Decoux, Jean. *A la barre de l'Indochine: Histoire de mon gouvernement général 1940–1945*. Paris: Plon, 1952.

Doré, Amphay. *Le partage du Mékong*. Paris: Editions de l'Encre, 1980.

(Général) Ely, Paul. *L'Indochine dans la tourmente*. Paris: Plon, 1964.

Hendache, Henri. ed. *Ho Chi Minh,* special issue of *Planète Action*. Paris: Mars, 1970.

Johnson, Lyndon Baines. *The Vantage Point*. London: Weidenfeld and Nicholson, 1972.

Santoli, Al Santoli. *To Bear Any Burden*. New York: Dutton, 1985. (Contains testimonies of former members of the South Vietnam Liberation Front.)

Sissouk, Na Champassak. *Tempête sur le Laos*. Paris: La Table Ronde, 1961.

(Prince) Souvanna Phouma, Mangkra. *L'Agonie du Laos*. Paris: Plon, 1976.

Tran, Dan Tien, and others. *Avec l'Oncle Ho*. Hanoi: Editions en langues étrangères, 1972.

Truong, Nhu Tang. *Memoirs of a Vietcong*. New York: Harcourt Brace Jovanovitch, 1985.

Government Publications

Editions en langues étrangères. *Les peuples indochinois vaincront*. Hanoi, 1970. (Contains official documents on the Indochinese summit.)

————. *Le conflit Vietnam-Kampuchea*. Hanoi, 1979.

————. *Pour la paix et la stabilité en Asie du Sud-Est*. Hanoi, 1984. (Contains official communiques of the Indochinese summits.)

Foreign Languages Press, Beijing. *On the Vietnamese Foreign Ministry's White Book concerning Viet Nam-China Relations*. Beijing, 1979.

Ministère des Affaires étrangères de la République Socialiste du Viet Nam. *La Vérité sur les relations vietnamo-chinoises durant les trente dernières années*. Hanoi, 1979.

Ministère des Affaires étrangères du Kampuchea démocratique, Département de Presse et d'information. *Livre noir: Faits et preuves d'actes d'agression et d'annexation du Vietnam contre le Kampuchea*, Septembre 1978. Reprinted by Editions du Centenaire, Paris, 1979.

Ministry of Foreign Affairs, Thailand. *Documents on the Kampuchean Problem 1975–1985*. Bangkok, September 1985.

U.S. Ninety Seventh Congress, House of Representatives, Committee on Foreign Affairs, Hearings before the Sub-Committee on Asian and Pacific Affairs, October 15, 21, and 22, 1981, *US Policy toward Indochina since Vietnam's Occupation of Kampuchea*. Washington, D.C.: Government Printing Office, 1981.

Vietnam Courrier. *Kampuchea Dossier I,* Hanoi, 1978.

Books

Azau, Henri. *Ho Chi Minh, dernière chance*. Paris: Flammarion, 1968.

Ban Nghien Cuu Lich Su Dang, Tinh Uy Nghe Tinh (Historical Research Committee of the party, Nghe Tinh section). *Nhung mau chuyen ve doi nien thieu cua Bac Ho* (Stories about the youth of Uncle Ho). Hanoi: Nha Xuat Ban Su That, 1970.

Brimmell, J. H. *Communism in Southeast Asia, A Political Analysis.* London: Oxford University Press, 1959.

Broinowski, Alison, ed. *Understanding Asean.* London: MacMillan, 1982.

Brown, MacAlister (and Joseph J. Zasloff). *Communism in Indochina.* Lexington, Mass: D.C. Heath and Co, 1975.

Charlton, Michael (and Anthony Moncrieff). *Many Reasons Why, The American Involvement in Vietnam.* London: The Solar Press, 1978.

Chawla, Sundershan (Melvin Gurtov, Alain-Gerard Marsot). *Southeast Asia under the New Balance of Power.* New York: Praeger, 1974.

Chen, K. C. *Vietnam and China 1938–1954.* Princeton, N.J.: Princeton University Press, 1969.

Colbert, Evelyn. *Southeast Asia in International Politics 1941–1946.* 1977. Ithaca: Cornell University Press, 1977.

Daniels, Robert V. *A Documentary History of Communism,* Vol. 2. New York: Vintage Russian Library, 1960.

Desanti, Dominique. *L'Internationale Communiste.* Paris: Payot, 1970.

Devillers, Philippe. *Histoire du Vietnam de 1940 à 1952.* Paris: Seuil, 1952.

———— (et Jean Lacouture). *La fin d'une guerre, Indochine 1954.* Paris: Seuil, 1960.

Drachman, Edward R. *United States Policy Towards Vietnam 1940–1945.* Rutherford: Farleigh Dickenson University Press, 1970.

Drachovitch, Milovan (and Branko Lazitch). *Lenin and the Comintern,* Vol. I. Stanford: Hoover Institution Press, 1972.

Duiker, William J. *The Comintern and Vietnamese Communism.* Ohio University Center for International Studies, Papers on International Studies, Southeast Asia Series, No 37. 1975.

————. *The Rise of Nationalism in Vietnam 1900–1940.* Ithaca: Cornell University Press, 1976.

————. *The Communist Road to Power in Vietnam.* Boulder, CO: Westview Press, 1981.

————. *Vietnam, Nationalism and Revolution.* Boulder, CO: Westview Press, 1983.

————. *China and Vietnam, The Roots of Conflict.* Berkeley: Berkeley Institute of East Asian Studies, 1986.

Dyke, John M. Van. *North Vietnam's Strategy for Survival.* Palo Alto, CA: Pacific Book Publishers, 1972.

Elliott, David, ed. *The Third Indochina Conflict.* Boulder, CO: Westview Press, 1981.

Ellsbree, William. *Japans' Role in Southeast Asian National Movements 1940 to 1945.* New York: Russell and Russell, 1953.

<mark>242</mark><mark>Bibliography</mark>

Eudin, Xenia Joukoff, and Robert C. North. *Soviet Russia and the East 1920–1927: A Documentary Survey*. Stanford: Stanford University Press, 1957.

Fall, Bernard B. *Le Viet-Minh*. Paris: Armand Colin, 1960.

———. *The Two Vietnams, A Political and Military Analysis*. New York: Praeger, 1963.

———. *Last Reflections on a War*. New York: Doubleday, 1964.

Fallaci, Oriana. *Interview with History*. Boston: Houghton Mifflin, 1967.

Farrell, Robert, and Robert A. Rupen, eds. *Vietnam and the Sino-Soviet Dispute*. New York: Praeger, 1967.

Feijto, François. *Chine-URSS, de l'alliance au conflit 1950–1973*. Paris: Seuil, 1978.

Fifield, Russell. *The Diplomacy of Southeast Asia 1945–1958*. 1958, New York: Harper, 1958.

———. *Americans in Southeast Asia*. New York: Thomas Y. Crowell, 1973.

Frank, Pierre. *Histoire de l'Internationale communiste 1919–1943*. Paris: Editions de la Brèche, 1979.

Galloway, John. *The Kennedys and Vietnam*. New York: Facts on File, 1971.

Georges, Alfred. *Charles de Gaulle et l'Indochine*. Paris: Nouvelles éditions latines, 1974.

Goodman, Allan E.. *The Lost Peace, America's Search for a Negotiated Settlement of the Vietnam War*. Stanford: Hoover Institution Press, 1978.

Gourfinkel, Nina. *Lénine*. Paris: Seuil, 1973.

(Général) Gras, Yves. *Histoire de la guerre d'Indochine*. Paris: Plon, 1979.

Gravel (Senator Gravel Edition).*The Pentagon Papers*, Vol. 1. Boston: Beacon Press, 1971.

Grimal, Henri. *La décolonisation 1919–1963*. Paris: Armand Colin, 1963.

Grosser, Alfred. *La IV République et sa politique étrangère*. Paris: Armand Colin, 1967.

Gurtov, Melvin, Sundershan Chawla, and Alan-Gerard Marsot. *Southeast Asia under the New Balance of Power*. New York: Praeger, 1974.

Halberstam, David. *Ho Chi Minh*. Paris: Editions Buchet-Chastel, 1972.

Herring, George C. *The Secret Diplomacy of the Vietnam War*. Austin: University of Texas Press, 1983.

Hoang, Van Chi. *From Colonialism to Communism: A Case History of North Vietnam*. New York: Praeger, 1964.

Hodgkin, Thomas. *Vietnam: The Revolutionary Path*. London: MacMillan, 1981.

Honey, J. P. *Communism in North Vietnam, Its Role in the Sino-Soviet Dispute*. Westport, CT: Greenwood Press, 1963.

Hong Ha. *Bac Ho tren dat nuoc Le-nin (Uncle Ho in Lenin's land)*. 1980, Hanoi: Nha Xuat Ban Thanh Nien, 1980.

Huynh, Kim Khanh. *Vietnamese Communism 1924–1945*. Ithaca: Cornell University Press, 1982.

Institut Charles de Gaulle. *Le Général de Gaulle et l'Indochine*. Paris: Plon, 1982.

Isaacs, Harold R. *No Peace for Asia*. London: MacMillan, 1947.

Joyaux, François. *La Chine et le premier règlement du premier conflit d'Indochine*. Paris: Publication de la Sorbonne, 1979.

Kapur, Harish. *The Awakening Giant, China's Ascension in World Affairs*. Alphen aan den Rijn, The Netherlands: Sitjhoof and Noordhoof, 1981.

Lach, Donald F., and Edmund S. Wehrle. *International Politics in East Asia since World War II*. New York: Praeger, 1975.

Lacouture, Jean et Philippe Devillers. *La fin d'une guerre: Indochine 1954*. Paris: Seuil, 1960.

———. *Le Vietnam entre deux paix*. Paris: Seuil, 1965.

———. *Ho Chi Minh*. Paris: Seuil, 1969.

Lazitch, Branko, and Milovan Drachkovitch. *Lenin and Comintern*, Vol. I. Stanford: Hoover Institution Press, 1972.

Lenin, V. I. *Speeches at Congresses of the Communist International*. Moscow: Progress Publishers, 1972.

———. *Letters on Tactics*. Moscow: Progress Publishers, 1976.

———. *Selected Works in Three Volumes*. Moscow: Progress Publishers, 1977.

Levesque, Jacques. *L'URSS et sa politique internationale de 1917 à nos jours*. Paris: Armand Colin, 1980.

McKenzie, Kermit. *Comintern and World Revolution, 1928–1943, The Shaping of Doctrine*. New York: Columbia University Press, 1964.

McLane, Charles B. *Soviet Strategies in Southeast Asia (An Exploration of Eastern Policy under Lenin and Stalin)*. Princeton, N.J., Princeton University Press, 1966.

McVey, Ruth. *The Calcutta Conference and the Southeast Asian Uprisings*. Ithaca: Cornell University, 1958 (mimeo).

Marsot, Alain-Gerard, Sundershan Chawla, and Melvin Gurtov. *Southeast Asia under the New Balance of Power*. New York: Praeger, 1974.

Moncrieff, Anthony and Michael Charlton. *Many Reasons Why, The American Involvement in Vietnam*. London: Solar Press, 1978.

Munier, Bruno Pierre. *La politique chinoise vis-à-vis l'Indochine*, doctoral thesis, Graduate Institute of International Studies, Geneva, 1968 (mimeo).

Nguyen, Khac Huyen. *Vision Accomplished, The Enigma of Ho Chi Minh*. New York: MacMillan, 1971.

Nguyen, The Anh and Vu, Ngo Chieu. *Another School for Nguyen Tat Thanh*. Paris: Tu Sach Van Hoa, 1983.

Nguyen, Van Canh. *Vietnam under Communism 1975–1982*. Stanford: Hoover Institution Press, 1982.

North, Robert C., and Xenia Joukoff Eudin. *Soviet Russia and the East 1920–1927, A Documentary History*. Stanford: Stanford University Press, 1975.

Novosti (Agence de Presse). *Stratégie et tactique du léninisme*. Moscou, 1969.

Payne, Robert. *Lenin*. New York: Simon and Schuster, 1964.

Pedrazzini, Jean Michel. *La France en Indochine, de Catroux à Sainteny*. Paris: Arthaud, 1972.

Pike, Douglas. *History of Vietnamese Communism 1925–1976*. Stanford: Hoover Institution Press, 1978.

Porter, Gareth, ed. *Vietnam, A History in Documents*. New York: New American Library, 1981.

Randle, Robert F.. *Geneva 1954, The Settlement of the Indochinese War*. Princeton, NJ: Princeton University Press, 1969.

Reznikov, A. *The Comintern and the East, Strategy and Tactics*. Moscow: Progress Publishers, 1978.

Richer, Philippe. *L'Asie du Sud Est, indépendances et communismes*. Paris: Imprimerie Nationale, 1981.

———. *Jeu de quatre en Asie du Sud-Est*. Paris: Presses Universitaires de France, 1982.

Rupen, Robert A., and Robert Farrell. *Vietnam and the Sino-Soviet Dispute*. New York: Praeger, 1967.

Ruscio, Alain A.. *La C.G.T. et la guerre d'Indochine 1945–1954*. 1984, Paris: Institut C.G.T. d'histoire sociale, 1984.

Scalapino, Robert, ed. *The Communist Revolution in Asia*. Englewood Cliffs, NJ: Prentice Hall, 1969.

Shawcross, William. *Sideshow, Kissinger, Nixon, and the Destruction of Cambodia*. New York: Simon and Schuster, 1979.

Shub, David. *Lenin, A Biography*. New York: Mentor Book, 1948.

Smith, R. B.. *An International History of the Vietnam War*, Vol. I. New York: St. Martin's Press 1983.

Smith, R. Harris. *OSS The Secret History of America's First Intelligence Agency*. Berkeley: University of California Press, 1972.

Smyser, W. R.. *The Independent Vietnamese, Vietnamese Communism Between Russia and China*. Papers on International Studies, Southeast Asia Series, No. 55. Athens, OH: Ohio University Center for International Studies, 1980.

Stalin, Joseph. *Foundations of Leninism*. New York: International Publishers, 1977 (1939).

Suant, Jacques. *Vietnam 45–72*. Paris: Arthaud, 1972.

Taylor, Jay. *China and Southeast Asia: Peking's Relations with Revolutionary Movements*. New York: Praeger, 1974.

Traeger, Frank. *Marxism in Southeast Asia, A Study of Four Countries*. Stanford: Stanford University Press, 1965 (1957).

Turner, Robert F.. *Vietnamese Communism, Its Origin and Development*. Stanford: Hoover Institution Press, 1975.

Weatherbee, Donald W. *Southeast Asia Divided, The Asean-Indochina Crisis*. Boulder, CO: Westview Press, 1985.

Wehrle, Edmund S., and Donald F. Lach. *International Politics Since World War II*. New York: Praeger, 1975.

Vu, Ngo Chieu and Nguyen The Anh. *Another School for Young Nguyen Tat Thanh*. Paris: Tu Sach Van Hoa, 1983.

Zagoria, Donald S.. *Vietnam Triangle: Moscow, Peking, Hanoi*. New York: Pegasus, 1967.

Zasloff, Joseph J., and MacAlistair Brown. *Communism in Indochina*. Lexington, MA: D. C. Heathe, 1975.

Zinoviev, G. *Le léninisme,* Paris: Bibliothèque Communiste, 1926.

Index

About the Author

Dr. Ton That Thien was born in Hue, the former imperial capital of Vietnam. He went to secondary school there, and completed his education in London and Geneva. He earned a B.Sc. (economics) degree from the London School of Economics, majoring in International Relations, and received his Doctorate in Political Science from the Graduate Institute of International Studies of Geneva.

Dr. Ton That Thien has been active in political, academic and journalistic affairs.

He was a participant in the events that shook his country in 1945 and thereafter. He had a direct experience of the Bao Dai, Ho Chi Minh, Ngo Dinh Diem and Nguyen Van Thieu governments. He took part in the Geneva Conferences on Indochina in 1954 and on Laos in 1961. He was thus able to gain valuable insight concerning Vietnamese politics.

He was professor of economic development at the Vietnamese National Institute of Administration; professor of political science and dean of the Faculty of Social Sciences of the (Buddhist) Van Hanh University in Saigon, and associate dean of the Graduate School of Business and Government of the (Catholic) Dalat University; visiting professor at the Graduate Institute of International Studies, Geneva, and visiting fellow of the Information and Resource Center, Singapore.

He was director general of Vietnam Press; senior editor of *The Saigon Daily News* and *The Vietnam Guardian;* correspondent of *The Economist* (London), and *The Far Eastern Economic Review* (Hongkong), *The Gazette de Lausanne* and *24 Heures* (Lausanne). He won the Raymond Magsaysay Award for Journalism, Literature and the Communication Arts in 1968.

Dr. Ton That Thien is author of *India and Southeast Asia 1946–1960* (Droz, Geneva, 1963); *The Deadly Trap: How Hanoi Negotiates,* and *Moscow's Shadow over Vietnam* (Information and Resource Center, Singapore, 1987 and 1988 respectively); and co-author of *Vietnam, du delta du Mekong au Song Ben Hai* (Kummerly and Frey, Berne, 1970). He has written many studies on the political and cultural problems of Vietnam.

Dr. Ton That Thien is currently professor in the Department of Modern Languages of the Universite du Quebec at Trois Rivieres, Canada.